Temple Beth David

6100 Hefley Street
Westminster, CA 92683
(714) 892-6623

Light Jewish
Holiday Desserts

Light

Jewish

Holiday

Desserts

Penny Wantuck
Eisenberg

WILLIAM MORROW AND
COMPANY, INC.
NEW YORK

It is the policy of William Morrow and Company, Inc., and its imprints and affiliates, recognizing the importance of preserving what has been written, to print the books we publish on acid-free paper, and we exert our best efforts to that end.

Library of Congress Cataloging-in-Publication Data

Eisenberg, Penny Wantuck.
    Light Jewish holiday desserts / Penny W. Eisenberg. —1st ed.
        p.   cm.
    ISBN 0-688-15985-0
    1. Desserts. 2. Cookery, Jewish. 3. Fasts and feasts—Judaism.
    4. Low-fat diet recipes. I. Title.
    TX773.E36   1999
    641.8'6'089924—dc21   99–30745
                                                              CIP

Printed in the United States of America

First Edition

1 2 3 4 5 6 7 8 9 10

BOOK DESIGN BY RICHARD ORIOLO

www.williammorrow.com

For my mother,
Roslyn Wantuck,
an inspired and adventurous cook,
who continues to share her love of
food and cooking with me

Acknowledgments

I would like to thank my editor, Justin Schwartz, for his continued confidence in me, for keeping me rooted in reality, and for making sure that my writing is concise and clear. Thanks also to the copy editor, Karen Fraley, for her attention to detail, and to Christy Stabin for editorial assistance. To the design team and the rest of the Morrow staff who helped produce, market, and distribute this book, my sincere thanks. Thanks also to my agent, Harvey Klinger, for his continued efforts on my behalf. To Mary Ellen Bartley, who photographed my desserts, to Brett Kurzweil, who baked them, and to Barb Fritz, for her prop styling, it was a great pleasure to work with you and your staff Thank you for translating my work into such beautiful art.

The taste-testers who good-naturedly tried my successes as well as my failures were: Tanya Metzler and the hairstylists at Norman Russell Salon, the teachers at Charlotte Country Day School, the baseball moms, congregants of Temple Beth El, and my family and friends. Thank you all for your willingness to be guinea pigs.

To Sara Schreibman, Jan Weiner, Ahlam Albaba, and Alice Medrich, thank you for allowing me to use and/or adapt your wonderful recipes.

For their love and support I would like to thank my family, Roslyn and Ralph Wantuck; Leslie and Jordan

Weiner; Karen Wantuck and Eric Taylor; Bernie and Ruth Eisenberg; Lee, Nan, Josh, Matthew, and Kate Eisenberg; Florence, Debby, Marc, and Hope Wantuck; and Jeremy Schneider. To my inner circle of friends, Lisa Wohl, Jackie Stutts, Michelle Perlmutter, Chris Beloni, Margot Blackwell, and Linda Perlman, my heartfelt thanks for your friendship over the years. My continued gratitude goes to Roberta Massey for attending to my kitchen as if it were her own.

Lastly, to my husband, Carl, and to our children, Beth and Eric, the sun would not rise without you. All my love.

Acknowledgments

Contents

Jewish Holiday Overview

For exact dates through 2009, see the calendar on page 326.

HOLIDAY	TIME OF YEAR	FOODS TO EAT
Days of Awe (Rosh Hashanah and Yom Kippur—eaten at the Break-the-Fast)	September or October	honey, apples, carrots, dates, round cakes and cookies, seeds, sweet desserts, new fruits of the season
Sukkot	September or October—2 weeks after Rosh Hashanah	citrus fruits, fall fruits, dates, figs, grapes, star fruit, stuffed foods
Simkat Torah	October—8 days after Sukkot	round or rolled cookies and cakes, Sukkot desserts
Chanukah	November or December	fried desserts, foods made with oil, cheese and dairy dishes, menorah-, Maccabee-, or dreidel-shaped cookies
Tu b'Shevat	January or February	fruits and nuts of Israel, desserts with fruit and nut combinations
Purim	February or March	hamantashen, poppy seeds, triangular and ear-shaped cookies, small cakes and bars to give away
Pesach (Passover)	March or April	desserts made with matzo, without leavening or flour and certified kosher for Passover

HOLIDAY	TIME OF YEAR	FOODS TO EAT
Yom ha-atzma'ut	April or May	Israeli products, Israeli produce, typical Jewish desserts
Shavuot	May or June	first fruits of the season, cheese and dairy products, white foods, spices, rose water, and honey
Shabbat	Friday sundown through Saturday sundown	all desserts that are particularly enjoyable, traditional Jewish fare, Israeli foods, seeds, braided and round cookies and cakes, sweet spices

For thousands of years, adherence to Jewish dietary law (the laws of kashrut) was essential to the practice of Judaism. Then, as now, this was not an easy task and required meticulous daily attention to food procurement, preparation, service, and cleanup. Kashrut has made food a major part of Jewish life, a preoccupation that has had a profound effect upon Jewish culture. Because Jews could not eat food prepared by outsiders, and could only eat certain foods and/or food combinations, our cuisine has remained distinct, despite incorporation of new foods and techniques from the lands to which we have been displaced. Perhaps intentionally, these laws have set the Jewish people apart in a fundamental way.

The Torah teaches us, indeed commands us, to celebrate our holidays with joyous feasting, to eat certain foods at certain times of the year, to honor our history and our God by eating symbolic foods. In the Torah we are also counseled to be mindful of our physical health as well as our spiritual health. As human beings, we are genetically programmed to seek out foods that are sweet and fatty. As Jews, we may eat these foods because they add immeasurably to our enjoyment of life, and because they are comfort foods that connect us to our past. We are a people with a long and joyful culinary history!

In the United States, most Jews are of Germanic, Russian, or Eastern European descent (Ashkenazi Jews). Our traditional foods reflect this. But Jewish cooking worldwide is as varied as the Jews who cook it and the places in which Jews have lived. Those who are unfamiliar with Sephardic cooking from the Mediterranean, through the Middle East, and into Asia might like to read Claudia Roden's wonderful anthology, *The Book of Jewish Food*. Throughout time Jews have adapted their cooking to the new lands in which they have found themselves, and that continues today as Jews move throughout the world. In this era, some maintain the laws of kashrut and some do not. We have less time for cooking; we spend less time together and more time working at nonphysical labor. Health professionals counsel us to cut back on foods high in fat and cholesterol, but these are often the traditional foods to which we cling for comfort and historic connection. How can we make our desserts healthier and still maintain our culinary cultural identity? What will distinguish Jewish food from food just cooked by Jews?

I believe that the true essence of Jewish food is that it tells a story about who we are and where we have come from. Throughout the centuries Jews have been storytellers, passing along culture and values through words, song, and food. Although recipes may change over time, the symbolism of the food itself remains constant. By linking ingredients to stories, people, events, or values, we can continue to have food that will be quintessentially Jewish, even as it reflects our particular time and place in history. It does not matter if we serve honey cake, chiffon honey cake, or lowfat honey cake on Rosh Hashanah. What is important is that we recognize and talk about the significance of the honey.

The recipes in this book were created by using fat reduction techniques that I learned from reading some of the wonderful lowfat books previously published. Susan Purdy's *Let Them Eat Cake* and Alice Medrich's *Chocolate and the Art of Lowfat Desserts* were particularly helpful. Shirley Corriher's fabulous book, *Cookwise*, was also an indispensable aid in expanding my knowledge about food science. Nutritional values were calculated using Mastercook Deluxe and are included for information only. Each recipe was tested again and again to create the best dessert with the least amount of fat. To satisfy the palate and the soul, however, some fat has been retained to preserve the mouth-feel and flavor of our beloved food. I hope these recipes will please you physically (they taste good!), intellectually (they're better for you!), and spiritually (they all contain the requisite symbolic ingredients). The chapters are arranged by holiday with explanations of the foods to eat for each celebration. Recipes are marked as pareve (containing neither meat nor dairy), dairy, or both, meaning that the choice is yours. Although representing different Jewish customs, each recipe uses traditional ingredients to tell a story, link us to our past, and celebrate our Jewishness. Enjoy!

I welcome your questions and comments. You can E-mail me at p2bakes@aol.com.

To achieve the greatest success with baking these recipes, please follow these basic guidelines:

1. Read each recipe through before beginning to bake.

2. If possible, measure flour by weight. Because it is prone to packing, flour is difficult to accurately measure by the cup. I have had cups of flour that have weighed 105 grams, and others that have weighed 130 grams (using the exact same kind of flour)—that's about a three-tablespoon difference in just one cup! Weighed flour, on the other hand, will always be the same, no matter how it is scooped or packed. If this is not possible, measure dry ingredients in dry measuring cups which come in sets with specific sizes: 1 cup, ½ cup, etc. Shake the flour off a spoon into the measuring cup (in the recipes I call this lightly sprinkling) to the top of the cup, and level off the ingredient with a knife, or chopstick. Semisolid ingredients, such as sour cream, should also be measured in dry measuring cups.

3. When measuring wet ingredients, use a liquid measuring cup. These glass or plastic cups have multiple measurements on them. Do not measure to the top. Get your eye down to the level of the ingredient, so that you are really seeing how full the cup is.

4. When a "method" comes before a recipe ingredient, such as ½ cup sifted flour, first perform the action (sift) and then measure. When the method comes after the ingredient, such as ½ cup nuts, chopped, measure first and then perform the action (chop).

5. Do not use substitutes for essential ingredients (fat, flour, sugar, liquid) unless the recipe says you may do so. Results may vary considerably if you change the basic components.

6. Read about the ingredients and equipment used in these recipes beginning on page 303.

7. A list of suppliers can be found on page 324.

Rosh Hashanah, celebrated on the first and second days of Tishri (September or October), marks the beginning of the Days of Awe, the holiest days of the Jewish year. Throughout the world, Jews celebrate Rosh Hashanah, the Jewish New Year, in daylong synagogue services and at home with family and friends. It is said that divine judgment is made on Rosh Hashanah and delivered on Yom Kippur, the Day of Atonement, which concludes the holiday. Throughout the week, we think about our past deeds, ask for forgiveness, and pray for a sweet and

Rosh Hashanah and Yom Kippur

prosperous New Year. Feasting is an integral part of Rosh Hashanah, and symbolism is abundant. Honey is eaten to express our wishes for a sweet New Year, and apples dipped in honey are symbolic of the Garden of Eden. Carrots (*mehren* in Yiddish) are eaten because *mehren* also means to increase, which conveys our wishes for prosperity. Dates may be eaten because their Hebrew name sounds like a part of the blessing in which we ask to be cleansed of sin. Seeds are symbolic of fertility or prosperity (and also our covenant with God), and round foods represent a well-rounded year, or the circle of life. On the second night of Rosh Hashanah it is customary to partake of a new fruit of the season. Pomegranates are usually eaten in Israel, but in the United States, one might choose grapes.

The conclusion of the holy days is Yom Kippur, the Day of Atonement. Celebrated on the tenth of Tishri, it is a day of fasting and synagogue worship. At the conclusion of the fast, we join with our friends and family to celebrate at a "break-the-fast" meal which usually includes light dairy foods. Desserts are often the same as those for Rosh Hashanah.

Symbolic foods for the Days of Awe are:

Honey

Apples

Carrots

Dates

Round cakes and cookies

Seeds

Sweet desserts

New fruits of the season—perhaps pomegranates or grapes

Lekach

Honey Cake

Unlike traditional honey cake, this lowfat version is not overly sweet. Although it has one-fourth the fat of most honey cakes, it is still moist and delicious. I like it best with almonds, but those who do not eat nuts can eliminate them.

MAKES 2 LOAVES, 10 SERVINGS EACH

2 tablespoons canola oil

½ cup plum/apple or prune/apple baby food

6 large egg whites, at room temperature

1 cup honey

1½ cups firmly packed light brown sugar

3 cups (360 grams) all-purpose flour, lightly sprinkled into
   measuring cup

1 teaspoon baking soda

2 teaspoons baking powder

⅛ teaspoon salt

2 teaspoons cinnamon

1 teaspoon nutmeg

½ cup finely chopped almonds

⅔ cup brewed coffee, at room temperature

¼ cup sliced almonds (optional)

1. Preheat the oven to 350°F, with a rack in the lower third of the oven. Spray-grease and flour two 9 × 5-inch loaf pans.

2. Place the oil, baby food, egg whites, honey, and brown sugar in a large mixing bowl. Beat with an electric mixer, on medium speed, for 3 minutes.

continued

ALSO SERVE ON
*Shabbat,
Yom ha-atzma'ut*

PAREVE

NUTRITIONAL
NOTES
(per serving with nuts)

208 calories

4g fat (16%)

0mg cholesterol

41g carbohydrates

4g protein

149mg sodium

1g fiber

RDA %

1% vitamin A

0% vitamin C

6% calcium

8% iron

Rosh Hashanah
and Yom Kippur

3. In a small mixing bowl, thoroughly mix together the flour, baking soda, baking powder, salt, cinnamon, nutmeg, and chopped almonds. Alternately, stir the flour mixture and the coffee into the sugar mixture, beginning and ending with the flour. Do not overmix. The batter will be very thin.

4. Pour the batter into the prepared pans. Rap the pans sharply on the counter several times to break any large bubbles. Sprinkle ⅛ cup of sliced almonds on the top of each loaf.

5. Place the cakes in the oven and bake for 55 to 65 minutes, until a toothpick inserted into the center of the cake comes out with no moist crumbs attached. Set pans on a rack to cool completely. Run a knife around the edges of the pans, and invert to release the cakes from the pans. For best flavor, make the cakes 1 day ahead, wrap in aluminum foil, and store at room temperature. The cakes will keep for 3 days at room temperature or may be frozen for up to 3 months.

Honey Coffee Chiffon Cake

A cross between a sponge cake and a chiffon, this cake is fluffy and fine-textured. It's easy to make, can be prepared in advance, and keeps well. In addition, it is festive and visually appealing.

MAKES 16 TO 20 SERVINGS

1 cup (120 grams) all-purpose flour, lightly sprinkled into measuring cup

²⁄₃ cup (70 grams) sifted cake flour, lightly sprinkled into measuring cup

½ teaspoon baking soda

½ teaspoon baking powder

¼ teaspoon salt

1 teaspoon cinnamon

½ teaspoon cloves

½ teaspoon ginger

½ cup plus 3 tablespoons sugar, divided

⅓ cup canola oil

2 whole eggs, at room temperature, separated

½ cup brewed coffee, at room temperature

¼ cup honey

4 large egg whites, at room temperature

Coffee Honey Glaze

1 cup powdered sugar

1 teaspoon honey

2 tablespoons brewed coffee, at room temperature

1 teaspoon vanilla extract

¼ cup finely chopped walnuts (optional)

continued

ALSO SERVE ON
Yom ha-atzma'ut, Shabbat

PAREVE

NUTRITIONAL NOTES
(per serving with nuts)

160 calories

5g fat (30%)

20mg cholesterol

26g carbohydrates

2g protein

94mg sodium

0g fiber

RDA %

1% vitamin A

0% vitamin C

1% calcium

4% iron

Rosh Hashanah and Yom Kippur

1. Preheat the oven to 300°F, with a rack in the middle of the oven. Have ready an angel food pan or an unfluted 9- or 10-inch tube pan (do not grease either pan).

2. Mix both flours, baking soda, baking powder, salt, cinnamon, cloves, ginger, and ½ cup sugar in a large mixing bowl. Add the oil, egg yolks, coffee, and honey and beat on medium for 1 minute.

3. Put the egg whites in a clean, grease-free bowl. Using clean, dry, grease-free electric beaters, beat the egg whites on high speed until frothy. Gradually beat in the remaining 3 tablespoons of sugar. Beat until the egg whites are stiff but not dry. Stir one-quarter of the whites into the batter to lighten it. Gently fold in the remaining whites. Spoon the batter into the prepared pan.

4. Bake for 55 to 65 minutes, or until a toothpick inserted into the center of the cake comes out with no moist crumbs attached.

5. Cool the cake upside down. (Angel food pans have little feet to rest on. If using a tube pan, invert the cake onto the neck of a bottle.) When the cake is completely cool, run a knife around the sides of the pan, the inner tube, and under the whole bottom of the pan. Invert onto a cooling rack, place a cardboard round, slightly smaller than the cake, on the bottom, and reinvert.

6. For the glaze, combine the powdered sugar, honey, coffee, and vanilla in a small bowl. Whisk until smooth. It should be thin enough to brush. Brush the glaze onto the top of the cake. Sprinkle lightly with the chopped nuts. Brush the sides of the cake. Hold the cake up on the palm of one hand (on its board) and pat the remaining nuts onto the sides of the cake. Let it stand at room temperature until the glaze is firm. Place in a covered cake holder and store at room temperature until ready to serve. Can be made 1 day ahead. Do not freeze.

Carrot Pineapple Bundt Cake

*D*ense, moist, and fruity, this cake is richly satisfying. Easy to
make, it's also great for the busy holiday season because it can be
made several days ahead or frozen. High in beta-carotene and iron, it's
not only delicious but nutritious as well. If you don't care for whole
wheat or cannot find whole wheat pastry flour, try one of the variations
at the end of the recipe. For best results make the cake one day ahead.

MAKES 16 TO 20 SERVINGS

1 cup (120 grams) all-purpose flour, lightly sprinkled into
   measuring cup

⅔ cup (70 grams) sifted cake flour, lightly sprinkled into
   measuring cup

1¾ cups (130 grams) whole wheat pastry flour, lightly sprinkled into
   measuring cup

1 tablespoon pumpkin pie spice, or combine 2 teaspoons cinnamon,
   ½ teaspoon ginger, ¼ teaspoon nutmeg, and
   ¼ teaspoon ground cloves

2 teaspoons baking soda

¼ teaspoon salt

1 cup raisins

½ cup walnuts, chopped into ⅛-inch pieces

¼ cup canola oil

3 tablespoons water

2 cups firmly packed light or dark brown sugar

1 large egg, at room temperature

One 8-ounce can crushed pineapple, in its own juice

3 cups packed finely grated carrots (about 4 large)

Powdered Sugar (optional)

continued

ALSO SERVE ON
Sukkot, Shabbat

PAREVE

**NUTRITIONAL
NOTES**
(per serving)

226 calories

5g fat (21%)

0mg cholesterol

43g carbohydrates

4g protein

184mg sodium

2g fiber

RDA %

91% vitamin A

5% vitamin C

3% calcium

9% iron

**MUST BE MADE 1 DAY
AHEAD**

Rosh Hashanah
and Yom Kippur

1. Preheat the oven to 325°F, with a rack in the middle of the oven. Spray-grease and flour a 12-cup fluted tube (Bundt) pan.

2. Sift together all three flours, the spices, baking soda, and salt. Stir in the raisins and nuts. Set aside.

3. Place the oil, water, and brown sugar in a large mixing bowl. Beat for 1 minute on medium speed. Beat in the egg until well blended. On low, beat in the pineapple with its juice, and the carrots.

4. On low, or by hand, beat in the flour mixture in 3 additions, mixing just until the flour is incorporated. The batter will be fairly thick.

5. Spoon the batter into the prepared pan, and bake for 60 to 70 minutes, or until a tester inserted into the center of the cake comes out with no moist crumbs attached. Remove the cake to a rack and cool completely. Invert the cake onto a serving platter and sprinkle with powdered sugar, if desired.

6. The cake must be made at least 1 day ahead, but can be made 2 days in advance. Wrap in foil and store at room temperature. May also be frozen for up to 3 months.

VARIATIONS: If you prefer a moister, more cakelike texture, delete the whole wheat flour, and use a total of 1¾ cups (210 grams) all-purpose flour and 1¾ cups (185 grams) sifted cake flour. Also add ¼ cup more grated carrots. For a drier tea cake, delete the whole wheat flour, and use 2⅓ cups (280 grams) all-purpose flour and 1⅛ cups (120 grams) sifted cake flour.

Apple Date Bundt Cake

This is a very sweet, rich-tasting, classic Jewish cake. Don't be alarmed at the thickness of the batter. As the sugar melts and caramelizes, and as the apples soften and produce juice, the cake will bake up into a moist and dark treat.

MAKES 18 TO 20 SERVINGS

2¾ cups (330 grams) all-purpose flour, lightly sprinkled into measuring cup

½ teaspoon salt

1 tablespoon baking soda

1 tablespoon cinnamon

¾ cup chopped dates (not prechopped)

¾ cup walnuts, coarsely chopped

2⅔ cups sugar

2 large eggs, at room temperature

2 large egg whites, at room temperature

⅓ cup canola oil

⅓ cup applesauce, at room temperature

1 tablespoon vanilla extract

2 medium apples, preferably Fuji or Granny Smith

1 tablespoon fresh lemon juice

1. Preheat the oven to 325°F, with a rack in the middle of the oven. Spray-grease a 12-cup fluted tube (Bundt) pan.

2. In a bowl, sift together the flour, salt, baking soda, and cinnamon. Stir in the dates, nuts, and sugar.

3. In a large mixer bowl, beat the eggs, egg whites, oil, applesauce, and vanilla until well blended.

continued

ALSO SERVE ON
Shabbat, Sukkot,
Tu b'Shevat,
Yom ha-atzma'ut

PAREVE

NUTRITIONAL
NOTES
(per serving)

262 calories

6g fat (18%)

20mg cholesterol

51g carbohydrates

3g protein

283mg sodium

1g fiber

RDA %

0% vitamin A

2% vitamin C

1% calcium

7% iron

Rosh Hashanah
and Yom Kippur

4. Peel, core, and chop the apples into ⅛-inch dice, sprinkling with lemon juice as you cut them (to keep them from turning brown).

5. Stir the flour mixture into the eggs. The batter will be extremely thick. Stir in the apples.

6. Spoon the batter into the prepared pan and bake for 65 to 75 minutes, or until a toothpick inserted into the center of the cake comes out with no moist crumbs attached.

7. Cool the pan on a rack for 20 minutes and then invert to release the cake from the pan. The cake can be made 2 days in advance or frozen for up to 3 months.

Apple Mousse Layer Cake

Light, tasty, and beautiful, this cake is a great way to celebrate the holidays. All cakes with multiple components are time consuming to make, but the work can be done on different days to make it easier to handle. This dessert will be worth the effort. For best results the cake should be assembled a day in advance.

MAKES 16 TO 20 SERVINGS

Browned Butter Genoise
2 tablespoons unsalted butter, cut into chunks
3 large eggs, at room temperature
4 large egg whites, at room temperature
1 cup sugar
*½ cup (60 grams) all-purpose flour, lightly sprinkled into
    measuring cup*

½ cup plus 1 tablespoon (60 grams) sifted cake flour,
    lightly sprinkled into measuring cup

½ teaspoon vanilla extract

Baked Apples

1 medium lemon

2–3 medium apples, preferably Fuji or Granny Smith

3 tablespoons sugar

1 teaspoon canola oil

Apple Mousse

⅓ cup cornstarch

⅓ cup sugar

1½ cups apple juice

1⅛ cups applesauce

1 tablespoon fresh lemon juice

½ cup reduced-fat sour cream, preferably Breakstone's

Soaking Syrup

¼ cup apple juice

1 tablespoon sugar

1 tablespoon applejack brandy, or other kosher liqueur or brandy
    (optional)

Glaze (optional)

2 tablespoons apricot jam

1 teaspoon apple juice or water

1. Preheat the oven to 375°F, with a rack in the middle of the oven. Spray two 10-inch round pans with cooking spray, and line them with parchment paper or nonstick Teflon liners (for suppliers, see page 324). Spray-grease and flour the pans.

2. For the genoise, place the butter in a small skillet and cook over medium-high heat, swirling the pan occasionally until dark flecks appear

NUTRITIONAL
NOTES
(per serving with glaze)

194 calories

3g fat (13%)

39mg cholesterol

41g carbohydrates

3g protein

29mg sodium

1g fiber

RDA %

2% vitamin A

12% vitamin C

1% calcium

4% iron

Rosh Hashanah
and Yom Kippur

in the butter and the color darkens to a medium-amber (about 2 minutes after the butter starts to simmer). Scrape the butter into a medium microwavable bowl and set aside to cool.

3. Bring about 2 inches of water to boil in the bottom of a double boiler. Reduce the heat, and keep the water simmering. Place the eggs and egg whites in the top of the double boiler or in a metal mixer bowl (not over the hot water). With a wire whisk, lightly whisk the eggs. Gradually whisk in the sugar. Place the eggs over the water and whisk until the eggs are about 110°F (warm, but not hot to the touch).

4. Take the bowl off the double boiler, and beat the eggs with an electric mixer, on high, until they are very thick and billowy, 5 to 7 minutes.

5. Mix together both flours. Sift half of the flour over the egg mixture and gently fold together. Repeat with the remaining flour.

6. Microwave the reserved brown butter for 10 to 20 seconds. Add the vanilla to the butter.

7. Fold about 2 cups of batter into the butter. Fold this gently into the remaining batter. Divide the batter between the two pans. If necessary, carefully spread the batter to the edges of the pans. Do not tap the pans to remove bubbles.

8. Bake the cakes, in the middle of the oven, for 9 to 13 minutes, or until lightly browned and springy (unlike full-fat genoise, they will not shrink from the sides of the pans). Place a piece of waxed paper or parchment, and a cakeboard, over each cake. Invert to remove the cakes from the pans, and leave the cakes with the bottom side up. When the cakes are cool, place a 9-inch cake pan or a 9-inch cakeboard on top of the cakes and cut around the form to make the cakes into 9-inch rounds.

9. Take the cake pieces that you have cut off and bake them at 350°F for 5 minutes. Crumble the toasted cake into small crumbs and continue baking until the crumbs are browned and dry. If the crumbs are over-browning, but are not yet dried out, reduce the temperature to 200°F, and continue to cook until the crumbs are dry. The cakes can be made 1 day ahead or frozen for up to 3 months (wrap tightly in foil; defrost in foil

at room temperature). The crumbs can be stored at room temperature for several days, in an airtight container, or frozen (defrost the crumbs, uncovered, at room temperature).

10. For the baked apples, preheat oven to 425°F.

11. Squeeze ½ of the lemon into 4 cups of cold water. Peel, halve, and core the apples. Dice 2 of them into ¼-inch pieces, dip into the lemon-water, drain, and set aside. If making the apple flower, cut the remaining apple into ¹⁄₁₆-inch slices and drop into the lemon-water.

12. Drain the sliced apples, squeeze the remaining ½ lemon over them, and put them into a 9 × 12-inch nonreactive baking pan (preferably nonstick). Add the diced apples, keeping them separate from the sliced apples. Sprinkle all the apples with the sugar, drizzle on the oil, and toss the apples to coat evenly. Cover with foil and bake for 10 to 12 minutes, or until the apples are crisp-tender. Remove them from the oven, remove the foil, and let cool. The apples can be prepared 2 days ahead. Store, covered, in the refrigerator.

13. For the apple mousse, place the cornstarch and sugar in a medium, nonreactive pot. Stir in the apple juice, a little at a time. Stir in the applesauce and lemon juice. Bring the mixture to a boil.

14. Reduce the heat, and let the mixture simmer for 1 minute. Cool the puree to room temperature, or make it up to 2 days ahead and refrigerate until ready to use. Whisk the sour cream into the apple puree.

15. Drain the cooked apples, reserving the juice in a microwavable bowl. To make the soaking syrup, add the apple juice, sugar, and brandy to the reserved baked apple juice. Microwave on medium heat for 1 minute.

16. To assemble the cake: Set 1 genoise layer on a cakeboard that is the same size as the cake or smaller. With a pastry brush, pat on ¼ cup of the soaking syrup. Use a cake-decorating spatula to spread a thin layer of apple mousse over the top of the cake. Spoon the apple chunks evenly over the cake. Top with ¾ cup of the apple mousse. Set the other cake layer on top of the mousse. Brush it with the soaking syrup, and spread about 1 cup of the mousse over the top of the cake. Use the remaining mousse to thinly cover the sides and to fill the space between the 2 cakes.

continued

Rosh Hashanah and Yom Kippur

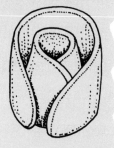

17. Hold the cake up on the cakeboard, and use the other hand to pat cake crumbs onto the sides of the cake. Sparsely sprinkle some cake crumbs over the top of the cake.

18. For a more decorative presentation, make an apple flower for the center of the cake. Prepare the glaze by heating the apricot jam and juice together until melted. Strain and then brush the glaze over the reserved apple slices. Make the flower as follows: Start the flower with the center bud by rolling up one of the smaller, outside slices of apple. Turn it upside down, so that the base is fatter than the top. Wrap 2 or 3 slices around the bud, overlapping slices, slightly. Continue, as above, staggering the rows of petals until the flower is the size you want.

19. Refrigerate the cake for at least 4 hours, preferably overnight, or up to 2 days ahead (do not freeze assembled cake). For a different presentation, score the cake into 16 or 20 wedges (after it has been refrigerated overnight). Roll up each apple slice and cut off the bottom of each slice so that the roll is ½ to ¾ inch high. Set one of these tiny rose apples on each partition.

Tayglach

I think these lowfat tayglach are slightly more crisp and tastier than full-fat ones. A little sugar has been added to the dough for flavor, and the nuts are put in right before molding, which prevents them from overcooking and tasting burnt. Seeds, nuts, and candied fruits, to taste, can be added. With today's wonderful nonstick pots, making tayglach is no longer a messy job, as the sugar syrup comes right off the surface. Make the dough in the food processor and in less than thirty seconds it's ready to be pinched off and cooked. Tayglach can be made ahead and stored at room temperature or frozen.

MAKES 65 CONFECTIONS

2 large eggs, at room temperature

2 cups (240 grams) all-purpose flour, lightly sprinkled into measuring cup

1 tablespoon sugar

1 teaspoon baking powder

½ teaspoon ground ginger

Salt

Syrup

¾ cup honey

½ cup sugar

1 teaspoon ground ginger

½ cup chopped unsalted nuts (optional; walnuts are traditional)

¼ cup sesame seeds (optional)

¼ cup candied fruit (optional)

continued

PAREVE

NUTRITIONAL
NOTES
(per piece)

45 calories

1g fat (14%)

6mg cholesterol

9g carbohydrates

1g protein

9mg sodium

0g fiber

RDA %

1% vitamin A

0% vitamin C

1% calcium

3% iron

Rosh Hashanah and Yom Kippur

1. Spray-grease 3 nonstick cookie sheets or jelly roll pans. Set aside.

2. Place the eggs in a processor bowl and pulse, just to blend them.

3. In another bowl, combine the flour, sugar, baking powder, ginger, and a pinch of salt. Mix the ingredients well, and add them to the processor bowl. Pulse-process until the dough comes together in a ball, then continue to process for 10 seconds.

4. Cut the dough into 8 sections. Keep all of the dough, except the portion you are working with, wrapped in plastic. On an unfloured board, roll 1 section of dough with your hands into a ¼-inch-thick string, about 15 inches long. Cut or pull off ¼-inch pieces of dough, and set aside on a cookie sheet. Repeat with the remaining dough.

5. For the syrup, in a Dutch oven or deep, wide skillet (preferably nonstick), combine the honey, sugar, and ginger. Bring the syrup to a boil over medium-high heat. Add all of the dough pieces, and reduce the heat to medium-low, just enough to keep the syrup simmering. Let the dough cook for 5 minutes, then stir to coat all of the dough with syrup. Simmer 20 more minutes, stirring every 5 minutes to keep the pieces coated with syrup and browning evenly. Remove 1 piece of dough and cut it open. Let it cool for a moment and then taste it. The dough should be dry all the way through. If not, cook 5 minutes more. The dough and syrup should be golden brown. Stir in the nuts, seeds, and fruit, if using. Turn the dough out onto one of the greased pans. Immediately scoop up tablespoons of dough, place on 1 of the other cookie sheets, and shape the dough into 1-inch mounds. Repeat with all of the dough. Wet your hands with cold water and then shape any mounds that don't look attractive. (Alternatively, the *tayglach* can all be molded together into a large mound, which gets cut or torn apart for eating. I prefer these individual pieces which are neater to eat.) Let the *tayglach* cool completely before storing in an airtight tin. To clean the pot, fill it with water and set on the stove to boil. Use a wooden spoon to scrape up excess syrup. Dump the water out, and clean as usual. Utensils can also be immersed in boiling water to get rid of sticky syrup.

Honey Spice Thumbprints

These soft, lightly spiced cookies are a colorful addition to the holiday buffet table. With honey, spice, apples, and sweet fillings, they are perfect for both Rosh Hashanah and Yom Kippur break-the-fast. The cookies look prettiest filled with raspberry jam but also taste great with apricot jam or apple butter.

MAKES 35 COOKIES

¼ cup unsalted butter or unsalted pareve margarine, softened

⅓ cup unsweetened applesauce

⅓ cup sugar

½ cup plus 1 tablespoon honey

3 cups (360 grams) all-purpose flour, lightly sprinkled into measuring cup

½ teaspoon baking soda

¼ teaspoon salt

½ teaspoon ground ginger

1½ teaspoons cinnamon

¼ teaspoon nutmeg

¾ cup raspberry or apricot jam, or apple butter

1. Place the butter, applesauce, sugar, and honey in a food processor. Process until well blended.

2. In another bowl, mix together the flour, baking soda, salt, ginger, cinnamon, and nutmeg. Add the flour mixture to the processor bowl, and pulse-process until the dough forms a ball. Wrap in plastic wrap and refrigerate overnight.

3. Preheat the oven to 350°F, with a rack in the middle of the oven. Line a cookie sheet with parchment paper or a Teflon liner.

continued

ALSO SERVE ON
Havdalah, Sukkot,
Purim, Yom
ha-atzma'ut

DAIRY OR
PAREVE

NUTRITIONAL
NOTES
(per cookie)

91 calories

1.5g fat (15%)

4mg cholesterol

19g carbohydrates

1g protein

37mg sodium

0g fiber

RDA %

1% vitamin A

1% vitamin C

1% calcium

3% iron

Rosh Hashanah
and Yom Kippur

4. Form the dough into 1-inch balls. Using your thumb, make an indentation in each ball and then shape the dough, just as if it were clay, making a little "pot" with a ⅛-inch rim and ¾-inch well. Fill each well with a rounded ½ teaspoonful of filling. Bake for 8 to 10 minutes, until the cookies are just set. They will be soft and not yet brown. Let the cookies cool on the parchment paper on a cooling rack. Cookies taste best if made 1 day ahead, and will keep for 1 week in an airtight tin, or frozen for up to 3 months.

Apple Tart Normandy

A thin film of lowfat custard surrounding apple slices makes this simple tart a truly elegant dessert.

MAKES 8 SERVINGS

One 9-inch tart shell (page 290)

1 medium lemon, squeezed into 8 cups cold water

4 large apples, preferably Fuji or other firm variety

2 tablespoons unsalted butter, melted

2 tablespoons firmly packed light brown sugar

Custard

2 tablespoons (15 grams) all-purpose flour

½ cup sugar

1 large egg

½ cup 2% milk

1 teaspoon vanilla extract

1 tablespoon Calvados (apple brandy), brandy, rum, or water

DAIRY

NUTRITIONAL NOTES
(per serving; trimmed dough is not counted)

217 calories

7g fat (30%)

24mg cholesterol

36g carbohydrates

2g protein

104mg sodium

2g fiber

R D A %

6% vitamin A

2% vitamin C

2% calcium

5% iron

Light Jewish
Holiday Desserts

20

Glaze

¼ cup apple or red currant jelly

1 tablespoon Calvados, or water

1. Prepare and bake the tart shell up to 8 hours ahead. Before assembling the tart, preheat the oven to 375°F, with a rack in the middle of the oven.

2. Peel, core, and cut the apples into ⅛-inch-thick slices, placing them in the lemon-water as each is cut. Drain the apples and pat them dry. Place the slices in the tart crust in concentric circles, with the rounded edges of the apples not quite parallel to the perimeter of the tart. The slices should be overlapping one another. After the first ring, fill the center so that the second ring will be raised above the first. For the last row, fan the slices like a pinwheel, going in the opposite direction from the first 2 circles. Brush the apples with butter and sprinkle on the brown sugar. Bake for 30 minutes.

3. For the custard, combine the flour and sugar in a medium bowl. In a separate bowl, whisk the egg lightly and then discard all but 1 tablespoon of the egg. Whisk in the milk, vanilla, and Calvados. Gradually stir the milk mixture into the flour mixture until smooth. Pour this batter over the baked apples. Bake 10 minutes more, or until a knife inserted into the custard comes out clean.

4. For the glaze, melt the jelly with the Calvados. Brush over the apples. Serve the tart at room temperature or cold.

Rosh Hashanah
and Yom Kippur

Apple-Grape Potpies

*E*verything but the actual baking of these wonderful one-crust individual pies can be done ahead. The dough can be rolled and frozen; or the pies can be assembled and cooked later; or they can be assembled, frozen, and then cooked a few hours before serving.

NUTRITIONAL
NOTES
(per serving,
includes crust)

268 calories

9g fat (29%)

10mg cholesterol

46g carbohydrates

4g protein

115g sodium

2g fiber

RDA %

5% vitamin A

8% vitamin C

3% calcium

8% iron

MAKES 8 SERVINGS

Nut Pastry Crust, for 8 rounds (page 292)

2 medium lemons

6 medium apples, preferably greenish Golden Delicious, or other medium-firm variety

2 cups whole red seedless grapes

½ cup firmly packed light brown sugar

1 teaspoon cinnamon

2 tablespoons cornstarch

1. Make the Nut Pastry Crust and refrigerate it for at least 30 minutes or up to 2 days in advance.

2. Roll the dough so that it fills a jumbo zip-top bag (it will be about ¹⁄₁₆ inch thick). Using a 4-inch round cookie cutter (I use a Tupperware container), cut the dough into 8 rounds. Use a small cookie cutter or the back of a decorating tip to cut out a ½-inch hole in the center of each round. (These can be made 8 hours ahead, or frozen for up to 3 months. If freezing, place the rounds in a single layer until frozen, and then stack with waxed paper between the layers. In all cases, allow the dough to come to room temperature before continuing.)

3. Squeeze 1 lemon into a large bowl of cold water. Peel, halve, core, and cut the apples into 1-inch chunks. Drop them into the bowl of lemon-water. Drain the apples well, and transfer them to a large bowl. Add the grapes, sugar, cinnamon, and cornstarch. Squeeze the remaining lemon

Light Jewish
Holiday Desserts

over the apples. Toss well, and then divide the filling among eight 1-cup ramekins (3½ inches in diameter). Make sure to evenly divide the liquid and sugar, which may have collected on the bottom of the bowl. The filling should be mounded slightly, and there will be about 2 teaspoons of liquid per serving.

4. Place a dough round atop each filled ramekin. Press the pastry so that it adheres to the sides of the ramekin. Refrigerate for 15 minutes. Alternatively, prepare the ramekins 8 hours ahead, cover with plastic wrap, and place in the refrigerator, or freeze for up to 3 months.

5. When ready to bake, preheat the oven to 400°F, with a rack in the middle of the oven.

6. Set the ramekins on a baking sheet, and bake unfrozen ramekins for 30 to 40 minutes (if you like softer fruit, cook for 45 to 60 minutes, covering the pastry with foil when it is nicely browned). Frozen ramekins cook for 45 to 50 minutes, or until the pastry is cooked through and brown. Remove the pastries and set them on a rack to cool for at least 1 hour. These can be made 4 hours ahead. Store at room temperature. To serve, reheat at 350°F for 15 minutes. The fruit should be just warm. If desired, dollop a heaping teaspoon of Light Whipped Cream (page 299) or a small scoop of lowfat frozen yogurt onto the crust.

Apple Butter Puff Tarts

*A*lthough puff pastry is usually thought of as a high-fat dessert, each of these tarts uses such a small amount of pastry that they do fit well into a healthy diet. An elegant dessert, these tarts are high on flavor and extremely satisfying.

ALSO SERVE ON
Sukkot, Shabbat, or for Shavuot see variation

DAIRY OR PAREVE

NUTRITIONAL NOTES
(per serving)

207 calories

8g fat (30%)

0mg cholesterol

34g carbohydrates

3g protein

77mg sodium

1.5g fiber

RDA %

0% vitamin A

5% vitamin C

3% calcium

4% iron

MAKES 8 SERVINGS

1 sheet of Pepperidge Farm frozen puff pastry sheets

Baked Apple Slices

1 medium lemon, squeezed into 8 cups water

4 medium apples, preferably greenish Golden Delicious, or other firm variety

1 teaspoon canola oil

3 tablespoons sugar

Filling

½ cup nonfat yogurt

½ cup apple butter

1 teaspoon honey (or more to taste)

1. Preheat the oven to 425°F, with a rack in the middle of the oven.

2. Defrost the sheet of puff pastry for 30 minutes, according to package directions.

3. While the puff pastry is defrosting, peel, halve, core, and cut each apple into slices about 1/16 inch thick, dropping each into the lemon-water as it is cut.

4. Remove the apples from the water and pat them dry. Place the oil in a Pyrex or nonstick pan, add the apple slices, and toss until all are coated

with oil. Spread the slices out so that they're overlapping as little as possible and sprinkle with the sugar.

5. Cover the pan with foil and bake for 15 minutes or until the apples are tender. Remove the pan from the oven. Uncover, and let the apples cool. Reduce the oven temperature to 400°F.

6. Unfold the thawed puff pastry on a floured work surface. If using homemade dough, roll it out on a floured surface to a 10 × 10-inch square, 1/16 inch thick. Cut the dough into four 5-inch circles (I use an inverted storage container top as a guide). Line a cookie sheet with parchment paper, place the pastry on it, and freeze for at least 15 minutes (can be frozen up to 3 months ahead—freeze in a single layer and then transfer to a plastic bag).

7. Bake for 25 to 30 minutes or until nicely browned. Remove the pastries from the parchment paper and place on a rack to cool completely.

8. Make the filling by placing the yogurt, apple butter, and honey in a processor. Blend until completely smooth.

9. To serve, cut each pastry in half horizontally, so that you now have 8 rounds of pastry. Place 1 on each plate with the cut side up. Divide the filling among the 8 pastries (about 2 tablespoons per pastry). Arrange the apples on the filling in a "flower" pattern, with the apples in overlapping concentric circles, slightly rotated, so that centers of the slices in the second row are at the junction of 2 slices of the first row (see Apple Tart Normandy, page 20). Roll up 1 slice for the very center of the flower.

VARIATIONS: Substitute canned or freshly poached figs for the apples. For Shavuot, substitute raspberry jam for the apple butter, and top with fresh raspberries or mixed berries.

Apple Honey Strudel

*B*ecause of the way in which this strudel is assembled, it can be made ahead without getting soggy, a wonderful advantage over traditional strudel. The strudel contains very little butter and no sugar, making it exceptionally light and nonfilling—the perfect dessert for the conclusion of a big holiday meal.

MAKES 10 SERVINGS

ALSO SERVE ON
Sukkot, Shabbat, Yom ha-atzma'ut

DAIRY OR PAREVE

NUTRITIONAL NOTES
(per serving; based on 10 servings plus 2 ends)

174 calories

6g fat (30%)

3mg cholesterol

29g carbohydrates

2.5g protein

150mg sodium

1g fiber

RDA %

1% vitamin A

3% vitamin C

1% calcium

6% iron

½ package defrosted phyllo dough (see directions below)

1 medium lemon

3 medium apples, preferably greenish Golden Delicious or other dry, sweet variety

¼ cup raisins

1 tablespoon cornstarch

½ teaspoon cinnamon

1 tablespoon sliced almonds

1 tablespoon honey

8 whole lowfat graham crackers

2 tablespoons unsalted butter, or unsalted pareve margarine

2 tablespoons canola oil

4 tablespoons powdered sugar

2 tablespoons finely chopped unsalted pecans or walnuts

Powdered sugar, for sprinkling

1. The night before assembling, place the unopened box of phyllo dough in the refrigerator. In the morning, at least 2 hours before using, remove it from the refrigerator and let it stand, unopened, for 2 to 4 hours.

2. Preheat the oven to 375°F, with a rack in the middle of the oven.

3. Squeeze half of the lemon into a large bowl of cold water. Peel, halve, core, and cut the apples into ½-inch chunks. Drop them into the bowl of

Light Jewish Holiday Desserts

lemon-water. Drain well. Add the raisins, cornstarch, cinnamon, almonds, and honey.

4. Process the graham crackers into fine crumbs. Measure out 1 cup and discard the remainder.

5. Place the butter and oil in a microwavable bowl, and heat it on high until the butter melts.

6. Tape together 2 pieces of waxed paper into a section measuring at least 19 × 16 inches. Repeat, twice, so that you have 3 of these sheets. Once the phyllo has been unwrapped, it must be used quickly and kept covered with waxed paper, or it will dry out and crumble like dried leaves. Before opening the box, gather together the apple mixture, graham crumbs, melted butter mixture, powdered sugar in a sprinkler (or a small strainer), nuts, the waxed paper sheets you have assembled, cookie sheet, pastry brush, and a sharp, nonserrated knife.

7. Place 1 of the waxed paper sheets on the counter with the tape side down. Remove the phyllo from the box and unfold it onto the waxed paper. Remove half of the stack, reroll the remainder, and place back in the plastic sleeve, or in a zip-top bag. Refrigerate or refreeze it for another use (if you want to make 2 strudels you can double the recipe, but place the phyllo for the second strudel back in the plastic so that it doesn't dry out).

8. Cover the remaining phyllo with a waxed paper sheet. To prevent the phyllo from drying out, keep it covered whenever you are not removing a leaf of pastry. Place the remaining waxed paper with the long end facing you.

9. Remove 1 phyllo leaf (1 sheet of pastry) and set it on the paper. Brush it with a very light coating of the melted butter mixture. Place another pastry sheet on top of this. Brush it with butter, sprinkle with powdered sugar (about 2 teaspoons), and then sprinkle with about 1½ tablespoons of graham cracker crumbs. Repeat this layering of pastry, butter, sugar, and crumbs 5 more times. The last piece of pastry should be buttered only.

10. Leaving clean 3½ inches along the long side closest to you, and 2 inches at each short end, spread the remaining graham cracker crumbs in a strip, 2½ inches wide, on top of the 7-layer stack.

continued

Rosh Hashanah
and Yom Kippur

11. Sprinkle the nuts on the crumbs, and then place the apples on the nuts in a mound 1½ inches high. Fold the 3½-inch unsprinkled side over the filling and then fold in the short ends. After the short ends are folded in, brush them with butter to keep them moist. Roll up the pastry, lengthwise, jelly roll fashion.

12. Transfer the pastry to a baking sheet. Make diagonal cuts, about ½ inch deep, every 1¼ inches. Brush the strudel with the butter mixture and bake for 35 to 45 minutes, until nicely browned. Set the baking sheet on a rack to cool for 45 minutes.

13. Serve the strudel slightly warm, lightly sprinkled with powdered sugar. Strudel can be made 8 hours in advance if left at room temperature, uncovered. Reheat in a 350°F oven for 15 minutes. Strudel may also be frozen, unbaked. Let the strudel freeze on a tray before wrapping first in foil and then in a plastic bag. Unwrap and bake frozen strudel at 350°F for 30 minutes. Increase the heat to 425°F, and bake for 10 minutes or until golden. Let cool 45 minutes before serving.

VARIATION: If you are not kosher, you can enhance the flavor by using lowfat pecan sandies instead of graham crackers. Add 2 tablespoons of sugar to the apple filling.

Chocolate or Nut Baklava

ALSO SERVE ON
*Yom ha-atzma'ut,
Purim*

**DAIRY OR
PAREVE**

Light Jewish
Holiday Desserts

All peoples of the Middle East and the Mediterranean region, regardless of religion, eat baklava. The recipe may vary depending upon the country of origin, or even by family. Middle Easterners are partial to flavoring their honeyed treats with orange blossom or rose flower water, while Greeks might prefer cinnamon and orange juice. Flower waters taste quite perfumy and are definitely an acquired taste. You might want to taste a syrup flavored with the flowers before pouring it over your baklava. Traditionally, baklava is very high in fat, due to the large quantities of nuts and butter or oil. I've substituted toasted oatmeal and graham crackers for most of the nuts, a combination that gives just the right amount of texture and taste. Chocolate chips and cocoa are a delightful twist on the classic pastry. The baklava must be made one day ahead.

MAKES FORTY 1-INCH DIAMONDS

1 pound phyllo dough, defrosted overnight according to
directions below

Syrup

2¼ cups sugar

1¼ cups water

⅔ cup honey

1 whole cinnamon stick

3 whole cloves

2 tablespoons orange juice, orange liqueur, or 2 teaspoons orange
blossom water mixed with 2 tablespoons water

Filling

1 cup old-fashioned oats

10 (whole) lowfat graham crackers

1 tablespoon cinnamon

2 tablespoons sugar

1 tablespoon unsweetened cocoa powder

2 tablespoons unsalted butter or unsalted pareve margarine

3 tablespoons canola oil

1 cup miniature chocolate chips (or pareve chocolate chips
cut into smaller bits)

continued

NUTRITIONAL
NOTES
(per serving; reflects 1
tablespoon leftover
butter)

126 calories

3 fat (22%)

1mg cholesterol

24g carbohydrates

1g protein

81mg sodium

1g fiber

RDA %

2% vitamin A

1% vitamin C

2% calcium

6% iron

MUST MAKE
1 DAY AHEAD

Rosh Hashanah
and Yom Kippur

1. Leave the phyllo dough in the box and defrost it in the refrigerator overnight. Remove it from the box, but leave it in its inner sleeve, and let sit at room temperature for 2 hours.

2. Preheat the oven to 350°F, with a rack in the middle of the oven.

3. For the syrup, combine the sugar, water, honey, spices, and orange juice in a large pot (the mixture will almost double in volume when it starts to boil). Heat over medium heat to dissolve the sugar. Raise the heat to bring the mixture to a boil, and then reduce the heat to low and allow the syrup to simmer for 10 minutes. Remove from the heat and reserve. The syrup can be made 2 weeks ahead. Refrigerate, but bring to room temperature before using.

4. For the filling, place the oats on a cookie sheet and bake for 5 minutes, until lightly browned. Set aside to cool.

5. Place the grahams in a processor bowl and process until finely ground. Transfer to a large bowl. Stir in the cinnamon, sugar, cocoa powder, and toasted oats.

6. Place the butter and oil in a covered microwavable bowl. Microwave on medium for 2 minutes or until the butter is completely melted.

7. Once the phyllo has been unwrapped, it must be used quickly and kept covered with waxed paper, or it will dry out and crumble like dried leaves. Before opening the box, gather together: waxed paper, large cutting board on which to cut the phyllo, long knife, 8 × 12-inch baking pan (do not use nonstick, as you will have to cut the pastry in the pan), pastry, brush, spray bottle filled with water, the graham mixture, and chocolate chips. Remove the phyllo from the box and inner plastic bag, place it on the cutting board, and unfold it. Cut the pastry stack in half, widthwise (along the line where the pastry has been folded, so that each stack will be 8 inches wide). Using the 8 × 12-inch baking pan as a guide, cut the phyllo to the same size as the pan (removing about ¾ inch from each stack, which can be discarded). Place waxed paper over the phyllo.

8. Slide 1 sheet of phyllo into the bottom of the pan. Brush with the lightest coating of butter mixture that you can (after assembling there should be about 1 tablespoon of butter/oil mixture left, which I have in-

cluded so that you don't run out in the middle of assembly). Slide another sheet of phyllo on top of the first. Brush again, and repeat this process until there are 15 sheets of phyllo in the bottom of the pan. Don't worry about tears. Try alternating sheets so that ripped spots are covered by solid spots from the next sheet.

9. Sprinkle ¾ cup of the graham mixture over the pastry. Sprinkle with ⅓ cup of the chocolate chips. Add 6 sheets of pastry, brushing the butter/oil mixture between each. Sprinkle on another ¾ cup of graham mixture and ⅓ cup of the chocolate chips. Add 6 sheets, brushing between each, add the remaining filling and chocolate chips. Layer on the remaining sheets of pastry, brushing between each leaf with the butter/oil mixture. Do not butter the top sheet of pastry.

Parallel cuts at 1-inch intervals

10. Cut the phyllo diagonally, from one corner of the pan to the opposite corner, and then make parallel cuts at 1-inch intervals on both sides of the first diagonal cut. Hold the pastry down on either side of the knife to make it easier to cut. To make diamonds, the next cuts should be perpendicular to the long side of the pan at 1-inch intervals (you will end up with 40 nice diamonds, plus the end pieces).

Perpendicular cuts at 1-inch intervals

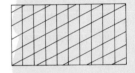

11. Spray the top of the baklava with water. Bake for 55 to 65 minutes, or until golden. Remove the baklava from the oven. Take the cinnamon stick and cloves out of the syrup and immediately pour the room temperature syrup over the baklava. When the baklava is cool, cover it with foil and let it stand at room temperature at least overnight.

12. Store at room temperature, covered with foil, for up to 1 week. The baklava can be frozen before or after baking. Unbaked frozen baklava should be kept frozen and baked for 1 hour at 350°F and 45 minutes more at 325°F or until brown. Frozen baked baklava can be defrosted at room temperature.

VARIATION: For regular baklava, omit the cocoa and chocolate chips. Add ½ cup nuts (I use pecans and almonds, but walnuts and pistachios are also traditional).

Rosh Hashanah
and Yom Kippur

Kadaif or Konafa

Middle Eastern Shredded Wheat Pastries

ALSO SERVE ON
*Shabbat, Yom
ha-atzma'ut*

**DAIRY OR
PAREVE**

**NUTRITIONAL
NOTES**
(per serving)

160 calories

4g fat (30%)

9mg cholesterol

30g carbohydrates

1g protein

41mg sodium

1.5g fiber

RDA %

3% vitamin A

0% vitamin C

1% calcium

4% iron

*T*hese delicacies have many different names, depending on the country of origin. The traditional recipe calls for more than twice as much butter and at least twice as many nuts. The result is a small pastry with a whopping 12 grams of fat. To reduce the butter, special techniques must be used in constructing the pastries, so follow the directions even if you are used to making them differently. Although many shapes are possible with the traditional recipe, this lower-fat version works best as nests or squares. If you like the pastries on the crispy side, serve them within 30 minutes of baking them, and don't make them on humid days. The sweetness can be adjusted by cutting down on the amount of honey in the syrup. Although I prefer to use Grand Marnier in mine, for a real Middle Eastern flavor, use a drop of orange blossom or rose water.

MAKES 40 PIECES

Syrup

3 cups sugar

2 cups water

½ cup honey

1 whole cinnamon stick

*3 tablespoons Grand Marnier liqueur, orange juice, or 1 teaspoon
orange blossom water mixed with 3 tablespoons water*

Nut Filling

¼ cup chopped pecans

½ cup shelled pistachio nuts

¼ cup sugar

Light Jewish
Holiday Desserts

1 teaspoon cinnamon

2 whole lowfat graham crackers, crushed

1 pound kataifi shredded wheat dough (found in Middle Eastern and Sephardic grocery stores)

13 tablespoons unsalted butter or unsalted pareve margarine, melted

1. Preheat the oven to 375°F, with a rack in the middle of the oven. Spray-grease a rimmed cookie sheet.

2. To make the syrup, combine the sugar, water, honey, cinnamon stick, and Grand Marnier in a medium pot. Bring to a simmer over medium heat. Remove and set aside to cool. The syrup can be made 2 weeks ahead and stored in the refrigerator. Bring to room temperature before using.

3. For the nut filling, chop the nuts medium fine and mix them together in a bowl.

4. In another bowl, combine the sugar, cinnamon, and graham cracker crumbs. Set aside.

5. To make the nests, remove the pastry from the box, unfold it, and cut it into sections that are about 6 × 1½ inches. Place the strands back in the plastic bag, and remove 1 section.

6. When making a full-fat recipe of *konafa*, the butter is poured over the entire batch of dough. Because so much butter is used there is no danger of ending up with dry patches. With this lower-fat version, the butter will be poured onto each pastry as it is formed, ensuring that each will be well moistened. Spoon 1 teaspoon of butter over the section, and work the butter into the strands so they are evenly coated. Curl the strands into a little nest, tucking the end under the nest and slightly into the center. Place on the cookie sheet. Press down into the center of the nest and out toward the edges to make a spot for the filling. Cover with foil. When the tray is filled with nests, place ½ teaspoon of nuts into each nest. Top with ½ teaspoon of the crumb mixture (putting the nuts at the bottom will prevent them from overbrowning).

7. Bake for 25 to 35 minutes or until nicely browned. Remove from the oven and immediately spoon a tablespoon of syrup over each nest. Let

cool for 20 to 30 minutes and serve. If the pastries are to be eaten out of hand, they can be served in paper candy or muffin cups. They can be stored at room temperature in a loosely covered tin for 2 days, but are best when freshly made. They can be frozen unbaked, and then baked (do not defrost) at 375°F for 25 to 30 minutes, or they can be frozen already baked—defrost, uncovered, at room temperature.

8. Invariably, you will have strands that are too short for nests, or pieces that just won't work for nesting. Save these to make into bars. Cut the strands into 1-inch pieces. Moisten with butter (about 1 teaspoon per 6 × 1½-inch piece). Spray-grease an 8- or 9-inch square pan. Make a ½-inch layer of dough on the bottom of the pan. Sprinkle on the nut mixture to make a very thin (⅛-inch) layer. Spread on another ½-inch layer of shredded dough. Bake in the middle of the oven for 25 to 35 minutes until nicely browned. Pour on about 1 cup of syrup. Let the pastry cool, turn out onto a board, and cut into small squares.

Ataif bi loz

Nut-Filled Syrian Pancakes

ALSO SERVE ON
Sukkot, Purim

PAREVE

*A*taif *are Syrian pancakes that are eaten by people of various religious traditions. While Muslims might serve them for Ramadan, Jews eat them at Rosh Hashanah, Purim, Sukkot, Chanukah, or Shavuot, depending upon the filling used. There are yeast and baking powder versions, pareve and dairy recipes, those using only flour, and fried variations. There are probably as many variations as there are Syrians! Syrian pancakes, especially those made without*

Light Jewish
Holiday Desserts

milk, tend to be a little mushy. To toughen them, I use bread flour, and add a little salt. If you would like even more texture, use Middle Eastern semolina (smead) instead of Cream of Wheat. For a wonderful dairy yeasted version, please see Syrian Cheese Pancakes (Ataif bi jibn) on page 116.

MAKES 36 PANCAKES, OR 9 SERVINGS

2 large egg whites

2 cups plus 3 tablespoons water

1 cup (125g) bread flour, lightly sprinkled into measuring cup

1 cup Cream of Wheat, or smead (see page 116)

⅛ teaspoon salt

1 teaspoon baking powder

Sugar Syrup

2 cups sugar

1 cup water

2 tablespoons orange juice, or 1 teaspoon orange flower water

Pistachio Filling

⅔ cup finely chopped pistachios, walnuts, or pecans

⅓ cup lowfat graham cracker crumbs (about 2½ crackers)

1. In a food processor, process the egg whites and water just until well mixed. In a bowl, combine the flour, Cream of Wheat, salt, and baking powder. Add it to the processor bowl. Process until the batter is well mixed, about 20 seconds. Transfer the batter to a storage container, cover, and refrigerate for at least 1 hour (can be made 1 day ahead).

2. To make the sugar syrup, combine the sugar, water, and orange juice in a medium pot. Heat and stir over medium heat until the sugar dissolves. Bring to a boil, then reduce the heat and simmer for 5 minutes without

NUTRITIONAL NOTES
(per 4 pancakes with a glazing of sugar syrup; the sodium can be reduced by eliminating the salt)

256 calories

5g fat (19%)

1mg cholesterol

45g carbohydrates

8g protein

134mg sodium

2g fiber

RDA %

1% vitamin A

4% vitamin C

12% calcium

39% iron

Rosh Hashanah and Yom Kippur

stirring. The syrup can be made 2 weeks ahead and refrigerated. Reheat before using.

3. For the filling, in a bowl, combine the nuts, graham cracker crumbs, and ½ cup sugar syrup.

4. Preheat the oven to 350°F, with a rack in the middle of the oven.

5. To make the pancakes, heat a griddle, or nonstick frying pan over high heat until a droplet of water will roll in the pan. Reduce the heat to medium-high. Spoon in the batter by tablespoons to make pancakes that are about 2½ inches in diameter. Do not do more than 4 at a time. Cook the pancakes until the bottoms are well browned and the tops have just barely dulled. Transfer them to a work surface with the uncooked sides up. Place a rounded half-teaspoonful of filling into the center of each pancake. Fold the pancakes in half to form half-moons. Pinch the edges closed. Make and fill all of the pancakes. Set them in a nonstick baking pan (a 9 × 12-inch jelly roll pan is ideal) and cover with foil. They can now be rewarmed in the oven for 10 to 15 minutes, or they can be refrigerated (up to 1 day ahead) and then reheated before eating. After the pancakes have been heated, spoon warm syrup over each pancake. Turn them to coat with the syrup. Transfer the pancakes to individual plates or to a large platter. The remaining syrup can be passed separately.

Two weeks after Rosh Hashanah, on the fifteenth of Tishri, Jews around the world build temporary huts or sukkot within which they will eat, study, pray, and perhaps even sleep for seven days. Sukkot is a time to again remember our deliverance out of the desert. "You shall live in huts seven days . . . in order that future generations may know that I made the Israelite people live in huts when I brought them out of the land of Egypt . . . " (Leviticus 23: 42, 43). It is also a celebration of the autumn harvest. "You shall celebrate the festival of ingathering, at the end of the year, when you gather in your labors out of the field'' (Exodus 23:16). In ancient times, farmers would tend to their crops in outlying areas and return to the village for evening protection, but during the busy fall harvest, they would make temporary huts in the fields. In Leviticus (23:40) we are commanded to gather four kinds of growing things (represented by the *etrog* and *lulav*) and to praise God for what he has given us. In appreciation, we lavishly decorate our *sukkot* with autumn fruits such as citrus (to represent the *etrog*), pears, apples, cranberries, and fruits from Israel. Besides these foods, stuffed foods, such as turnovers or *varenikes* (dumplings), are eaten as a symbol of prosperity.

Make desserts using the following foods:

Citrus fruits to represent the etrog

Fall fruits such as pears, apples, and cranberries

Fruits of Israel such as dates, figs, star fruit, grapes

Stuffed foods such as turnovers, pies, and varenikes

Zucchini Pear Loaf

This delightful "tea cake" is quick and easy to make. The combination of flours and rising agents is designed to provide the best texture and to limit the amount of browning, which otherwise would be excessive. Although the cake has only a small amount of oil, it is moist and tender.

MAKES 14 SERVINGS

12 ounces zucchini (about 3 medium)

1 cup sugar

1 cup (105 grams) sifted cake flour, lightly sprinkled into measuring cup

1⅓ cups (160 grams) all-purpose flour, lightly sprinkled into measuring cup

1 teaspoon cinnamon

1 teaspoon baking powder

1 teaspoon baking soda

¼ teaspoon salt

½ cup coarsely chopped walnuts

2 tablespoons canola oil

⅓ cup pear baby food

2 large eggs, at room temperature

1. Preheat the oven to 325°F, with a rack in the middle of the oven. Spray-grease and flour a glass 9 × 5-inch loaf pan.

2. Peel the zucchini and shred it with a food processor shredding disk. Remove the shredder and insert the metal blade. Pulse-process the zucchini 2 or 3 times, just to shorten the zucchini strands. Measure out

ALSO SERVE ON
Shabbat

PAREVE

NUTRITIONAL
NOTES
(per serving)

169 calories

5g fat (26%)

26mg cholesterol

29g carbohydrates

3g protein

163mg sodium

1g fiber

RDA %

2% vitamin A

3% vitamin C

4% calcium

8% iron

Sukkot

2¼ cups and discard (or save) the remainder. Place the zucchini back in the processor or in a medium bowl. Add ½ cup of the sugar. Set aside.

3. In a mixing bowl, sift together both flours, cinnamon, baking powder, baking soda, and salt. Stir in the remaining ½ cup of sugar and the nuts.

4. In a large mixing bowl, beat the oil, baby food, and eggs until well blended. Stir in the zucchini, making sure to scrape the bowl so that all of the sugar is mixed in.

5. Gently stir the flour mixture into the egg mixture, mixing just until all of the flour is moistened.

6. Spoon the batter into the prepared pan and bake for 75 to 85 minutes or until a toothpick inserted into the center of the cake comes out with a few moist crumbs attached. Cool the cake on a rack for 10 minutes. Loosen the edges with a blunt knife, and then turn the cake out of the pan. Cool the cake completely on a rack. The cake can be made 1 day ahead. Store at room temperature, wrapped in aluminum foil, or freeze for up to 3 months. (Defrost the cake in its foil at room temperature overnight.)

Orange-Cranberry Tea Loaf

*T*his homey loaf has half the fat of a traditional "quick bread." The combination of cranberries, the quintessential autumn fruit, and citrus, symbolic of the etrog, makes it a perfect cake for Sukkot. This great combination also provides a large quantity of vitamin C.

MAKES 10 SERVINGS

½ cup (50 grams) sifted cake flour, lightly sprinkled into
  measuring cup

1⅓ cups (160 grams) all-purpose flour, lightly sprinkled into
  measuring cup

½ teaspoon baking soda

1½ teaspoons baking powder

½ teaspoon salt

1 cup plus 2 tablespoons sugar, divided

⅔ cup fresh cranberries, washed and halved

¼ cup chopped pecans

1 large egg, at room temperature

2 tablespoons canola oil

2 tablespoons pear baby food

⅔ cup orange juice, at room temperature

1. Preheat the oven to 325°F, with a rack in the middle of the oven. Spray-grease a 9 × 5-inch loaf pan.

2. In a large bowl, sift together both flours, baking soda, baking powder, and salt. Stir in 1 cup of the sugar and the cranberries and nuts.

3. In another bowl, blend together the egg, oil, baby food, and orange juice. Stir this into the dry ingredients. Mix well. Pour the batter into the pan.

continued

NUTRITIONAL
NOTES
(per serving)

212 calories

5g fat (22%)

18mg cholesterol

39g carbohydrates

3g protein

230mg sodium

1g fiber

RDA %

1% vitamin A

15% vitamin C

6% calcium

8% iron

Sukkot

4. Sprinkle the remaining 2 tablespoons sugar over the top of the loaf. Bake for 50 to 60 minutes or until a toothpick inserted into the center of the cake comes out with no moist crumbs attached. Cool on a wire rack for 15 minutes and then loosen the edges of the cake and unmold it. Cool completely. For best taste and texture, wrap in plastic wrap and allow to mellow overnight. Do not freeze.

Lemon Mousse Charlotte

This spectacular show-stopper has only 1 gram of fat per serving. Lots of fresh lemon juice creates a burst of tangy flavor. Lemon extract and zest provide a slight bitter edge, but these can be omitted for a more mellow taste. The mousse has been lightened by adding soft meringue, a variation of Alice Medrich's recipe from Chocolate and the Art of Low-Fat Desserts. *The ladyfingers are also delicious by themselves.*

MAKES 16 SERVINGS

Lemon Ladyfingers

1 cup all-purpose flour (120 grams), lightly sprinkled into measuring cup

½ cup plus 1 tablespoon (60 grams) sifted cake flour, lightly sprinkled into measuring cup

1½ teaspoons baking powder

¼ teaspoon salt

7 large egg whites, at room temperature

2 teaspoons fresh lemon juice

¾ cup sugar, divided

4 large eggs yolks, at room temperature

ALSO SERVE ON
Chanukah, Shavuot, Shabbat, Yom ha-atzma'ut

DAIRY

NUTRITIONAL NOTES
(per serving)

184 calories

1g fat (5%)

45mg cholesterol

38g carbohydrates

5g protein

126mg sodium

0g fiber

1 teaspoon lemon extract (optional)

Powdered sugar

Lemon Soaking syrup

⅓ cup water

⅓ cup sugar

⅓ cup fresh lemon juice (about 2 lemons)

Lemon Mousse

1½ teaspoons unflavored kosher gelatin (Kolatin only,
   see page 317), or regular unflavored gelatin

½ cup fresh lemon juice (about 3 lemons)

7 ounces nonfat, sweetened condensed milk

1 cup nonfat yogurt

1 teaspoon finely grated lemon zest (optional)

Soft Marshmallow Meringue

4 large egg whites, at room temperature

½ cup sugar

2 tablespoons water

1. To make the ladyfingers, preheat the oven to 400°F, with the racks in the middle and lower third of the oven. Cut parchment paper to fit two 10 × 15-inch jelly roll pans. Turn the paper curl side up. On each piece of parchment paper, draw a 9-inch circle and 2 rectangles, each 8 × 2½ inches. Place the parchment on the cookie sheets, with the curl side down so that the drawings will not come in contact with the batter. (If you plan to make charlottes or ladyfingers often, you can save a lot of time by using 2 precut 9-inch nonstick Teflon liners and 4 strips, each 8 × 2½ inches, which you cut from a rectangular piece of Teflon. Set them on the cookie sheets or on top of a piece of parchment, and pipe directly onto them. These are a snap to clean and can be used again and again.)

2. Mix together both flours, baking powder, and salt. Set aside.

3. In a clean, grease-free bowl with clean, grease-free beater blades, beat the egg whites on high until the beater marks are just starting to show,

Sukkot

and the eggs are very foamy and thickened. Add 1 teaspoon of the lemon juice. With the beater going, gradually add ¼ cup of the sugar. Beat on high until the egg whites just form stiff peaks but are not dry. Set aside.

4. Place the egg yolks in a large mixer bowl, and beat on high speed, gradually adding the remaining ½ cup sugar. Continue to beat for 2 to 4 minutes, until the egg yolks are pale yellow and very thick. Lower the speed and beat in the lemon extract and the remaining 1 teaspoon of lemon juice. Sift the flour mixture over the egg yolk mixture, but do not stir together. Add ⅓ of the whites to the egg yolk batter and gently fold-stir them in. Gently fold in the remaining whites.

5. Place a ½-inch plain or fluted pastry tip in a large pastry bag. To pipe the circles, start at the perimeter of each and pipe rings or a spiral toward the inside of each circle. To pipe ladyfingers, begin with the tip about ¼ inch from 1 of the lines. As you squeeze the tube, the ladyfinger batter will spread up toward the line and then down toward the other line. Pipe the ladyfingers ⅛ inch from one another. Sprinkle all of the shapes with the powdered sugar. After the sugar disappears, sprinkle them again. Bake for 5 minutes. Switch the pans top to bottom, and continue to bake for another 4 to 5 minutes, or until golden brown. Remove the pans from the oven, slide the parchment onto racks, and let cool completely. (The cakes can be made 1 day ahead, or frozen for 3 months. Wrap tightly in foil for storage.)

6. Peel the cakes off the parchment. Place a cardboard cake round into the bottom of a 10-inch springform pan. Arrange the ladyfingers around the inside perimeter, with the rounded sides pressing against the pan sides. Place 1 round cake into the bottom of the pan. The cake can be trimmed with scissors, if necessary. It should fit snugly against the lady-fingers. Remove the cake, and trim the second cake to the same size. Re-place 1 of the cake layers inside the pan to hold the ladyfingers in place.

7. To make the soaking syrup, combine the water, sugar, and lemon juice in a small saucepan. Stir over medium heat until the sugar dissolves. Re-move the syrup from the heat.

8. To make the mousse, place the gelatin in a small microwavable bowl. Stir in ¼ cup lemon juice, and let the mixture stand for 5 minutes, to

soften. Heat the gelatin mixture in a microwave oven, on high power, for 45 seconds. Stir the liquid and check to see if the gelatin is dissolved. If not, reheat in 10-second bursts until it is dissolved.

9. In a large bowl, stir together the condensed milk, yogurt, and lemon zest. Stir the gelatin into the milk mixture, a little at a time. Stir in the remaining ¼ cup lemon juice. Set the bowl near the stove so that you can stir it as you make the meringue.

10. To make the soft marshmallow meringue, fill a large skillet with 1 inch of water. Bring the water to a simmer. In a small metal bowl, whisk the egg whites with the sugar and 2 tablespoons water. Have a rubber scraper, an instant-read thermometer, a timer, another mixing bowl, and a beater near the stove.

11. Place the bowl with the egg white mixture into the simmering water, and rapidly stir with the rubber scraper for 20 seconds. Remove the bowl from the simmering water and check the temperature of the egg white mixture. The temperature needs to be 160°F to kill salmonella, but not much higher, or the eggs will overcook. The time that it takes depends upon the type of bowl and pot that are being used—I've had it take from 20 to 80 seconds using different types of pots and bowls. If the eggs are not yet hot enough, heat them for 10 seconds more. Remove the bowl from the water, dip the thermometer into the boiling water, and then retest. Repeat the process if necessary. As soon as the eggs reach 160°F, transfer them to a cool bowl and beat at medium-high speed until they are just barely stiff (overheating the eggs will make the mousse too spongy).

12. Stir 1 cup of the meringue into the milk mixture to lighten it, and then fold in the remaining meringue.

13. With a pastry brush, pat the syrup onto the cakes and ladyfingers. Use most of the syrup, going back over the cakes as the syrup is absorbed. Spoon half of the mousse into the cake pan. Place the second cake on top of the mousse, and press lightly to level it. Add the remaining mousse. Gently shake the pan from side to side to level the mousse. Refrigerate overnight. When the mousse is set, the cake can be covered with foil. Garnish the cake with a candied lemon rose, page 302. The cake can be made 2 days in advance, or frozen for 3 months.

Sukkot

Maple Baked Apples

Baked apples are not only delicious as a dessert but can be served as a sweet component of any meal. I recommend Fuji, Golden Delicious, or Stayman apples because they are firm varieties that hold up very well when baked. Granny Smiths, which most people use for pies, exploded when I baked them, leaving me with wonderful applesauce! If you haven't ever tried maple syrup with apples, you'll be thrilled. This dessert is great for Sukkot because apples are at their very best during the fall harvest season.

MAKES 4 SERVINGS

4 medium apples, medium-firm to firm variety such as Fuji, Stayman, or Golden Delicious

¼ cup dried raisins or currants

2 tablespoons chopped pecans

¼ cup pure maple syrup

½ teaspoon cinnamon

⅓ cup apple cider

1. Preheat the oven to 350°F, with a rack in the middle of the oven.

2. Use a melon baller to core the apples, leaving ½ inch of apple at the bottom and forming a ½- to ¾-inch cavity in the apple. Remove a 1-inch strip of peel from the top of the apples. Place the apples in a baking dish.

3. In a small bowl, combine the raisins, nuts, maple syrup, and cinnamon. Fill the cavities with this mixture. Use some of the maple syrup left in the bottom of the bowl to brush the tops of the apples. Pour the apple cider into the bottom of the pan. Cover with foil and bake the apples for 30 to 50 minutes depending on the variety and size of the apples used. Test for doneness by piercing the apple with a knife to see if it is tender

ALSO SERVE ON
Rosh Hashanah,
Tu b'Shevat,
Yom ha-atzma'ut,
Shabbat

PAREVE

NUTRITIONAL NOTES
(per serving)

174 calories

2g fat (8%)

0mg cholesterol

42g carbohydrates

1g protein

3mg sodium

4g fiber

RDA %

1% vitamin A

13% vitamin C

3% calcium

5% iron

Light Jewish
Holiday Desserts

(the degree of tenderness is a matter of taste). Be careful not to push the knife in too far, or the syrup in the cavity will leak out.

4. Cool the apples to lukewarm, and serve with the juices and a little milk or frozen yogurt. Baked apples are also delicious cold.

VARIATIONS: Use a different kind of nut, or substitute ground cookies for the nuts. Substitute dried cranberries or dried cherries for the raisins. The spice can also be altered. Ginger, nutmeg, and clove are commonly used. The liquid in the bottom of the pan can also be diet ginger ale, water, orange juice, or raspberry juice.

Pear Varenikes (Kreplach) in Chocolate Sauce

This dessert is traditional for Hoshanah Rabbah (the seventh day of Sukkot), Yom Kippur, and Purim. When filled with cheese, these are also suitable for Chanukah or Shavuot. Pasta may not seem like a very interesting dessert, but prepared this way it is quite attractive, with a simple elegance. Rather than the traditional 3-inch half-moon shape, these varenikes are giant 6-inch rounds. The top dough forms pleats, and when cooked, the sealed edges around the pear create a ruffle, making the varenikes look like hats. This is a dessert that will surely stimulate conversation! The recipe is very easy and quick to make, because eggroll wrappers are used instead of homemade dough. Those cooks who prefer to make everything from scratch can use the homemade recipe, included with Peach Melba Varenikes, on page 254. The chocolate sauce has a richer flavor than store-bought fat-free

ALSO SERVE ON
*Yom Kippur,
Shabbat, and filled
with cheese on
Chanukah or Shavuot*

PAREVE OR
DAIRY

Sukkot

47

272 calories

2g fat (7.5%)

5mg cholesterol

60g carbohydrates

6g protein

346mg sodium

4g fiber

RDA %

1% vitamin A

5% vitamin C

6% calcium

11% iron

chocolate sauce and contains no preservatives. It can be eaten cold or warm. If you need to save time, the varenikes will still be delicious with store-bought, fat-free sauce.

MAKES 6 SERVINGS

Chocolate Sauce

¼ cup Dutch-processed cocoa, preferably Droste

2 tablespoons (½ ounce) chopped semisweet chocolate or chocolate chips

1 teaspoon cornstarch

1 teaspoon sugar

½ cup skim milk or water

¼ cup light corn syrup

½ teaspoon vanilla extract

Varenikes

3 ripe Bosc pears

1 medium lemon, squeezed into 4 cups cold water

2 teaspoons cinnamon

1 tablespoon sugar

½ teaspoon nutmeg

2 whole lowfat graham crackers, crushed

12 eggroll wrappers

Cinnamon-sugar for sprinkling

1. Place the cocoa and chocolate in the top of a double boiler. Set it aside.

2. Fill the bottom of the double boiler with 2 inches of water. Set over high heat, and bring it to a boil. Cover the pot, reduce the heat to low, and keep the water warm.

3. Combine the cornstarch and sugar in a small pot. Gradually add the milk, stirring to make the mixture smooth. Stir in the corn syrup. Place the pot over medium heat and stir until the sugar has dissolved. Increase

the heat to medium-high (high if using water) and continue to cook and stir until the mixture comes to a boil. Cook for 30 seconds.

4. Remove the pot from the heat. Gradually pour the hot liquid into the cocoa, stirring to make it smooth. Set the pot over the boiling water, cover, and let it cook for 1 minute. Stir in the vanilla. Strain the mixture through a medium-mesh strainer into a storage container. Let the mixture cool for a few minutes, cover, and let it cool to room temperature. Refrigerate until cold. (The sauce will continue to thicken for about 6 hours.) Can be made 2 weeks ahead.

5. To make the *varenikes,* fill a pasta or soup pot with water and add a pinch of salt. Cover and bring to a boil. Reduce the heat to keep the water at a simmer.

6. Peel, halve, and core the pears. Dip the pears in the lemon-water. Pat dry with paper towels. Cut off the stem end of the pears so that they are round, like apples. Slice ⅛ inch off the flat side of each pear to reduce the thickness of the pears.

7. In a small bowl, combine the cinnamon, sugar, and nutmeg, and sprinkle this onto the pears. Sprinkle the crushed grahams on both sides of the pears.

8. Cut 6 eggroll wrappers into 6-inch rounds (I use the metal box that my cookie cutters come in, but a storage container also works well). Place a pear half in the center of each wrapper rounded side up. Using your finger, or a pastry brush, moisten the perimeter of each round with water. Cover each pear with one of the remaining whole eggroll wrappers. It will form several pleats as it falls over the pear. Place the cutter over the pear and cut the top wrapper to the same size as the bottom. Press down on the edges to seal. If any of the pleats are not sealed, wet them slightly and pinch to seal. *Varenikes* can be made 2 hours ahead. To store, place in a lightly floured pan and cover tightly with plastic wrap.

9. Bring the water back to a rolling boil. Gently slide in the *varenikes* and cook for 3 to 4 minutes until the dough is translucent. Remove the pasta with a slotted spoon and place 1 on each dessert plate. Sprinkle the *varenikes* with cinnamon-sugar, and drizzle about a tablespoon of chocolate sauce over each dumpling. Serve immediately.

ALSO SERVE ON
Shabbat, Tu b'Shevat
(add nuts)

PAREVE

NUTRITIONAL NOTES (PER SERVING)

175 calories

3g fat (14%)

0mg cholesterol

38g carbohydrates

1g protein

30mg sodium

3g fiber

RDA %

4% vitamin A

6% vitamin C

1% calcium

3% iron

Sukkot

49

Apple Cranberry Cornmeal Cobbler

ALSO SERVE ON
Shabbat

DAIRY

NUTRITIONAL NOTES
(per serving)

228 calories

3g fat (13%)

49g carbohydrates

4mg cholesterol

3g protein

226mg sodium

4g fiber

RDA %

2% vitamin A

13% vitamin C

15% calcium

8% iron

I love cranberries for Sukkot, as they are one of the few fruits available exclusively in the fall. Living in the New World, I think it is also appropriate to include cornmeal in the cobbler batter.

MAKES 9 SERVINGS

1 small lemon

8 medium apples, mixed varieties (I use Fuji, Stayman, Golden Delicious, and Granny Smith)

1 cup fresh cranberries

¾ cup sugar

2 teaspoons cinnamon

1 tablespoon cornstarch

Cobbler Batter

1 cup (105 grams) sifted cake flour, lightly sprinkled into measuring cup

⅓ cup (40 grams) white cornmeal (not self-rising)

6 teaspoons sugar, divided

1 teaspoon baking powder

1 teaspoon baking soda

3 tablespoons (1.5 ounces) lowfat cream cheese, such as Philadelphia ⅓ Less Fat

¾ cup nonfat or lowfat buttermilk

1 tablespoon canola oil

½ teaspoon vanilla extract

Light Jewish
Holiday Desserts

1. Preheat the oven to 425°F, with a rack in the middle of the oven. Have ready an 8 × 10-inch baking pan.

2. Squeeze the lemon into a large bowl. Peel, halve, core, and cut the apples into ¾-inch chunks. Toss the apples with the lemon juice. Wash the cranberries and remove any soft or decayed ones, and any other debris. Stir them along with the sugar, cinnamon, and cornstarch into the apples. Spoon mixture into the pan. Cover with aluminum foil (shiny side down) and bake for 30 minutes.

3. While the apples are baking, measure out the ingredients for the cobbler batter, but do not make it yet. When the apples are done, remove them from the oven and uncover.

4. To make the cobbler batter, mix the flour, cornmeal, 5 teaspoons of sugar, baking powder, and baking soda in a large bowl. Using a pastry blender or 2 knives, cut the cream cheese into the dry ingredients until the pieces are about the size of sunflower seeds. Mix together the buttermilk, oil, and vanilla extract. Make a well in the center of the flour and pour in the buttermilk mixture. Stir until the flour is completely moistened.

5. Drop the batter by tablespoonfuls over the fruit and then spread the batter to almost completely cover the fruit (if using a larger pan, the batter will not cover the apples but should be spread about ⅛ inch thick). Sprinkle the remaining teaspoon of sugar over the batter. Bake for 20 to 25 minutes or until the cobbler is nicely browned. Remove it from the oven and cool until the cobbler is just barely warm, about 30 minutes. The cobbler can be made 1 day ahead. Cover with foil and bake at 350°F until just warm, 10 to 15 minutes. Serve with frozen yogurt, if desired.

VARIATIONS: If you want to eliminate the extra step of cooking the fruit first, you cannot use fresh cranberries, as they are too firm and tart when not cooked long enough. Instead, substitute dried cranberries, dried cherries, or fresh grapes. The apples should also be cut into smaller pieces, and the firmer varieties, such as Fuji, should not be used. Cobbler topping also works well with pears, berries, or peaches (see Summer Fruit Cobbler, on page 284).

Sukkot

Deep-Dish Pear-Cherry Gratin

ALSO SERVE ON
*Shabbat, for Tu
b'Shevat add nuts*

PAREVE

**NUTRITIONAL
NOTES**
(per serving)

175 calories

3g fat (14%)

0mg cholesterol

38g carbohydrates

1g protein

30mg sodium

3g fiber

RDA %

4% vitamin A

6% vitamin C

1% calcium

3% iron

*This is not a true gratin, because the fruit layer is very thick.
However, the character of the dessert is closer to a gratin than to a
brown Betty, a similar dessert that has interior bread crumbs as well as
crumbs on top. To maximize crunch, the buttered bread crumbs are
baked separately and sprinkled on the fruit just before serving. Dried
tart cherries and a hint of vanilla provide the unusual flavoring.*

MAKES 4 SERVINGS

3 medium Bosc pears, firm but ripe

½ medium lemon, squeezed into 4 cups cold water

3 tablespoons granulated sugar

⅛ teaspoon cinnamon

1 tablespoon cornstarch

⅛ teaspoon vanilla

¼ cup dried tart cherries

Bread Topping

3 slices Vienna bread, or other pareve, nonspongy white bread

2 teaspoons firmly packed light brown sugar

2 teaspoons canola oil

1. Preheat the oven to 350°F, with a rack in the middle of the oven.

2. Peel, halve, core, and cut the pears into ½-inch chunks. Place the pears
into the lemon-water as each one is cut. Drain the pears and place them
back in the empty bowl. Stir in the sugar, cinnamon, cornstarch, vanilla,
and cherries. Spoon the fruit into 4 individual ramekins or into an ovenproof serving dish. Cover with foil, and bake the fruit for 30 to 40 minutes, or until tender. Remove from the oven, and let cool until warm.

(The fruit can be baked up to 1 day ahead. Cover and refrigerate. Warm for 15 minutes in a 350°F oven before continuing with the recipe.)

3. While the fruit is cooling (or just before reheating), prepare the topping. Cut off the bread crusts, tear the bread into large pieces and place in a food processor bowl. Pulse-process until the bread is in crumbs. There should be some small crumbs and some larger pieces in about ⅛-inch cubes.

4. Toss the bread crumbs with the brown sugar. Sprinkle with oil and toss again with a fork until the crumbs are lightly coated with oil. Place the crumbs on a foil-lined cookie sheet and bake at 350°F for 10 minutes, or until nicely browned. Sprinkle the crumbs over the top of the fruit, and serve immediately. If you prefer crumbs that are not as crispy, sprinkle the baked crumbs on the fruit 5 minutes before serving.

Apple Plum Rice Crisp

NUTRITIONAL NOTES
(per serving)

200 calories

4g fat (15%)

5mg cholesterol

44g carbohydrates

2g protein

81mg sodium

4g fiber

RDA %

13% vitamin A

30% vitamin C

5% calcium

5% iron

For a casual dessert, nothing beats warm fruit crisp. So easy and quick to prepare, it can be made on a moment's notice. Hard plums cook into slightly tart, soft fruits that make a wonderful counterpoint to the sweet, toothy apples. High in vitamin C and fiber, this is a dessert you will want to serve often.

MAKES 6 SERVINGS

Crispy Rice Topping

1 cup Rice Krispies cereal

1 tablespoon unsalted butter, or unsalted pareve margarine

1 teaspoon canola oil

1 tablespoon all-purpose flour

1 tablespoon firmly packed light brown sugar

½ teaspoon cinnamon

Apple-Plum Filling

½ small lemon

4 medium apples, preferably greenish Golden Delicious, or other medium-firm variety

10 prune plums or 5 medium purple plums

½ teaspoon cinnamon

Pinch of allspice and nutmeg

⅓ cup firmly packed light brown sugar

1 to 3 teaspoons cornstarch

1. Preheat the oven to 350°F, with a rack in the middle of the oven. Line a cookie sheet with parchment paper or a nonstick Teflon liner.

2. Place the Rice Krispies in a medium bowl. Place the butter in a small microwavable bowl, cover, and microwave until melted (or melt in a pot on the stove). Add the oil to the butter and pour the mixture over the rice cereal. Toss lightly to coat the cereal.

3. In a small bowl, mix together the flour, brown sugar, and cinnamon. Sprinkle onto the cereal. Toss again to coat the cereal with the flour mixture. Spread the cereal on the prepared cookie sheet. Bake for 8 to 10 minutes, until the crumbs are golden brown. Set aside to cool. The crumbs can be stored in a covered container for up to 3 days.

4. To make the filling, squeeze the lemon into a large bowl. Peel, core, and cut the apples into ½-inch chunks. Toss the apples with the lemon juice. Cut the plums off the stones into ½-inch chunks. Mix them into the apples, with the cinnamon, spices, and brown sugar. Add the smaller quantity of cornstarch if you like your fruit very juicy, and more for a firmer dessert. Spoon the fruit into an 8-inch square baking pan.

5. Cover the fruit with foil, and bake for 45 to 50 minutes, or until the fruit is as tender as you like it. For best flavor let the fruit cool at least 30 minutes, preferably several hours, and up to 1 day ahead (refrigerate, covered, if serving the next day).

6. If the fruit is no longer warm when you want to serve it, reheat it at 350°F for about 15 minutes, or until heated through. Spoon the fruit into individual bowls, and sprinkle with the topping. The topping will be very crunchy. If you prefer it softer, you can let the topping sit on the fruit for 5 minutes before serving. For a dairy dessert, the crisp tastes great with a small scoop of nonfat vanilla ice cream.

VARIATIONS: Use with other crumb toppings, such as Streusel (Crumb) Topping on page 296 or Graham Cracker Topping on page 295.

Cranberry Pear *Fluden*

ALSO SERVE ON
Shabbat

DAIRY

NUTRITIONAL
NOTES
(per 2-inch square)

99 calories

3g fat (28%)

11mg cholesterol

17g carbohydrates

1g protein

31mg sodium

1g fiber

RDA %

1% vitamin A

7% vitamin C

12% calcium

2% iron

F luden, *a Franco-German Jewish pastry from the tenth century, means "flat cake." Typically it is made from a rich pastry dough or yeast dough. It may have many layers, or like this one, may be simply a flat, rectangular pie. A traditional* fluden *may have 12 to 30 grams of fat, depending on how many layers of pastry there are and what is in the filling. This rich-tasting, yet lowfat dough is a variation of one used by my grandmother, Ray Wantuck. It creates a wonderful* fluden *that is easy to cut into small pick-up-size squares but is low enough in fat to serve in large squares, as a plated dessert. If your kids don't enjoy cranberries, try substituting dried cherries or raisins.*

MAKES 20 TO 35 SERVINGS

Cranberry-Pear Filling
6 medium Bosc pears, ripe but firm
1 medium lemon, juiced
2 cups fresh cranberries, washed and picked over
2 tablespoons orange juice
¾ cup sugar
3 tablespoons cornstarch
1 recipe Sour Cream Muerbe Teig Pastry, page 294
Powdered sugar

1. Preheat the oven to 400°F, with a rack in the middle of the oven. Have a 9 × 13-inch baking pan ready.

2. Peel, core, and chop the pears into large chunks. Toss the pears with the lemon juice. Place the pears in a food processor bowl. Add the cranberries,

orange juice, sugar, and cornstarch. Pulse-process until the fruit is coarsely chopped. Spoon the fruit into the baking pan, cover with foil, and bake for 30 minutes. Remove the pan from the oven, uncover it, and let the fruit cool to room temperature. Refrigerate until cold, or overnight.

3. The next day, preheat the oven to 425°F. Spray-grease a 10 × 15-inch jelly roll pan.

4. Between sheets of floured plastic wrap, roll 1 piece of dough into a 12 × 17-inch rectangle. Transfer the dough to the prepared pan. Spread the reserved cold filling on the dough.

5. Roll the second piece of dough to the same size, and place on top of the filling. Press the edges of the bottom and top crust together. Cut off excess dough so that it is just even with the edge of the pan. Pinch the edges again and roll them forward slightly to seal the crust. Prick the dough all over with a knife tip (I make 6 rows of 5 slits).

6. Bake for 20 to 25 minutes or until the crust is nicely browned all over. Remove the pastry from the oven and let it cool in the pan, on a wire rack, until completely cool. Sprinkle the pastry with powdered sugar and cut it into 2-inch squares. If the pastry is not part of a dessert buffet, it can be served warm. To present the whole *fluden*, transfer it to a serving platter using a jumbo spatula or a rimless cookie sheet. If you do not have either of these, consider lining the pan with foil, so that you can lift the pastry out of the pan, and then slide the pastry off the foil onto a decorative platter. The *fluden* can also be cut into 4-inch squares and plated in the kitchen. Serve with frozen yogurt, if desired.

Brandied Nutmeg Pear Tart

ALSO SERVE ON
Chanukah, Shavuot, Shabbat

DAIRY

NUTRITIONAL NOTES
(per serving; reflects 84 grams of trimmed-off dough)

187 calories

7g fat (33%)

40mg cholesterol

28g carbohydrates

3g protein

91mg sodium

1g fiber

RDA %

6% vitamin A

3% vitamin C

2% calcium

6% iron

A thin layer of brandied custard makes this tart extremely satisfying. Usually this type of filling contains up to ¼ cup of butter, and sometimes even cream. Neither is necessary for good taste and texture. The nutritional information takes into account excess dough trimmed from the tart, so be sure to follow the rolling instructions, or you will end up with more fat than you want.

MAKES 8 SERVINGS

One 9-inch tart shell, page 290

Pear Topping

2 large Bosc or Bartlett pears, firm but ripe

1 medium lemon, squeezed into 4 cups cold water

1 teaspoon sugar

Brandied Nutmeg Custard

1 tablespoon all-purpose flour

¼ cup sugar

¼ cup whole milk (do not use skim)

1 large egg

¼ teaspoon fresh nutmeg, plus additional for garnish

¼ teaspoon vanilla extract

1 teaspoon cognac, brandy, or rum

2 tablespoons apricot jam (optional)

1. Make and prebake the tart shell.

2. Preheat the oven to 425°F, with a rack in the middle of the oven.

Light Jewish Holiday Desserts

3. Peel the pears and place in the lemon-water. One at a time, cut the pears in half lengthwise, remove the core, and cut them, lengthwise, into 1/16-inch slices. Place the slices in the lemon-water as each pear is cut. Drain the pears and blot dry with paper towels. Transfer to a Pyrex or nonstick baking pan. Sprinkle with sugar, cover with foil, and bake for 15 to 30 minutes (depending on the ripeness of the pears and variety used) until tender. Remove the pan from the oven, lift off the foil, and let the pears cool until they can be handled.

4. Reduce the oven temperature to 350°F.

5. To make the custard, combine the flour and sugar in a medium bowl. In a separate bowl, whisk together the milk, egg, nutmeg, vanilla, and cognac. Gradually stir the milk mixture into the flour mixture to form a smooth batter. Pour this into the baked crust.

6. Arrange the pears over the filling with the fat tips of the pear slices perpendicular to the perimeter of the pie and with the slices overlapping each other. The pear slices should cover most of the custard.

7. Make another ring of pears using the shorter slices.

8. Fill the center with a rolled sliver of pear. Generously grate fresh nutmeg over the tart. Place the tart on an insulated cookie sheet (or 2 nested sheets) and set in the oven.

9. Bake the tart for 30 minutes or until the custard is set. Remove from the oven and let the tart cool on a rack. The tart can be eaten at room temperature, but I prefer to chill it for at least 1 hour before serving. If making more than 2 hours ahead, heat the apricot jam with about 1/2 teaspoon water, strain if very lumpy, and brush over the pears.

VARIATION: Ginger Pear Tart—omit the vanilla, cognac, and nutmeg. Sauté 1 tablespoon of freshly grated ginger in 2 teaspoons butter until the butter browns. Strain the butter into the egg/milk mixture of the filling. Top with the pears. Sprinkle the pears with 1 teaspoon of sugar mixed with 1/8 teaspoon powdered ginger.

First ring of pears

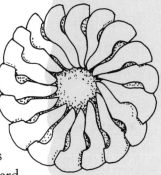

Second ring of pears and rolled center piece

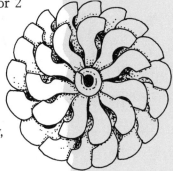

Sukkot

Apple Rhubarb Lattice Pie

NUTRITIONAL
NOTES
(per serving; reflects 110
grams of trimmed-off
dough)

315 calories

8g fat (23%)

8mg cholesterol

59g carbohydrates

4g protein

112mg sodium

2g fiber

RDA %

4% vitamin A

6% vitamin C

3% calcium

9% iron

Rhubarb appears sporadically throughout the year but is usually available around Sukkot. It adds color and an interesting twist to a standard apple pie. When apples are baked uncovered (as in a lattice pie), they tend to toughen somewhat. This provides a nice contrast to the soft apples and rhubarb within. To ensure a crisp bottom crust, partially bake the crust and then fill it and top with the lattice. The results will be worth the extra effort. The Nut Pastry Crust is a little more crumbly and harder to work with than the Tart Pastry Dough. To compensate, follow the directions for a simple lattice top rather than a woven one.

MAKES 8 SERVINGS

1 recipe **Tart Pastry Dough**, for lattice pie, page 290, refrigerated

or

1 recipe **Nut Pastry Crust**, for lattice pie, page 292, refrigerated

1 medium lemon

5 medium apples, preferably greenish Golden Delicious, or other medium-firm variety

4 ounces rhubarb (about 1 large stalk)

1 cup sugar

3 tablespoons cornstarch

½ teaspoon cinnamon

1. Spray a 9-inch pie plate with cooking spray.

2. Remove the larger piece of dough from the refrigerator. In a floured, jumbo zip-top bag, roll it into a 12-inch circle, about 1/16 inch thick. Flip the bag over periodically while rolling, liberally flouring each side of the dough. Transfer the dough to the pie plate, and press it firmly into and up the sides of the pan. Using scissors, trim the dough 1/16 inch past the rim. (Add the trimmings to the second, smaller piece of dough in the refrigerator.) With a finger on each side of the dough, make a decorative edge, by pressing the dough together to make a slightly raised rim. (The idea is to have a nice rim but to use less dough than with a traditionally pinched crust.) Freeze the crust for 15 minutes.

3. Preheat the oven to 375°F, with a rack in the middle of the oven.

4. Place a piece of heavy-duty foil into the pie so that it extends a couple of inches higher than the plate. Fill it with dried beans, pie weights, or a metal dog chain (purchased especially for use in the kitchen). Bake the crust for 15 minutes. Remove the foil and weights. If the dough is still shiny and raw-looking, bake a few more minutes. Let the crust cool to room temperature, about 10 minutes.

5. To make the filling, squeeze half of the lemon into a bowl of cold water. Peel, halve, core, and cut the apples into 1/4-inch slices, dropping each into the lemon-water as it is cut.

6. Peel the rhubarb with a vegetable peeler. If using a large stalk, halve it lengthwise and then cut into 1/4-inch chunks. Thinner stalks can just be cut into chunks. Drain the apples well. Place them in a large bowl with the rhubarb, sugar, cornstarch, and cinnamon. Squeeze the remaining lemon half over the mixture. Mix well.

7. Repeat the rolling process (in step 2) for the second piece of dough. Use a fluted pastry cutter or a knife to cut the dough into 1/2-inch strips.

8. Fill the pie with the filling. It will be well mounded in the pan.

continued

Sukkot

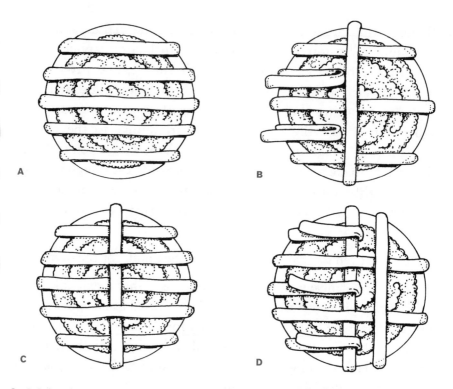

A B

C D

9. Make the woven-lattice crust as follows: Place 5 strips evenly spaced across the top of the pie (A). Fold strips #2 and #4 in half. Place a long strip in the middle of the pie, perpendicular to the other strips (B). Unfold strips #2 and #4 so that they are now on top of the middle strip (C). Fold back strips #1, #3, and #5, and add a second perpendicular strip, about ½ inch from the center strip (D). Unfold strips #1, #3, and #5. Continue folding back alternate strips and weaving in the cross strips, doing first one side of the pie and then the other.

10. Cut off the strips even with the edge of the pan.

11. Alternatively, for a simple lattice, place the 5 strips in one direction, and at right angles place the remaining 5 strips over the other strips.

12. Put the pie on a cookie sheet. Bake for 45 minutes to 1 hour, until the apples are as tender as you like them. Cover the top with foil if the lattice is getting too brown. Let cool for 30 to 45 minutes before eating. The pie can be made 3 hours ahead. Before serving, reheat at 350°F for 15 minutes. Serve with nonfat frozen yogurt, if desired.

Key Lime Pie

This is one of those quirky desserts that people either love or hate. Although I rarely use food coloring, I do use it in Key Lime Pie—the color is always a topic of lively conversation. True Key limes are not readily available, but supermarket limes make a fine pie and are preferable to bottled Key lime juice. Traditional Key lime pie has twice the fat of this trimmed-down version. The reduction in egg yolk makes for a softer filling, which we actually prefer.

MAKES 10 SERVINGS

1 Graham Cracker Crust for 9-inch pie plate, page 295

3 large egg yolks

1 large egg white

1 tablespoon finely grated lime zest

One 14-ounce can nonfat sweetened condensed milk

½ cup fresh lime juice (4 to 6 limes)

Green food coloring (optional)

¼ cup whipping cream, whipped to stiff peaks with 1 teaspoon powdered sugar (garnish)

1. Preheat the oven to 325°F, with a rack in the center of the oven. Bake the Graham Cracker Crust for about 15 minutes, until lightly browned and fragrant. Transfer the pan to a wire rack and let cool to room temperature, about 20 minutes.

2. In a medium mixer bowl, place the yolks, egg white, and zest. Beat on low speed for 2 minutes. Beat in the condensed milk and then the lime juice. If you are unhappy with the color, add a couple of drops of green food coloring.

continued

Sukkot

3. Pour the lime filling into the crust. Bake until the center is set, about 20 minutes. The pie will ripple slightly, when it is moved. Let the pie cool on a wire rack. Refrigerate until well chilled, at least 3 hours, or up to 1 day ahead. (Can be covered with oil-sprayed plastic wrap laid directly on the filling.)

4. For the garnish, place the whipped cream in a pastry bag with a tiny fluted tip. Pipe parallel lines or a crosshatch design on the pie. The cream adds only 1 gram of fat per serving, but there is so little of it that the dessert won't suffer much if whipped cream substitute is used.

Little Lemon Tarts

Lemon lovers will swoon over these refreshing tarts. They are a perfect treat to have out in the sukkah or to bring to Temple. I like to serve them as part of a dessert buffet table. If you want to serve them alone, you might want to make them in 2½- to 3-inch individual tart pans. The filling is too soft to be used in a 9-inch tart pan, as it will not hold slices nicely.

MAKES 24 TARTS

Tart Pastry Dough, page 290, refrigerated at least 15 minutes

2 large eggs

1 cup sugar

¼ cup (25 grams) sifted cake flour, lightly sprinkled into measuring cup

1 teaspoon finely grated lemon zest

½ cup fresh squeezed lemon juice (about 3 lemons)

Powdered sugar (garnish)

ALSO SERVE ON
Shabbat, Yom ha-atzma'ut

DAIRY OR PAREVE

NUTRITIONAL NOTES
(per tart; does not include excess filling)

69 calories

3.5g fat (32%)

14mg cholesterol

11g carbohydrates

1g protein

27mg sodium

0g fiber

Light Jewish Holiday Desserts

1. Spray 2 mini-muffin pans with cooking spray.

2. Sprinkle flour inside a jumbo zip-top bag and place the dough into the bag. Using a rolling pin, roll the dough 1/16 inch thick. Cut off the top of the bag. Sprinkle dough with flour, flip the plastic over onto a floured cutting board. Peel the plastic off the dough, and sprinkle the dough with more flour if it is sticky. Cut the dough into 2½-inch rounds. For traditionally shaped tarts, push the rounds into the muffin cups so that dough is pressed flush up against the sides of the tin. The tarts can also be made with the top edge ruffled. Hold the dough round along its perimeter and then push toward the center of the muffin cup, and it will naturally form pleats or ruffles. Instead of pressing these out as you would normally, leave the pleats, and add some extra ones if the pleats have not formed all around the top of the tarts. The tarts will all be different and they will have a homemade look to them. Freeze the tarts for 15 minutes.

3. Preheat the oven to 375°F, with a rack in the middle of the oven. Set the pans on a cookie sheet and place in the oven. Bake the tarts for 8 to 10 minutes or until slightly browned. Remove the cookie sheet to a cooling rack and let it cool while you make the filling.

4. Reduce the oven temperature to 325°F.

5. Place the eggs in a medium-sized bowl and whisk lightly to blend. Gradually whisk in the sugar. Whisk-stir in the flour and lemon zest. Stir in the lemon juice. Spoon a teaspoonful of the filling into each tart (fill the tarts up to the top—there will be excess filling).

6. Bake the tarts for 8 to 10 minutes, just until the filling is set. Let the tart pans completely cool on a cooling rack. The tarts should lift right out of the pans. Serve at room temperature or cool. Sprinkle them with powdered sugar before serving. Can be made 1 day ahead, or frozen. (Defrost frozen tarts at room temperature for about 30 minutes or in the refrigerator for several hours.)

Sukkot

Simkat Torah, celebrated on the eighth or

ninth day after Sukkot (eighth in Israel,

and ninth elsewhere) is a joyous festival

that developed in the Middle Ages when it became

customary to read the entire Torah each year. At

Simkat Torah, the last chapters of Deuteronomy are

read, and then Genesis is begun again. The Torah

scrolls are removed from the ark, and the

congregants circle around the synagogue in joyful

song and dance. To honor the Torah, foods that are

rolled and look like scrolls are often eaten. Round

cookies and cakes represent the "circle of life," the

cyclical reading of the Torah, and the circling around the synagogue with the Torah.

These foods are symbolic for Simkat Torah:

Round cookies and cakes

Rolled cookies and cakes that look like Torah scrolls

Chocolate or Cinnamon-Raisin Babka

ALSO SERVE ON
*Shabbat,
Yom ha-atzma'ut*

DAIRY

NUTRITIONAL
NOTES
(per serving)

207 calories

3g fat (16%)

19mg cholesterol

38g carbohydrates

5g protein

177mg sodium

1g fiber

I used to dream about babka, but with 18 grams of fat per serving in my regular recipe, that's about all I did with it. Now I can enjoy it again as this version that has only 3 grams of fat per serving. Reduced-fat sour cream replaces almost all of the butter in the dough. Combined with a dense chocolate filling and topped with streusel crumbs, the babka seems as rich as its fat-laden counterpart. Preparation is very important to the success of the cake, so do not use your regular routine for making yeast bread. Sugar tends to prevent gluten formation, creating a soft dough that is difficult to roll. For babka you need a sweet dough that can be rolled, and at the same time is light and not too fine-textured. To accomplish these goals, I consulted Shirley Corriher's magnificent book, Cookwise. Her suggestions for adding crushed ice, and the fats after the dough has been kneaded, proved to be the perfect solution for increasing gluten formation, and maximizing rise, thereby making the texture of the baked babka perfect. Make sure to begin the dough one day ahead.

MAKES 2 LOAVES, 20 SERVINGS

⅓ cup evaporated skim milk

½ cup very warm water (120°F—not hot enough to sting your finger)

4⅓ cups (540 grams) bread flour, lightly sprinkled into measuring cup

1 tablespoon instant (not rapid rise) yeast, such as Fleischmann's Bread Machine Yeast (if using a different yeast, please consult page 319)

½ cup firmly packed light brown sugar

1¼ teaspoons salt

¼ cup crushed ice

2 large eggs, lightly whisked

½ cup reduced-fat sour cream, preferably Breakstone's

1 tablespoon unsalted butter, melted

Filling

½ cup sugar

6 whole lowfat graham crackers

¼ cup Dutch-processed cocoa powder, preferably Droste

3 tablespoons chopped semisweet chocolate or chocolate chips

2 large egg whites

2 tablespoons nonfat chocolate sundae syrup

Topping

2 tablespoons egg substitute (such as Egg Beaters), or 1 large egg white whisked with 1 teaspoon water

Streusel (Crumb) Topping, page 296

RDA %

1% vitamin A

0% vitamin C

2% calcium

10% iron

BEGIN DOUGH 1 DAY AHEAD

1. Place the milk, water, 1½ cups of the flour, and the yeast in a large mixer bowl. Beat on medium speed for 4 minutes. Cover the bowl with plastic wrap, and let the dough rise for at least 30 minutes or up to 2 hours. Add the remaining flour, sugar, salt, ice, and eggs. Beat for a couple of seconds just to mix everything, and then switch to a dough hook if you have one. Knead the dough for 10 to 15 minutes until it is smooth and elastic. Divide the dough into 4 pieces and place them back in the bowl. Mix the sour

Simkat Torah

cream and butter together, then add to the bowl and knead them into the dough by hand. The dough will be soft and sticky. Cover with foil or plastic wrap and let rise for 1 hour. Refrigerate the dough overnight.

2. To make the filling, combine the sugar, graham crackers, cocoa, and chocolate in a food processor. Process until the grahams and chocolate are finely ground. Add the egg whites and the sundae syrup. Process for a few seconds just to blend the ingredients together. Set aside.

3. Spray-grease and flour two 9 × 5-inch loaf pans.

4. Divide the dough in half. Cover 1 piece with a tea towel, and roll the other piece on a well-floured board into a 7 × 10-inch rectangle, about ¼ inch thick.

5. Pat on half of the filling, leaving ½ inch on the long sides, and 1 inch at the far, short end, without filling. Roll up the dough from the near short end, jelly roll style. Place the roll, seam side down, in one of the prepared pans. Brush the top and sides with the egg wash and sprinkle on half of the streusel crumbs. Repeat with the remaining dough. Cover the loaves with a tea towel, and let rise for 1 to 1½ hours, until the dough has risen to the top of the pan.

6. Preheat the oven to 350°F, with a rack in the middle of the oven. Bake the loaves for about 45 minutes, or until an instant-read thermometer stuck into the middle of the cake reads 200°F (usually bread is "tapped on the bottom" and is done when hollow sounding, but you can't do that with this cake). Let the cakes cool on a rack for 15 minutes, and then loosen the edges and turn the cakes out of the pans.

7. Cool completely before cutting. The cakes taste best when freshly made. On the second and third days, they will be slightly stale but still taste great with a cup of coffee. The cakes can be frozen, but there is a loss of taste and texture.

VARIATION: For cinnamon-raisin babka, plump ⅓ cup raisins in hot water for 5 minutes. Delete the cocoa and chocolate chips from the filling. Brush the rolled dough with the egg substitute, sprinkle with cinnamon-sugar, and then pat half of the raisins on each dough half. Pat on the filling. Proceed as for the chocolate babka.

Lemon Pistachio Roulade

This all-purpose lemon roulade can be served throughout the year for almost any occasion. Pistachios give it an unusual taste and a pleasing appearance.

MAKES 12 SERVINGS

Lemon Filling, page 300

½ cup plus 1 tablespoon (60 grams) sifted cake flour, lightly sprinkled into a measuring cup

¼ cup cornstarch

½ teaspoon salt

3 large egg whites, at room temperature

½ cup sugar, divided

2 large eggs, at room temperature

1 teaspoon vanilla extract, or lemon extract

1 teaspoon canola oil

Powdered sugar

Lemon Soaking Syrup

¼ cup water

2 tablespoons sugar

1 teaspoon fresh lemon juice

1 teaspoon orange liqueur (optional)

For Assembly

¼ cup shelled pistachio nuts, coarsely ground

Candied lemon rose (page 302) (optional)

continued

ALSO SERVE ON
Sukkot, Shabbat, Yom ha-atzma'ut

DAIRY

NUTRITIONAL NOTES
(per serving)

156 calories

2g fat (13%)

46mg cholesterol

31g carbohydrates

4g protein

128mg sodium

0g fiber

RDA %

2% vitamin A

15% vitamin C

3% calcium

3% iron

Simkat Torah

1. Make the Lemon Filling and refrigerate until cold.

2. To make the cake, preheat the oven to 400°F, with a rack in the middle of the oven. Spray-grease a 10 × 15-inch jelly roll pan, and line it with parchment paper or a nonstick Teflon liner. Spray-grease and flour the parchment and pan (spraying the pan first keeps the parchment paper in place so it doesn't lift up when you start to spread the batter).

3. In a bowl, whisk together the flour, cornstarch, and salt.

4. Place the egg whites in a clean, dry, and grease-free bowl. Beat on medium-high with clean, dry, and grease-free beaters until foamy and thickened. Continue beating, and gradually add ¼ cup of the sugar. Increase the speed to high and beat the egg whites until stiff but not dry. Set aside.

5. Place the whole eggs in a large mixer bowl. Gradually beat in the remaining ¼ cup of sugar. Beat on high for 5 minutes until thick, fluffy, and tripled in volume. Beat in the vanilla and oil. Sift a few tablespoons of the flour mixture over the egg yolk mixture, and gently fold together. Repeat until about ⅔ of the flour mixture has been added. Fold in ⅓ of the whites. Sift and fold in the remaining flour mixture. Gently fold in the remaining whites.

6. Spread the batter in the prepared pan. Bake in the middle of the oven for 7 to 9 minutes until the cake is lightly browned and springy.

7. Place a 20-inch piece of waxed paper on the counter. Sprinkle it liberally with powdered sugar.

8. Using a sharp, nonserrated knife, loosen the edges of the cake. While the cake is hot, turn the pan over onto the paper so that there is about 3 inches of paper showing on one of the short ends. Lift off the pan and remove the parchment paper. Fold the 3-inch piece of waxed paper over the cake, and roll the cake up. Cool completely. When the cake is cool, it can be filled, or frozen for future use. (Freeze it rolled in the paper, wrapped in foil, and then in a plastic bag.)

9. To make the soaking syrup, combine the water, sugar, lemon juice, and orange liqueur, if using, in a small pot. Heat over medium heat until the sugar dissolves, and then raise the heat and bring the mixture to a boil.

Let it cool before using (it can be made up to 3 weeks ahead, refrigerated, and brought to room temperature before using).

10. To assemble, unroll the cake and remove the waxed paper. Brush the syrup over the cake. Spread a ⅛-inch layer of the lemon filling over the cake, leaving 1 inch of a short end and ½ inch on both long ends free of filling. Sprinkle lightly with pistachios. Roll the cake up loosely, from one short end, toward the edge with no filling. The filling will spread outward and upward. Spread a very thin layer of lemon filling on the outside of the cake and sprinkle the cake with the remaining pistachios. If desired, garnish with a candied lemon rose. Refrigerate the cake for 1 to 2 hours (or up to 1 day ahead) before serving. To serve, cut with a serrated knife into ¾-inch pieces.

Chocolate Nut Torah Roulade

ALSO SERVE ON
Shavuot (use a dairy filling), Shabbat, Bar Mitzvah, Onegs

PAREVE

NUTRITIONAL NOTES
(per serving;
2 pieces–not including
tootsie rolls)

129 calories

3g fat (16%)

24mg cholesterol

23g carbohydrates

3g protein

101mg sodium

1g fiber

RDA %

1% vitamin A

0% vitamin C

1% calcium

3% iron

Light Jewish
Holiday Desserts

T his is one of those cakes that can make great memories for your family. It's fun to make, and the presentation is sensational. Two small chocolate rolls, placed side by side, are decorated to look like Torah scrolls. For a simpler presentation, make a single large, rolled cake. Kids love to help roll up the cake, sprinkle on the chocolate chips and nuts, and push in the Torah poles. When they see the finished product and recognize its shape, they are delighted. You and your guests will be delighted, too, as each serving has only 2 grams of fat!

MAKES 15 SERVINGS

½ cup (52 grams) sifted cake flour, lightly sprinkled into measuring cup

¼ cup Dutch-processed cocoa, preferably Droste

½ teaspoon salt

3 large egg whites, at room temperature

½ cup sugar, divided

2 large eggs, at room temperature

1 teaspoon vanilla extract

1 teaspoon canola oil

Powdered sugar

Soaking Syrup

¼ cup water

2 tablespoons sugar

1 teaspoon rum, or other liqueur, or orange juice

Filling and Topping

1 recipe Marshmallow Meringue, page 298

¼ cup finely chopped pecans

*2 tablespoons finely chopped semisweet chocolate, or miniature
  chocolate chips*

1 tablespoon finely ground pecans

Pretzel rods (optional)

1. Preheat the oven to 400°F, with a rack in the middle of the oven. Spray-grease a 10 × 15-inch jelly roll pan, and line the pan with parchment paper or a nonstick Teflon liner. Spray-grease and flour the parchment and the pan. (Spraying the pan first keeps the parchment paper in place so it doesn't lift up when you start to spread the batter.)

2. In a bowl, whisk together the flour, cocoa, and salt.

3. Place the egg whites in a clean, dry, and grease-free bowl. Using clean, dry, and grease-free beaters, beat on medium-high until foamy and thickened. Continue beating, and gradually add ¼ cup of the sugar. Increase the speed to high and beat the egg whites until stiff but not dry.

4. Place the whole eggs in a large mixer bowl. Gradually beat in the remaining ¼ cup of sugar. Beat on high for 5 minutes until thick, fluffy, and tripled in volume. Beat in the vanilla and oil. Sift a few tablespoons of the flour mixture over the egg yolk mixture, and gently fold together. Repeat until about ⅔ of the flour mixture has been added. Fold in ⅓ of the egg whites. Sift and fold in the remaining flour mixture. Gently fold in the remaining whites.

5. Spread the batter in the prepared pan. Bake for 7 to 9 minutes until the cake is lightly browned and springy.

6. Place a piece of waxed paper, at least 6 inches longer than the cake pan, on the counter. Sprinkle it liberally with powdered sugar.

7. Immediately, while the cake is hot, loosen the edges of the cake using a sharp nonserrated knife. Turn the pan over onto the waxed paper so that there is about 3 inches of the paper showing on one of the short ends. Lift off the pan and remove the parchment paper. Fold the 3-inch piece of waxed paper over the cake, and roll the cake up. Cool completely. When the cake is cool, it can be filled, or it can be frozen for future use (freeze it in the waxed paper, wrap in foil, and then in a plastic bag).

continued

Simkat Torah

8. While the cake is cooling, make the soaking syrup by combining the water, sugar, and rum in a small pot. Heat over medium heat, and stir until the sugar dissolves. Increase the heat to high and bring the syrup to a boil. Remove from the heat and let cool before using. It can be made 3 weeks ahead and refrigerated—bring to room temperature before using.

9. Make the Marshmallow Meringue. When the cake is cool, unroll it. Cut ⅜ inch off of each short end. Reserve these pieces. Now cut the cake in half (perpendicular to the long end) so that you have 2 pieces, each about 10 × 7 inches. Brush the soaking syrup over each piece (there will be 1 to 2 teaspoons excess syrup). Spread a ⅛-inch layer of the meringue over the cakes, leaving about 1 inch at the far, long end plain. Sprinkle half of the chopped nuts and half of the chopped chocolate over each cake. Roll the cakes up fairly tightly, starting from the long ends that do have filling on them. The filling will push out toward the plain ends and should fill them completely.

10. Spread a thin layer of the meringue on the outside of each cake. Cut each reserved scrap of cake in half, and wrap these around the top and bottom of each scroll. These will look like the spools on which the Torah is rolled. Sprinkle the scrolls with the ground nuts, leaving the spools plain. Set the cakes on a serving platter, next to each other so that they look like Torah scrolls. Cover the cakes and refrigerate for several hours or overnight.

11. Before serving, push pretzel rods or other pole-shaped food into the ends of each scroll to look like the Torah poles. Cut the cakes into ¾-inch pieces and serve 2 pieces per person.

Biscotchos

CRUNCHY ORANGE ALMOND COOKIES

These Sephardic cookies are served year-round at most Jewish holidays and for desayuno (Sabbath brunch). They may vary depending on the holiday, country of origin, or family preference (see variations, below). Most biscotchos are circular, a shape that has symbolic importance for many of the Jewish holidays, including Simkat Torah. My lowfat version has about one-fourth the fat of traditional biscotchos. Although they are quite crunchy, cake flour and corn syrup prevent them from being overly hard. They're not very sweet, but you can double the sugar if you like. Make the dough one day before baking.

MAKES 64 COOKIES

1⅔ cups (175 grams) sifted cake flour, lightly sprinkled into measuring cup

1¾ cups (210 grams) all-purpose flour, lightly sprinkled into measuring cup

1 tablespoon baking powder

Pinch of salt

1 cup orange juice

¼ cup sugar

¼ cup canola oil

¼ cup corn syrup or honey

1 large egg white, whisked with 1 teaspoon of water

¼ cup sliced almonds, finely chopped

Powdered sugar (optional)

1. In a large bowl, sift together both flours, baking powder, and salt. In another bowl, combine the orange juice, sugar, oil, and corn syrup. Stir

SERVE ON
all Jewish holidays and life-cycle events

PAREVE

NUTRITIONAL NOTES
(per serving)

37 calories

1g fat (25%)

0mg cholesterol

7g carbohydrates

1g protein

20mg sodium

0g fiber

RDA %

0% vitamin A

3% vitamin C

1% calcium

2% iron

START 1 DAY AHEAD

Simkat Torah

this into the flour mixture to make a medium-firm dough. Wrap in plastic wrap and refrigerate overnight.

2. Preheat the oven to 325°F, with racks in the middle and lower third of the oven. Line a couple of cookie sheets with parchment paper. On a floured work surface, shape the dough into a log with a 1-inch diameter. Cut the log into 32 equal pieces. Roll each piece into a rope, about ¼ inch thick and about 6 inches long. One at a time, transfer each rope to the cookie sheet and coil it into a circle. Pinch the ends to seal them together. Repeat with all of the ropes. Brush the tops of the rings with the egg white glaze, and sprinkle lightly with almonds.

3. Bake for 10 minutes, switching the position of the cookie sheets halfway through baking. The cookies should not be brown. Turn off the oven and let the cookies stay in the oven for another 10 minutes, or until lightly browned. When cool, the cookies should be hard. If not, they can be returned to the warm oven to harden. If desired, sprinkle with powdered sugar before serving.

VARIATIONS: For Purim the rings can symbolize Ester's bracelets. A nice combination is to use anise liqueur (ouzo or raki) instead of the orange juice, and to sprinkle the tops with poppy seeds instead of almonds. For Rosh Hashanah, use honey instead of corn syrup, and sprinkle with either sesame seeds or poppy in place of the nuts.

Chocolate Spiral Cookies

Despite having only 2 grams of fat each, these cookies are quite rich tasting. They're great to bring to Temple, for a snack, or as an accompaniment to a fruit dessert.

MAKES 62 COOKIES

10 tablespoons unsalted butter, or unsalted pareve margarine, at cool room temperature (68° to 70°F)

ALSO SERVE ON
Shabbat, Purim

DAIRY OR
PAREVE

Light Jewish
Holiday Desserts

78

1⅓ cups firmly packed light brown sugar

2 large eggs, at room temperature

3¼ cups (390 grams) all-purpose flour, lightly sprinkled into measuring cups, divided

½ teaspoon baking soda

¼ cup Dutch-processed cocoa, preferably Droste

NUTRITIONAL NOTES (PER SERVING)

55 calories

2g fat (34%)

11mg cholesterol

8g carbohydrates

1g protein

32mg sodium

0g fiber

RDA %

1% vitamin A

0% vitamin C

0% calcium

2% iron

1. In a mixing bowl, beat the butter and sugar until well mixed and lightened, about 3 minutes. Add the eggs and beat until well blended. Sift together 3 cups of the flour and the baking soda. Add the flour mixture all at once to the butter, and mix or beat on low until the dough comes together and is well mixed. Remove half of the dough. Add the remaining ¼ cup of flour to the dough in the bowl and mix or beat it in on low. Wrap in plastic wrap and refrigerate. Place the second portion of dough into the mixer bowl. Add the cocoa and mix well. Wrap in plastic wrap and refrigerate for 1 hour or longer.

2. If the dough is very firm, allow it to sit at room temperature until it is soft enough to roll.

3. Place the chocolate dough in a greased jumbo zip-top bag. Roll it out so that it fills the bag (12 × 15 inches) and is about ⅛ inch thick. Roll the white dough in another bag to the same size. Cut off the top side of the bags. Flip the chocolate dough onto a cutting surface. Flip the white dough on top of the chocolate dough, and press the two gently together. Cut the dough in half lengthwise, so that each piece is about 7½ inches wide by 12 inches long. Roll the dough up tightly, from the long side, into a roll. Freeze the dough for about 30 minutes or until firm enough to cut.

4. Preheat the oven to 375°F, with the racks in the center and lower third of the oven. Line 2 cookie sheets (preferably insulated, or 2 pans nested together) with parchment paper. Cut the cold dough into slices, about ⅜ inch thick. Place them on the cookie trays and bake for 4 minutes (3 minutes for uninsulated sheets). Switch the positions of the trays, top to bottom, and bake another 4 to 5 minutes (3 to 4 for uninsulated) until set but not brown. Slide the parchment onto racks, and let cookies cool completely.

5. Store cookies at room temperature for 2 days, or freeze.

Simkat Torah

Apricot or Chocolate Rugelach

ALSO SERVE ON
Shabbat,
Yom ha-atzma'ut,
Purim

DAIRY

NUTRITIONAL NOTES
(per serving)

104 calories

4g fat (31%)

17g carbohydrates

9mg cholesterol

2g protein

58mg sodium

0g fiber

RDA %

2% vitamin A

1% vitamin C

1% calcium

3% iron

The trick to making lowfat rugelach that are flaky, moist, and delicious is to use Shirley Corriher's (Cookwise) method for making flaky pastry, and to substitute sour cream for part of the traditional cream cheese. I also include browned butter in the dough and glaze, which fools the taste buds into believing that these cookies are richer than they are. The result is a cookie with two-thirds less fat than the original, but with texture and flavor that everyone will adore.

MAKES 36 CRESCENT COOKIES OR 40 RECTANGULAR COOKIES

Cream Cheese Dough

½ cup (1 stick) unsalted butter, cold, divided

1⅛ cups (120 grams) sifted cake flour, lightly sprinkled into measuring cup

1 cup (120 grams) all-purpose flour, lightly sprinkled into measuring cup

¼ cup powdered sugar

¼ teaspoon salt

4 ounces light cream cheese, such as Philadelphia ⅓ Less Fat

½ teaspoon vanilla extract

½ cup reduced-fat sour cream, preferably Breakstone's

Use one of these fillings, or half of each:
Apricot Filling and Topping

3 whole lowfat graham crackers

⅓ cup pecans

⅓ cup granulated sugar

1½ teaspoons cinnamon

Light Jewish
Holiday Desserts

12 ounces (1 jar) apricot preserves

¾ cup golden raisins

Chocolate Filling

3 whole lowfat graham crackers

⅓ cup pecans, toasted at 350°F until aromatic (about 5 minutes)

⅓ cup granulated sugar

½ teaspoon cinnamon

2 tablespoons chopped semisweet chocolate, or chocolate chips

2 teaspoons cocoa powder

¼ cup fat-free chocolate syrup

Glaze

1 large egg white, at room temperature

1 tablespoon reserved brown butter

1. Place ¼ cup of the butter in a small frying pan. Cook and stir over medium-high heat until the butter is fragrant and flecks of brown can be seen on the bottom of the pan. Remove the pan from the heat. Place 1 tablespoon in a small microwavable bowl and set it aside. Transfer the remaining browned butter into a small bowl and place it in the freezer.

2. In a large mixing bowl, combine both flours, powdered sugar, and salt. Mix to blend ingredients together.

3. Cut the remaining ¼ cup of butter into ½-inch chunks, and stir into the flour mixture. Place the bowl in the freezer for 10 minutes.

4. Remove both the flour mixture and the browned butter from the freezer. Dump the flour mixture onto a work surface. Scrape the browned butter out of the bowl and lightly toss it into the flour. With a rolling pin, roll over the mixture to flatten the butter and coat it with flour. Scrape any butter that gets stuck on the rolling pin back into the flour. Continue to roll and scrape until the butter is flattened. Scrape the flour back into the bowl and freeze for 10 minutes.

continued

Simkat Torah

5. Cut the cream cheese into ½-inch cubes. Remove the flour mixture from the freezer. Using 2 knives or a pastry blender, cut the cream cheese into the flour until the cream cheese pieces are no larger than lentils. Add the vanilla to the sour cream. Spoon the sour cream into the flour mixture and use a fork to evenly distribute it. Press the mixture together with the tips of your fingers and then the heels of your hands, until it will hold together in a ball. Flatten the ball, wrap in plastic wrap, and place in the refrigerator for at least 1 hour.

6. Preheat the oven to 350°F, with a rack in the middle of the oven. Line 2 cookie sheets (preferably insulated or 2 pans nested together) with parchment paper. Have a large (about 10 × 15-inch) piece of wax paper next to the work surface.

For apricot rugelach

7. Process the graham crackers until ground medium-fine (no chunks larger than ⅛ inch). Add the pecans, granulated sugar, and cinnamon and process until the nuts are chopped medium-fine. Remove ¾ cup, and grind the remaining filling until the nuts are finely chopped. Set both the fine and coarse mixtures near the work surface. Use the coarse mixture as filling, and the finer mixture as topping.

8. Spoon the preserves into a small bowl. Mash down on the jam with the back of the spoon to thin it, and to see if there are any large lumps of apricot present. Cut these into ⅛-inch pieces and return them to the jam. Prepare the glaze by microwaving the reserved tablespoon of browned butter, just until it liquefies (10 to 30 seconds). Make sure it is just barely warm, and then whisk it into the egg white. Set it by the piece of waxed paper.

9. Cut the dough in half. Remove 1 piece, and place the remaining dough back into the refrigerator. Cut open a jumbo zip-top bag so that it is hinged on one long side. Sprinkle the inside with flour, place the dough in the bag, and roll it into a 12-inch circle, about 1/16 inch thick (turn the dough over periodically, peel back the bag, and sprinkle with a little flour to keep it from sticking).

10. Transfer the dough to a cutting surface by holding the dough to the bag, inverting it onto the surface, and then peeling off the plastic bag. Reroll the dough lightly if it shrinks when it is moved. Spread about ½ cup of jam onto the dough. Distribute the apricot lumps evenly around the dough, as these will contribute to the moistness and flavor of each cookie. Sprinkle and pat on 4 tablespoons of the coarse crumbs so that the dough is well covered. Cut the dough into 16 equal wedges, wiping off the blade with a damp cloth between cuts. Place 2 to 3 raisins at the base of each triangle and then scatter another 2 to 3 raisins on each piece. Roll the cookies up, from the circle's perimeter toward the center. Don't worry about excess jam oozing out around the edges of the cookie—it will caramelize and taste great. Bend the cookies slightly to form crescents.

11. Transfer the rugelach to the waxed paper. Generously brush the tops and sides of the rugelach with the glaze, and sprinkle each, liberally, with the finely ground nut/graham mixture. Roll the cookies around to make sure that they are well coated with the nuts. Place the cookies on the parchment paper making sure that the tips are down, and bake in the middle of the oven for 25 to 30 minutes, or until nicely browned. Remove the pan from the oven, slide the parchment onto a cooling rack, and let the cookies cool completely before eating. While 1 tray of cookies is baking, repeat the procedure with the remaining dough.

For chocolate rugelach
12. Pulse-process the graham crackers until chopped medium-fine. Add the nuts, sugar, and cinnamon, and process until the nuts are chopped medium-fine. Remove ¾ cup. Grind the remaining mixture until the nuts and cookies are finely ground. Transfer mixture to a small bowl and set it near the work surface to be used as topping. Place 2 tablespoons of the reserved coarse crumbs back into the processor. Add the chocolate and cocoa. Process until the chocolate is finely grated. Add this to the rest of the coarse crumbs for use as filling. Roll the dough as in step 9 above. Instead of spreading the dough with jam, brush it liberally with the chocolate syrup. Fill, roll, glaze, and bake, as above.

continued

Simkat Torah

For rectangular rugelach

13. Divide the dough into quarters. Roll each piece about 1/16 inch thick into a 6 × 10-inch rectangle. Roll the long, far edge a little thinner, as this will be the edge that will seal the roll together. Spread the dough with apricot jam, leaving 1/4 inch along the thinner edge clean. Sprinkle the brushed part with filling (about 3 tablespoons), leaving the top 1/4 inch clean so that the rolls will seal well. Place raisins in a line on the long, brushed edge. Scatter another 2 tablespoons of raisins over the dough. Roll up tightly. Press down lightly on the roll so that the bottom edge will seal well. Place on waxed paper. Brush the tops and sides with the glaze, and sprinkle each with the finer topping. Cut the roll into 1-inch pieces. Transfer them to the parchment-lined baking sheet. Make sure that each piece is level, with the sealed edge toward the bottom, or they may fall over or open up during baking. Bake 25 to 30 minutes or until nicely browned.

Assibih bi loz

ALMOND PISTACHIO PHYLLO FINGERS

ALSO SERVE ON
All holidays except Pesach

DAIRY OR PAREVE

S *ome variation of these basic pastries is served throughout the Sephardic world. They are suitable for most holidays, can be given as* mishloah minot *(Purim gifts), and are often eaten by the women attending a bride at the* mikvah. *I've substituted cookie or cake crumbs for half of the nuts, and used oil for part of the butter, thus reducing the fat by 60 percent.*

MAKES 36 PASTRIES

Atar **(Sugar Syrup)**

2 cups granulated sugar

1 cup water

1 tablespoon orange juice

1 teaspoon fresh lemon juice

Pastry

½ box phyllo dough, unopened in the refrigerator

Pistachio-Cardamom Filling

8 whole Stella D'oro Almond Toast cookies, or dried ladyfingers

½ cup shelled pistachio nuts, walnuts, or pecans

½ cup sliced almonds

2 tablespoons powdered sugar

½ teaspoon ground cardamom or cinnamon

3 tablespoons orange juice

For assembly

2 tablespoons unsalted butter, or unsalted, pareve margarine

2 tablespoons canola oil

Powdered sugar

1. Combine the granulated sugar, water, and juices in a medium pot and heat over medium heat to dissolve the sugar. Bring the mixture to a boil, remove from the heat, and refrigerate until ready to use (can be made 2 weeks ahead).

2. Remove the defrosted phyllo dough from the box, leave it in its inner sleeve, and let it stand at room temperature for 2 hours.

3. Preheat the oven to 350°F, with a rack in the middle of the oven.

4. To make the filling, place the cookies in a food processor bowl. Pulse-process until the cookies are ground. Add the pistachios and pulse-process until finely chopped. Add the almonds, powdered sugar, and cardamom, and process until the nuts are finely chopped. Stir in the orange juice.

5. Place the butter and oil in a covered microwavable bowl. Microwave on medium for 2 minutes or until the butter is completely melted.

6. Once the phyllo has been unwrapped, it must be used quickly and kept covered with waxed paper, or it will dry out and crumble like dried leaves. Before opening the plastic bag, gather together: waxed paper,

Simkat Torah

large cutting board on which to cut the phyllo, long knife, pastry brush, and cookie sheets lined with parchment paper.

7. Remove the phyllo from the inner plastic bag. Place half of the stack onto a cutting board; wrap and refreeze the remaining pastry. Across the long end, cut the pastry into four 4-inch strips. Leave 1 strip on the work surface. Stack the rest of the strips on top of one another, and cover them with waxed paper.

8. Very lightly brush the pastry leaf on the work surface, with the butter-oil mixture (about ¼ teaspoon per sheet—I have given about 1 tablespoon extra butter-oil, as it is easier to work when you are not scraping the bottom of the pan to finish the job). If the butter gets too firm, microwave it for 10 seconds to reheat. Use a sugar shaker or a medium-mesh strainer to sprinkle the pastry with about 1 tablespoon of powdered sugar. Place 1 to 1½ teaspoons of filling in a ¼-inch line, about ¼ inch from the short end, leaving ¼ inch at the sides. Tightly roll up the pastry. After 3 turns, brush and fold in the edges just at the filling. (If the phyllo tears, it is okay.) The filling will be sealed in, but as you continue to roll, it will look like a cigarette with open ends. Continue to roll until ¼ inch from the end. Brush the end with butter, and finish rolling up the dough. Lightly brush butter on top. Set the "finger" on the cookie sheet, and make the remaining pastry in the same manner. Bake for 20 to 25 minutes, or until the fingers are nicely browned. While they are still hot, dip them into the cold syrup, or wait until they cool, and then sprinkle with powdered sugar.

Schnecken

Sticky Buns

Schnecken *(snails) were probably the inspiration for the pastry we now call sticky buns. Traditional sticky buns vary greatly in the amount of fat they have. My original recipe has 18 grams of fat per bun, but those made with brioche dough can have as much as 154 grams of fat per bun! I had to do a lot of research and development to get these down to 4 grams of fat each. Thank goodness for Shirley Corriher's book,* Cookwise, *a treatise about why foods and food techniques do what they do. I've used several of her techniques to keep my schnecken light and moist: baking powder in addition to yeast, vitamin C and a pinch of cinnamon for increased yeast activity, and ice for good gluten development. The honey and brown sugar help keep them fresh for more than one day. The real success, though, comes from the topping. Usually the "topping" is put in the bottom of the pan, and the buns are turned upside down when they come out of the oven. Because there is practically no butter in this topping, that approach does not work very well. Instead, the buns get lavishly brushed with the topping, and then toasted nuts get sprinkled on. Another benefit is that you won't have to worry about the topping and nuts sticking to the pan. The result is a sticky bun that will please the most ardent fan.*

MAKES 24 BUNS

continued

ALSO SERVE ON
*Shabbat,
Rosh Hashanah,
Yom ha-atzma'ut*

DAIRY

**NUTRITIONAL
NOTES (PER
SERVING)**

164 calories

4g fat (22%)

13mg cholesterol

29g carbohydrates

4g protein

133mg sodium

1g fiber

RDA %

1% vitamin A

10% vitamin C

4% calcium

7% iron

**PREPARE 1 DAY AHEAD
FOR BREAKFAST BUNS**

Simkat Torah

87

¾ cup very warm water (115° to 120°F—it should not be warm enough to sting your finger)

½ cup evaporated milk, warmed

½ cup potato flakes (make sure they do not contain onion)

3½ cups (437 grams) bread flour, lightly sprinkled into measuring cup

1 tablespoon instant yeast, such as Fleischmann's Bread Machine Yeast (if using another yeast, please consult page 319)

1 large egg

2 tablespoons unsalted butter, melted

2 tablespoons honey

1½ teaspoons baking powder

1 teaspoon salt

¼ cup firmly packed light brown sugar

125mg vitamin C tablet, crushed (halve or quarter a tablet as necessary)

¼ teaspoon cinnamon

¼ cup finely crushed ice

Filling

1 large egg white, whisked until foamy

½ cup firmly packed light brown sugar

1 teaspoon cinnamon

Topping

1 tablespoon skim milk, for brushing the buns

½ cup pecans

1 cup firmly packed light brown sugar

2 tablespoons light corn syrup or honey

¼ cup water

½ teaspoon cinnamon

1 tablespoon unsalted butter

1. In a large mixer bowl, stir together the water, milk, and potato flakes. Add 1 cup of flour and the yeast. Beat on medium (medium-high on a handheld mixer) for 5 minutes. Cover with plastic wrap and let rise, at room temperature, for 1 hour.

2. Add the egg, melted butter, and honey, and mix to blend. Reserve 1 tablespoonful of the flour. In another bowl, combine the remaining flour, baking powder, salt, sugar, vitamin C, and cinnamon. Add to the mixer bowl, and mix for a few seconds with the beater. Add the ice. Change to a dough hook and knead the dough for 5 to 10 minutes, until smooth. The dough will be very sticky. (If you do not have a dough hook, but your beater is heavy enough, you can beat the dough for 5 to 10 minutes. To knead the dough by hand, turn the dough out onto a floured board before adding the crushed ice. The dough will be extremely sticky as the crushed ice gets worked in. Sprinkle on the reserved tablespoon of flour, but no extra flour, and work the dough by pushing it against the board and then using a scraper to get it off the board when it becomes unmanageable. Knead for 5 to 10 minutes.)

3. Grease another large bowl with oil. Sprinkle the reserved tablespoonful of flour over the dough so that you can get the dough out of the mixer bowl. Transfer the dough to the greased bowl. Turn it over in the bowl several times to make sure that it is coated with oil. If necessary, sprinkle on a couple more drops of oil. Cover with plastic wrap and let rise for about 1 hour, until doubled in bulk.

4. Punch down the dough and turn it out onto a well-floured work surface. Shape it into a ball. (At this point, the dough can be placed in a plastic bag and refrigerated overnight. In the morning, place the dough onto a floured board and continue with the recipe.)

5. Cover the dough with a lint-free towel, or a greased piece of plastic wrap, and let it rest for 15 minutes. On a lightly floured work surface, roll the dough out into a rectangle, about ¼ inch thick, 6 to 8 inches wide, and 12 inches long (if using cold dough, roll it to about 15 inches long).

6. For the filling, brush the dough with the egg white. Combine the brown sugar and cinnamon, and pat it thickly onto the dough. Roll the dough up from one long end into a fairly tight jelly roll. The roll should

Simkat Torah

be about 2½ inches in diameter and should have stretched to about 20 inches long. Cut off and discard the ends of the roll, and then cut the remaining log into 24 pieces, each about ¾ inch thick. Place the rolls, cut side up (you will see the spiral of the dough and the sugar), in 2 greased 12-hole muffin pans. Brush the tops of the rolls with the milk. Spray a piece of plastic wrap with cooking spray, and cover the pans with the wrap. Let the rolls rise until they reach the tops of the pans, 45 to 60 minutes.

7. While the dough is rising, preheat the oven to 350°F, with a rack in the middle of the oven. Toast the pecans on a sheetpan in the oven for 7 minutes or until fragrant. Set aside to cool, and then finely chop.

8. Increase the temperature to 375°F. Bake the rolls in the middle of the oven for 10 to 15 minutes, until nicely browned and the interior temperature is at least 190°F to 200°F (if both pans won't fit on one rack, use the lower and middle racks, and switch the pans halfway through baking).

9. While the rolls are baking, make the topping by combining the sugar, corn syrup, water, and cinnamon in a medium saucepan. Cook over medium heat, stirring constantly, until the sugar dissolves. Bring it to a boil, and then remove from the heat and add the butter. Stir until the butter is melted, cover the pot, and set it aside.

10. When the rolls are cooked, remove the pans from the oven and set them on cooling racks. Stir the syrup. If it is not still warm and liquidy, heat it briefly, but do not let it simmer. Immediately brush the warm syrup over the rolls and sprinkle each with the chopped nuts. Let the rolls cool for a couple of minutes, and then remove them from the pans (don't invert the pans—just use a toothpick or skewer to loosen the edges and to lift up a corner so that you can lift them out of the pan). Serve the rolls slightly warm. They can be made 1 day in advance. Wrap in foil and leave them at room temperature until ready to reheat. Heat in the foil at 350°F for about 10 minutes or until warm. Baked rolls can also be frozen. Reheat them, frozen, wrapped in foil at 400°F for 10 to 15 minutes.

VARIATIONS: *Onegs and life-cycle events*—You can make 48 miniature *schnecken* using 4 mini-muffin pans. Divide the dough in half and roll each part into a 3 × 12-inch rectangle, ¼ inch thick. Cut each roll into 24 ½-inch-thick pieces. Bake and glaze as above. If you do not have 4 mini-pans, work with half of the dough at a time, keeping the remaining dough in the refrigerator so that it rises slowly. Once shaped, the cold dough will require more rising time.

Cinnamon Raisin Buns—Soak ½ cup raisins in hot water for 5 minutes. Drain well, and then scatter them over the sugar-cinnamon mixture on the dough. Roll up the dough. Instead of brushing the baked buns with the sticky syrup, make a thick white glaze by mixing 2 cups powdered sugar, 2 tablespoons skim milk, 1 teaspoon vanilla, and 2 teaspoons corn syrup. The glaze will be very thick but will thin as you spread it onto the hot buns.

Chocolate Schnecken—Use the same filling as that in Chocolate Babka (page 68). Use the white glaze for the top (see Cinnamon Raisin Buns above).

Apple Cherry Strudel

Stretching strudel can be a relaxing solitary activity, or a fun family affair. Kids are amazed as the dough gets thinner and thinner until it covers the entire table. Unlike phyllo strudel, this dough needs to have pure butter brushed on it, or it will not be tender and flaky. You'll need a good old-fashioned linen or cotton tablecloth on which to work, as the newer no-wrinkle fabrics slide around too much for this process.

MAKES 24 SERVINGS

continued

ALSO SERVE ON
**Rosh Hashanah,
Tu b'Shevat,
Shabbat,
Yom ha-atzma'ut**

DAIRY

Simkat Torah

**NUTRITIONAL
NOTES**
(per serving)

135 calories

4g fat (27%)

11mg cholesterol

23g carbohydrates

2g protein

34mg sodium

1g fiber

RDA %

2% vitamin A

2% vitamin C

0% calcium

5% iron

¾ *cup warm water*

1 large egg, at room temperature

2 tablespoons plus 1 teaspoon canola oil, divided

½ *teaspoon salt*

3 cups (360 grams) all-purpose flour, lightly sprinkled into measuring cup

Apple Cherry Filling

5 large apples, preferably Fuji or other semifirm tart variety

1 medium lemon

4 whole lowfat graham crackers

¼ *cup sugar*

½ *teaspoon cinnamon*

½ *cup dried cherries*

3 tablespoons unsalted butter, melted

½ *cup pecans, finely chopped*

Powdered sugar

1. In a large mixer bowl, whisk together the water, egg, 2 tablespoons of the oil, and salt. Add 1½ cups of the flour. Beat on low just to blend the ingredients into a batter. Change to a dough hook if you have one. Knead in 1¼ cups more flour. Add the remaining ¼ cup of flour as necessary to make a soft, smooth, and elastic, but not sticky, dough. Coat the dough all around, with the remaining 1 teaspoon of oil. Cover, and let rest for 10 minutes.

2. For the filling, peel, core, and grate the apples in a food processor or on a coarse grater. Squeeze the lemon over the apples and mix well. Cover and set aside.

3. Crush the grahams to fine crumbs. In a bowl, mix with the sugar and cinnamon. Set aside. In another bowl, soak the cherries in hot water for 5 minutes. Drain and set aside.

4. Place a lint-free, nonslick tablecloth on a table that is at least 3 × 4 feet. Heavily flour the tablecloth.

5. Remove all jewelry from your hands. Place the dough on the cloth and roll it with a rolling pin until it is about ¼ inch thick. To start, you can stretch the dough by holding it up, in the center of the dough, on top of the backs of your hands, and letting the weight of the dough stretch it. Pull the dough, in opposite directions, on the backs of your hands. Set the dough down on the tablecloth, and continue to stretch, on the backs of your hands, rotating around the dough so that it is stretched in all directions. Stretch the dough until it is so thin that you can see through it and it covers the table. Small tears will not matter. Cut off any thick edges on the sides of the dough (there will be a lot).

6. Brush the dough with the melted butter. Sprinkle the dough with the graham mixture, leaving about 1 inch on all sides unsprinkled. Squeeze the apples to remove all excess moisture. Scatter the apples on the lower third of the dough (not on the inch of plain dough). Top with the pecans and the dried cherries. Fold the first inch of dough over the apples. Pick up the end of the tablecloth and use the cloth to get the dough rolling. Roll the dough up all the way to the end. Cut the roll in thirds, and place them on a parchment-lined cookie sheet.

7. Cut the strudels, not all of the way through but about ⅓ down, on the diagonal, into 1-inch pieces. Brush the top with the melted butter. Refrigerate for 20 minutes.

8. Meanwhile, preheat the oven to 425°F, with a rack in the middle of the oven. Just before placing the strudels in the oven, lower the heat to 375°F. Bake for 30 to 40 minutes, until the strudels are golden brown. Remove from the oven and let cool until just warm. Sift powdered sugar over the strudel, and cut through the pieces to serve.

Strudel can be prepared, wrapped in foil, and frozen for up to 3 months (unwrap, bake at 350°F for 30 minutes, and then increase the heat to 425°F and bake for an additional 15 to 20 minutes or until the strudel is nicely browned).

Simkat Torah

Orange Crêpe Scrolls

ALSO SERVE ON
Sukkot, Shabbat, Yom ha-atzma'ut, and for Shavuot and Chanukah use the dairy version (flamed for Chanukah)

PAREVE OR DAIRY (SEE VARIATION)

NUTRITIONAL NOTES
(per serving; 2 pancakes)

277 calories

3g fat (9%)

45mg cholesterol

45g carbohydrates

4g protein

100mg sodium

3g fiber

RDA %

4% vitamin A

48% vitamin C

6% calcium

13% iron

With this recipe I set out to create something reminiscent of crêpes suzette, but without so much fat and alcohol. I also wanted a dessert that could be made ahead. This variation has two-thirds less fat than the traditional recipe. The sauce is a flavored sugar syrup that does not need to be prepared at the table. They can be made dairy or pareve to suit your needs. Blintz or crêpe batter made with water is a little thinner and a little less tasty than when made with milk. To compensate for this, I add more egg yolk, a little sugar, and cornstarch, which thickens the batter without making it tough. Kids love to help make and decorate the crepes to look like Torah scrolls. Orange Crêpe Scrolls are also terrific for brunch, and can be made for a big crowd (great for life-cycle events).

MAKES 16 PANCAKES, OR 8 SCROLLS

Crêpe Batter

2 large eggs

¼ cup egg substitute (such as Egg Beaters), or 2 egg whites, whisked

1 cup water

¼ teaspoon salt

¼ teaspoon granulated sugar

1 teaspoon canola oil

1⅛ cups (120 grams) sifted cake flour, lightly sprinkled into measuring cup

2 tablespoons cornstarch

Orange Cinnamon Sauce

1 cup granulated sugar

½ cup water

1 whole cinnamon stick

Light Jewish
Holiday Desserts

2 tablespoons frozen orange juice concentrate, thawed

1 teaspoon unsalted pareve margarine (or butter, for dairy)

Orange Filling

¾ cup powdered sugar, sifted

1 teaspoon canola oil (or melted butter, for dairy)

1 tablespoon orange juice

¼ teaspoon cinnamon

Garnish (optional)

2 medium oranges, peeled and sliced

3 medium bananas, sliced crosswise

1 teaspoon fresh lemon juice

1. To make the crêpe batter, place the eggs, egg substitute, water, salt, granulated sugar, and oil in a food processor bowl. Process until well blended. Add the flour and cornstarch, all at once. Process for 10 seconds to blend ingredients. Scrape down the bowl and pulse for 10 more seconds to blend well. Transfer the batter to a storage container. Refrigerate for at least 1 hour, or up to 3 days.

2. While the batter is chilling, make the sauce. Combine the granulated sugar, water, cinnamon stick, and orange juice concentrate in a small pot. Heat over medium heat, and stir until the sugar dissolves. Bring the syrup to a boil, reduce the heat, and without stirring, let the syrup simmer for 15 minutes. Set aside until ready to use. The sauce can be refrigerated for several months. (Remove the cinnamon stick if storing for more than 1 week.)

3. To make the crepes, heat a 6-inch, slope-sided, nonstick frying pan over high heat, until a droplet of water will roll in the pan. Stir the batter, as it will have settled while resting. Add a small ladleful (about 2 tablespoons) of batter to the pan. Immediately, pick the pan up off the burner, and swirl the pan around and around, so that the batter very thinly coats the bottom. Set the pan back on the burner and let the pancake cook for about 8 to 10 seconds, on only one side. Flip the pancake out onto a plate (you might have to use a fork to get it started). Repeat

Simkat Torah

with the remaining batter, adjusting the temperature of the burner if the crêpes are browning before cooking through. The crêpes can be stacked one on top of the other. They can be used immediately, or can be refrigerated for up to 3 days. If you want to freeze the crêpes, let them cool, then stack them with waxed paper between each crêpe (wrap securely in foil and freeze for up to 3 months). Thaw them in the refrigerator before using (filled crêpes can also be frozen, so you have a lot of flexibility).

4. To make the filling, whisk together the powdered sugar, oil, orange juice, and cinnamon. Set 1 crêpe on a work surface with the unbrowned side up. Spread 1 teaspoon of filling on the pancake. Roll it up tightly. If the bottom and top edges are not square, you can cut them so that they'll look more like scrolls. Repeat with all of the crêpes. The filled crêpes can be refrigerated in a covered container for up to 2 days, or frozen for 3 months. Thaw in the refrigerator before continuing.

5. When ready to serve, preheat the oven to 350°F. Place the crêpes in an ovenproof dish. Reheat the sauce, add the margarine, and stir until the margarine is melted and the sauce is hot. Spoon the sauce over the crêpes. Cover with foil, and bake the crêpes for 10 to 20 minutes, until warmed through. If using the optional garnish, wash and peel 1 orange, reserving the rind. Cut the rind into 28 slivers, each about 1 inch long and ⅛ inch wide. Set aside. Peel the remaining orange and the bananas and cut them into slices. Sprinkle the banana slices with the lemon juice to keep them from browning. The crêpes can be served directly from the baking dish or can be plated as follows: Spoon 1 to 2 teaspoons of sauce onto each plate. Place 2 crêpes right next to each other on each plate, so that they look like Torah scrolls. Stick the slivers of orange rind into the top and bottom of each roll to look like the Torah poles. Garnish each plate with a couple of orange and banana slices. Brush some sauce over the fruit and serve immediately.

VARIATION: If you prefer something more sophisticated, add a tablespoon of liqueur to the sauce. For a dairy dessert, use the blintz batter on page 118 for the crêpes, and substitute butter for the oil and pareve margarine, to create a richer, more complex flavor. For Chanukah, heat 2 tablespoons of rum or brandy in a small saucepan until steaming. Ignite it with a long match, and then pour this over the warm, sauced crêpes. Be careful that your hair, hands, and face are not in the way of the flames.

By the year 167 B.C.E., Israel had come to be

ruled by Hellenized Syrians under the rule

of Antiochus Epiphanes. Jewish ritual was

outlawed and the Jews were commanded to sacrifice

pigs in the Temple and to worship Greek gods.

Refusing to accede to these demands, Mattathias, an

old priest, and his five sons retreated to the

mountains and began a guerrilla war against the

Syrians and their Jewish allies. After the death of

Mattathias, his son, Judah the Maccabee

("Hammer"), continued the fight and eventually

liberated Jerusalem and reclaimed and rededicated

the Temple. To light the menorah, there was one cruze of oil, enough to last just one day, but a miracle occurred and the menorah burned for eight days.

Historically, Chanukah was a minor celebration not even mentioned in the Torah. Earliest accounts can be found in the First and Second Books of Maccabees, two histories that have been preserved by the Church in collections of Apocrypha literature (literature not considered divinely inspired but worthy of study). Additional information comes from Flavius Josephus (born Joseph Ben Matthias— A.D. 37–100), a Jewish scholar, historian, and author of *Antiquities of the Jews,* a Jewish history from Creation through A.D. 66.

In none of these writings, or in the *Mishnah* (the early rabbinic sources), is the miracle of the oil noted. It first appears in the *Gemara,* and scholars speculate that there may have been political reasons for the shift away from celebrating the holiday as a military victory. Perhaps this occurred because the Jews in Mishnaic times were living under Roman rule and did not want to incite Jews to revolt, or possibly they did not want to glorify the Hasmonians (Maccabees), who eventually became Hellenized and thereafter began to persecute the rabbis.

Today, the miracle of the oil and the wonderful story of the Maccabees are both important to our celebration, teaching, and enjoyment of Chanukah. We celebrate the holiday for eight days, lighting our menorahs as a memorial to the brave little band of Jews who fought and beat an empire. The miracle of the light within the Temple allows us to focus on issues of dedication and renewal, and other symbolic interpretations of darkness versus light. Fried foods and desserts made with oil remind us of the Temple. We may eat dairy foods, particularly cheese dishes, in honor of Judith who saved her town by feeding a Syrian general salty cheese and copious quantities of wine to quench his thirst. When he became drunk, she beheaded him, whereupon his troops fled and the town was saved. Cookies shaped like a menorah, Maccabee warriors, or dreidels are also popular treats. The letters on a dreidel stand for the

words *"nes godal hayah shom,"* which mean "A great miracle hap-
pened there."

To celebrate Chanukah, eat the following foods:

Foods made with oil

Foods fried in oil

Cheese and dairy dishes

Cookies and cakes shaped like menorahs, Maccabees, or dreidels

Sour Cream Coffee Cake

NUTRITIONAL
NOTES (PER
SERVING)

166 calories

4g fat (23%)

27mg cholesterol

29g carbohydrates

2g protein

165mg sodium

0g fiber

RDA %

3% vitamin A

0% vitamin C

2% calcium

7% iron

A simple, casual dessert or breakfast treat, sour cream coffee cake has always been one of my favorites. This one has all of the flavor and texture, but two-thirds less fat than my standard recipe. For a sophisticated twist, try the coffee variation.

MAKES 20 SERVINGS

1⅛ cups (120 grams) sifted cake flour, lightly sprinkled into measuring cup

1 cup (120 grams) all-purpose flour, lightly sprinkled into measuring cup

¾ teaspoon baking soda

½ teaspoon salt

1 cup firmly packed light brown sugar

¾ cup granulated sugar

¼ cup pear baby food, at room temperature (less than a 3-ounce jar)

½ cup reduced-fat sour cream, preferably Breakstone's, at room temperature

½ cup nonfat or lowfat buttermilk, at room temperature

1 teaspoon vanilla extract

¼ cup (½ stick) unsalted butter, at room temperature

2 large eggs, at room temperature

Streusel (Crumb) Topping, page 296

1. Preheat the oven to 350°F, with a rack in the middle of the oven. Spray-grease and flour a 9 × 12-inch pan.

2. Into a large mixer bowl, sift both flours, baking soda, salt, and the sugars.

3. In another bowl, combine the baby food, sour cream, buttermilk, and vanilla.

4. Add the butter and half of the buttermilk mixture to the dry ingredients. Beat on high (medium-high on a standing mixer such as a KitchenAid) for 2 minutes, until pale in color and light in texture. Scrape down the sides of the bowl and beat a few seconds more. Add the eggs to the remaining buttermilk mixture. Whisk to combine. Add this to the batter and beat on medium speed just to blend the ingredients. Scrape down the bowl and beat for a couple of seconds more. Spoon the batter into the pan.

5. Sprinkle the streusel over the top of the cake.

6. Bake for 30 to 40 minutes, until a toothpick inserted into the center of the cake comes out with no moist crumbs attached.

7. Cool the cake in the pan, on a wire rack. The cake can be made several days ahead or can be frozen for up to 3 months.

VARIATION: For a coffee-flavored cake, add 2 tablespoons finely ground instant coffee to the dry ingredients.

Devil's Food and Cream Cheese Sheet Cake

ALSO SERVE ON
Shavuot, Shabbat

DAIRY

NUTRITIONAL
NOTES
(per serving)

278 calories

6g fat (19%)

37mg cholesterol

56g carbohydrates

3g protein

196mg sodium

2g fiber

RDA %

4% vitamin A

0% vitamin C

4% calcium

9% iron

This fluffy and moist chocolate cake has three to four times less fat than most frosted chocolate cakes. It's tasty enough to please the most ardent chocolate lovers, and it's great to make for a crowd.

MAKES 20 SERVINGS

½ cup **Dutch-processed cocoa powder** (preferably Droste)

½ cup **boiling water**

¼ cup **plum-apple, or prune-apple baby food** (less than a 3-ounce jar)

1 cup (105 grams) **sifted cake flour,** lightly sprinkled into measuring cup

1 cup (120 grams) **all-purpose flour,** lightly sprinkled into measuring cup

¾ teaspoon **baking soda**

½ teaspoon **salt**

1 cup firmly packed **light brown sugar**

1 cup **granulated sugar**

⅔ cup **nonfat or lowfat buttermilk,** at room temperature

1 teaspoon **vanilla extract**

¼ cup (½ stick) **unsalted butter,** at room temperature

2 large **eggs,** at room temperature

Chocolate Cream Cheese Frosting

¼ cup **skim milk**

¼ cup **Dutch-processed cocoa,** such as Droste

¼ cup **miniature chocolate chips**

4 ounces lowfat **cream cheese,** such as Philadelphia ⅓ Less Fat, softened

1 teaspoon vanilla extract

3 cups sifted powdered sugar

1 tablespoon unsalted butter, at room temperature

1. Preheat the oven to 350°F, with a rack in the middle of the oven. Spray-grease and flour a 9 × 12-inch cake pan (if you will be unmolding the cake, place a piece of parchment paper or a Teflon liner in the bottom).

2. Place the cocoa in a medium bowl. Gradually stir in the boiling water. Stir in the baby food, and set the bowl aside to cool.

3. Sift both flours, baking soda, and salt into a large mixer bowl. Stir in the brown and granulated sugars.

4. In another bowl, combine the buttermilk and vanilla. Stir in the cocoa mixture. Add half to the dry ingredients along with the butter. Beat on low to blend the ingredients. Increase the speed to medium-high (high with a portable mixer), and beat for 2 minutes.

5. Mix the eggs into the remaining buttermilk mixture. Pour it into the batter, and beat on low speed until well blended.

6. Pour the batter into the prepared pan. Rap the pan on the counter several times to remove any large bubbles. Bake for 25 to 30 minutes, or until a toothpick inserted into the center of the cake comes out with no moist crumbs attached.

7. Set the cake pan on a wire rack until completely cool.

8. For the frosting, boil 2 inches of water in the bottom of a double boiler. Reduce the heat to low, cover, and keep warm.

9. Over medium-high heat, heat the milk in the top part of the double boiler until it boils. Remove the pan from the heat. Place the cocoa in a small bowl. Stir in the boiling milk a little at a time to form a smooth paste. Scrape it back into the double boiler top. Add the chocolate chips. Place the pan over the simmering water and stir until the chocolate chips

Chanukah

are melted and the mixture is smooth. Remove from the heat and let cool to room temperature.

10. In a medium mixer bowl, beat the cream cheese until smooth and lightened. On low speed, beat in the melted chocolate and vanilla until smooth. Beat in the powdered sugar, 1 cup at a time, scraping the bowl periodically. Beat in the butter.

11. The cake can be frosted in the pan for a homey dessert. For a more decorative presentation, run a knife around the outside of the cake. Place a piece of waxed paper, and then a cakeboard, over the cake pan. Invert the pan. Place a platter or another cakeboard over the cake and reinvert so the cake is right side up. Remove the waxed paper.

12. Spread the top with frosting. If the cake has been unmolded, you can reserve some of the frosting and use it for the sides. Refrigerate the cake until at least 15 minutes before serving. The cake tastes best when it is at room temperature. Cut the cake into 3 × 2-inch rectangles. To make the prettiest slices, use a damp knife, and wipe the blade off between cuts. The cake can be made 2 days in advance. Store in the refrigerator, but bring to room temperature before serving. If freezing, do not frost. Freeze the cake in the pan or unmolded.

Rum Raisin Cheesecake Squares

*E*ven though these bars have two-thirds less fat than regular cheesecake squares, they still have a great taste and texture. Resist the temptation to increase the amount of crumbs for the crust and topping. Thin layers on top and on bottom balance perfectly with the filling.

ALSO SERVE ON
Shavuot, Shabbat

DAIRY

NUTRITIONAL NOTES (PER SERVING)

106 calories

3g fat (29%)

19mg cholesterol

15g carbohydrates

3.5g protein

66mg sodium

0g fiber

RDA %

4% vitamin A

0% vitamin C

3% calcium

3% iron

MAKES 16 SERVINGS

Oatmeal Crust and Topping

⅓ cup (40 grams) all-purpose flour, lightly sprinkled into measuring cup

½ cup old-fashioned oats

¼ cup firmly packed light brown sugar

1 tablespoon unsalted butter, melted

2 teaspoons oil

2 teaspoons egg substitute (such as Egg Beaters), or 2 teaspoons whisked egg

Cream Cheese Filling

½ cup granulated sugar

4 ounces lowfat cream cheese, such as Philadelphia ⅓ Less Fat, at room temperature

4 ounces nonfat cream cheese, at room temperature

1 large egg, at room temperature

2 tablespoons skim milk

2 tablespoons light sour cream, preferably Breakstone's

½ teaspoon vanilla extract

1 tablespoon dark rum

⅓ cup raisins, soaked in hot water for 5 minutes

continued

Chanukah

1. Preheat the oven to 350°F, with a rack in the middle of the oven. Spray-grease an 8 × 8-inch square nonstick pan.

2. Place the flour, oats, and brown sugar in a food processor bowl and pulse until the oats are ground. Transfer the mixture to a medium bowl. Wipe out the processor bowl, and set aside.

3. Add the butter and oil to the flour mixture. Stir with a fork to distribute the fats. Add the egg substitute, a little at a time, using your fingers to push the mixture into crumbs. Use only as much as necessary to get the mixture to clump. Press half of the crumbs onto the bottom of the prepared pan. Bake 5 minutes. Remove from the oven and set on a cooling rack.

4. To make the filling, place the granulated sugar and the lowfat and nonfat cream cheeses in the processor bowl. Process until smooth. Add the egg, milk, sour cream, vanilla, and rum. Pulse-process until well blended. Scrape down the bowl and process for a few seconds. Drain the raisins and add them to the batter. Pour the mixture over the crust and sprinkle with the remaining crumbs. Bake for 25 minutes, or until a toothpick inserted into the center of the cake comes out with no moist cheese attached.

5. Cool for ½ hour and then refrigerate, uncovered, until completely cool. Cover and chill for several hours or overnight. Cut the cheesecake into 16 squares. The squares can be made 2 days ahead, or frozen for up to 3 months. Defrost in the refrigerator overnight.

Crème Caramel Cheesecake

Many people like this smooth cheesecake even better than regular cheesecake, because it is rich without being filling. The original recipe from my neighbor, Jan Weiner, had 14 grams of fat per serving. By using lowfat products and fewer eggs, I've been able to reduce fat and cholesterol by 75 percent. Caramel fans will love the way the flavor infuses the cheesecake. Making caramel can be a little tricky, but in her book Cookwise, Shirley Corriher simplifies the process for us by adding lemon juice and corn syrup, which prevents the sugar from recrystallizing.

MAKES 12 SERVINGS

Caramel Topping

1 cup sugar

⅓ cup water

3 tablespoons light corn syrup

⅛ teaspoon fresh lemon juice

Cheesecake Flan

8 ounces lowfat cream cheese, such as Philadelphia ⅓ Less Fat, softened

One 14-ounce can nonfat sweetened condensed milk

2 large eggs

1 large egg white

1 teaspoon vanilla extract

One 12-ounce can evaporated skim milk

1. Preheat the oven to 350°F, with a rack in the lower third of the oven. Have ready an 8-inch round cake pan and another pan that is as deep as

ALSO SERVE ON
Shavuot, Rosh Hashanah, Shabbat

DAIRY

NUTRITIONAL NOTES (PER SERVING)

236 calories

4g fat (16%)

42mg cholesterol

42g carbohydrates

8g protein

136mg sodium

0g fiber

RDA %

7% vitamin A

1% vitamin C

19% calcium

2% iron

Chanukah

the cake pan and at least 1 inch bigger all around. Boil water in a teakettle. Reduce the heat and keep warm.

2. To make the caramel topping, in a medium pot, cook the sugar, water, corn syrup, and lemon juice over medium heat, stirring until the sugar melts. Using a wet pastry brush, brush down any sugar crystals on the insides of the pan. Increase the heat and simmer until the syrup turns golden brown. Pour the syrup into the 8-inch round cake pan and immediately swirl the syrup to coat the bottom and sides of the pan. Let cool.

3. To make the flan, place the cream cheese in a food processor and pulse-process until smooth. Add the condensed milk, and pulse until blended. Add the eggs, egg white, vanilla extract, and evaporated milk. Process until blended. Pour the filling into the caramel-lined pan.

4. Place the filled cake pan into the larger pan. Pour the boiling water into the larger pan so that it comes halfway up the sides of the filled pan (this is called a *bain-marie*).

5. Bake for 30 minutes. Cover the cheesecake with buttered foil, shiny side down, and bake for 30 minutes more, or until a toothpick inserted into the center of the cake comes out with no moist cheese attached. The center will still shake when the pan is moved.

6. Remove the foil, and cool the pan on a wire rack. Chill it at least 3 hours before unmolding.

7. To unmold, run a knife around the sides of the cake. Place a large plate over the cheesecake, hold the two together, and invert. If the cheesecake does not fall out, heat the teakettle again and place the hot teakettle on the pan bottom. This should loosen the cake enough to fall out. To cut nice, clean slices, wipe off the knife blade with a wet cloth between cutting each slice. Serve slices with some of the caramel liquid. This cake can be made 3 days ahead. Keep refrigerated until serving. Do not freeze.

Mandarin Orange Cheesecake

This is a delicately flavored, creamy cheesecake. For those who prefer ungarnished cheesecake, it also tastes great without the oranges on top. To maintain a creamy texture, make sure to cook the cheesecake as indicated. The tender, almost fat-free crust is made with a soft mandel bread, which makes a crust similar to one made with cake crumbs. After trying this cheesecake, you'll never want to go back to full-fat cheesecake again.

MAKES 12 TO 14 SERVINGS

Mandel Bread Crumb Crust

12 Stella D'oro Almond Toast cookies

1 to 2 teaspoons egg substitute (such as Egg Beaters), or whisked egg

Orange-Scented Cheesecake

24 ounces nonfat cottage cheese, such as Light and Lively Free

8 ounces lowfat cream cheese, such as Philadelphia ⅓ Less Fat

1 cup sugar

2 large eggs, at room temperature

1 tablespoon Grand Marnier, other orange liqueur, or orange juice

Mandarin Orange Topping

¼ cup apricot jam

1 tablespoon Grand Marnier, other orange liqueur, or orange juice

Two 11-ounce cans mandarin oranges, in light syrup

1. Preheat the oven to 350°F, with a rack in the lower third of the oven. Boil water in a teakettle, reduce the heat, and keep warm. Have a baking dish, at least 10 × 10 inches, and an 8-inch springform pan ready. Wrap

ALSO SERVE ON
Shavuot, Sukkot,
Yom ha-atzma'ut

DAIRY

NUTRITIONAL NOTES (PER SERVING)

187 calories

4g fat (21%)

41mg cholesterol

26g carbohydrates

12g protein

260mg sodium

0g fiber

RDA %

6% vitamin A

6% vitamin C

9% calcium

3% iron

MAKE 1 DAY AHEAD

Chanukah

the outside of the springform with heavy-duty aluminum foil. Crimp the foil around the top of the pan so that it is watertight. (Heavy-duty foil is wider and will wrap around the pan without a seam.)

2. In a food processor, process the cookies until finely ground. Measure out 1 cup of crumbs, and reserve the remainder in a storage container. Place the cup of crumbs in a small bowl, and stir in 1 teaspoon of egg substitute. Use your fingertips to distribute the egg substitute throughout the mixture. If the crumbs will not hold together, add the remaining egg substitute, ½ teaspoon at a time, until they just hold together. Press the crumbs into the bottom of the 8-inch pan. Wipe out the processor bowl.

3. To make the cheesecake, place the cottage cheese in a large piece of cheesecloth. Draw up the sides of the cloth to form a "bag." Twist the top of the bag, and squeeze the cloth to expel liquid from the cheese. Wipe the liquid off the sides of the bag, then twist and squeeze until no more liquid comes out of the cheese. Transfer the cheese to the processor bowl. Process for about 3 minutes or until completely smooth, scraping down the bowl a few times. Add the cream cheese to the processor. Pulse-process until the cheeses are well blended. Add the sugar, and process for 1 minute to fully incorporate. Add the eggs and liqueur, and process for a few seconds to blend. Scrape down the bowl sides and process a few more seconds.

4. Scrape the batter into the prepared 8-inch pan. Put the cheesecake in the larger pan and place it on the oven rack. Pour boiling water into the larger pan so that it comes halfway up the sides of the cheesecake pan. Be careful not to splash water into the cheesecake.

5. Bake for 40 to 45 minutes, until the cheesecake is set but a toothpick inserted into the center of the cake will still come out with some moist cheese attached. Remove the cheesecake from the oven, lift it out of the water-bath, and let it cool on a wire rack. Cover the cake with foil, and chill overnight.

6. When ready to unmold the cake, run a damp knife around the edge of the cheesecake and then remove the springform sides. Press the reserved crumbs onto the sides of the cheesecake.

7. For the topping, melt the apricot jam with the liqueur (this can be done on the stove or in the microwave on high). Brush some of the warm glaze over the cheesecake top. Drain the oranges and pat them dry with paper towels. Arrange the fruit in slightly overlapping, concentric circles with the rounded edge of each slice parallel to the perimeter of the cheesecake, and with the slices tip to tip. (See illustration on page 21.) Using a pastry brush, glaze the oranges with the remaining apricot glaze. Keep the cake refrigerated until ready to serve. This cake can be made 2 days in advance, or frozen (without the oranges) for up to 3 months.

Butter Cookie Dreidels

ALSO SERVE ON
Shabbat, Yom ha-atzma'ut, and Yom Kippur (when made with a Jewish star cookie cutter)

DAIRY OR PAREVE

NUTRITIONAL NOTES
(per cookie)

60 calories

2g fat (29%)

9mg cholesterol

10g carbohydrates

1g protein

31mg sodium

0g fiber

RDA %

1% vitamin A

0% vitamin C

3% calcium

1% iron

Most butter cookies have 2 to 8 tablespoons more butter than these cookies. Despite having only 2 grams of fat, these have a rich, buttery taste. If you must, you can omit another 2 tablespoons of butter (add a little extra water), but because the recipe makes so many cookies, you'll only reduce the fat count by ½ gram per cookie. I love the way these look when frosted white with blue letters on them, but I think they taste best unfrosted. They're great to make with kids, at home, school, or Temple.

MAKES 50 COOKIES

2¼ cups (270 grams) all-purpose flour, lightly sprinkled into measuring cup

¼ teaspoon salt

½ cup sugar

½ cup chilled unsalted butter, or frozen unsalted pareve margarine

1 teaspoon vanilla extract

1 tablespoon water

1 large egg

Simple Icing

1½ cups powdered sugar

2 tablespoons skim milk, or water

1 teaspoon clear imitation vanilla extract (to keep icing white)

Sprinkles (jimmies) (optional)

Food coloring

1. Preheat the oven to 350°F, with racks in the middle and lower third of the oven. Have two nonstick cookie sheets available.

2. Place the flour, salt, and sugar in a food processor bowl. Process for a few seconds to mix the dry ingredients.

3. Cut the butter into ½-inch chunks and scatter on top of the flour. Pulse-process until the butter is cut into the flour so that the mixture looks like coarse meal.

4. In a small bowl, combine the vanilla extract, water, and egg. Whisk lightly to blend. With the processor running, add the egg mixture through the feed tube. Continue to process until the dough just starts to clump together. If the dough is too dry to come together, add more water, 1 teaspoon at a time. The dough won't ball up in the bowl, but it should start to clump, and should come into a ball with the heat of your hands as you push it together. Wrap the dough in plastic wrap and let it rest for 15 minutes.

5. Roll the dough (I like to roll in a floured jumbo zip-top bag) to a scant ⅛ inch thick. Cut with a dreidel-shaped cookie cutter, and place on the cookie sheets. Bake for 5 minutes, switch the cookie sheets top to bottom, and bake another 4 to 7 minutes, until the edges are just starting to brown. Remove the cookies from the pan, and cool them on a wire rack.

6. For the icing, sift the powdered sugar into a medium bowl. Whisk in the milk and vanilla until smooth. The icing should be very thick but thin enough to spread. If it is not thin enough, add more milk by the ½ teaspoonful until the icing is the right consistency. Spread the cookies with icing (a small decorating spatula works best). If you are going to use sprinkles, sprinkle them on while the icing is still wet so they will stick well. If not using sprinkles, let the icing dry. Add color to the remaining icing (I like to use a rich blue) and paint on the dreidel letters using a fine artist's brush. For a great-looking accent, sprinkle small, fine sprinkles, such as multicolored tiny balls, on the wet lettering (larger sprinkles, such as chocolate sticks, will obscure the letters). If you prefer, the dreidel letters can be painted on un-iced cookies. In all cases, let the decorations dry before storing the cookies. Cookies can be made 1 day ahead, or frozen for up to 3 months. These are the Hebrew letters that appear on a dreidel:

שׁ ה ג נ

Chanukah

Apple Latkes

DAIRY

NUTRITIONAL
NOTES (PER
SERVING)

181 calories

3g fat (13%)

0mg cholesterol

35g carbohydrates

6g protein

137mg sodium

1g fiber

RDA %

1% vitamin A

4% vitamin C

4% calcium

7% iron

*P*ancakes are a Chanukah tradition, but they really don't need to be cooked in much oil to maintain their symbolic meaning. These grilled miniatures have the same texture as breakfast pancakes and make a nice family dessert.

MAKES 6 SERVINGS (24 PANCAKES)

1 large apple, Fuji, Golden Delicious, or similar variety

1 medium lemon

1 cup (120 grams) all-purpose flour, lightly sprinkled into measuring cup

¼ teaspoon salt

4 tablespoons sugar, divided

4 large egg whites, divided

½ cup skim milk

1 tablespoon canola oil

Extra sugar, for sprinkling

1. Peel, core, and cut the apple into large chunks. Squeeze the lemon over the apple chunks to keep them from turning brown. Place the chunks in a food processor bowl and pulse-process until they are finely chopped. Measure out 2 cups and discard the remainder. Wipe out the processor bowl.

2. Place the flour, salt, and 3 tablespoons of sugar in the processor bowl. Pulse to blend.

3. Add 2 of the egg whites, the skim milk, and oil. Process until smooth. Stir in the apple.

4. In a clean, dry, and grease-free mixer bowl, beat the remaining 2 egg whites on high speed until very foamy. Sprinkle in the remaining 1 table-

spoon of sugar and continue to beat until stiff peaks form. Push the egg whites to one side, and scrape the batter into the other side. Fold gently together.

5. Spray a large nonstick frying pan with cooking spray and heat over medium-high heat until a drop of water rolls in the pan. Reduce the heat to medium. Make 2-inch pancakes by spooning batter by the tablespoonful into the pan. Cook until the underside is browned, about 40 seconds. Turn the pancakes over, press down lightly on them, and continue to cook until the bottoms are brown and the pancakes are cooked through, about 40 seconds. Reduce the heat if the pancakes are browning before the centers are cooking, or raise the heat if they are not browning enough. Sprinkle the pancakes with sugar and serve 3 to 4 per person. These are also wonderful for breakfast served with maple syrup or honey.

Chanukah

Ataif bi jibn

Syrian Cheese Pancakes

DAIRY

NUTRITIONAL
NOTES
(per 4 pancakes; reflects
just a glazing of the sugar
syrup)

244 calories

3.5g fat (14%)

13mg cholesterol

42g carbohydrates

11g protein

110mg sodium

1g fiber

RDA %

4% vitamin A

4% vitamin C

25% calcium

35% iron

This wonderful recipe was given to me by a neighbor, Ahlam Albaba. Because they contain semolina, the pancakes have a nice "tooth." This is not the semolina flour that is used in pasta dough but a finer flour that can be bought in Middle Eastern or Sephardic grocery stores. It is also called smead. *If you are unable to find it, you can use Cream of Wheat, but the pancakes won't be as chewy as these. Ataif are not only delicious for dessert, they are also terrific for breakfast or brunch. For a parev nut version, see Ataif bi loz, page 34.*

MAKES 9 SERVINGS (4 PANCAKES PER PERSON)

1 cup (125 grams) bread flour, lightly sprinkled into measuring cup

1 cup Middle Eastern semolina

¼ teaspoon instant yeast, such as Fleischmann's Bread Machine Yeast (for other yeasts, please see page 319)

2½ cups skim milk, warmed (not hot enough to sting your finger)

Syrian Cheese Filling

¾ cup shredded lowfat mozzarella cheese

½ cup lowfat ricotta cheese

2 teaspoons sugar

Sugar Syrup

2 cups sugar

1 cup water

2 tablespoons orange juice, or 1 teaspoon orange flower water

1 cinnamon stick

Garnish

2 tablespoons ground pistachio nuts (optional)

1. Place the flour, semolina, and yeast in a food processor bowl. Pulse for a few seconds to blend the ingredients. Pour in the milk. Process for 5 seconds to mix the ingredients well. The batter will be very thin. Transfer the batter to a small bowl, cover, and let rise for 1 hour. Wipe out the processor bowl.

2. Meanwhile, to make the cheese filling, place the mozzarella, ricotta, and sugar in the processor bowl. Process until the cheeses are blended together. Transfer to a small bowl, cover, and refrigerate until ready to use. (This can be made 2 days ahead.)

3. To make the sugar syrup, combine the sugar, water, orange juice, and cinnamon stick in a medium pot. Heat and stir over medium heat, until the sugar dissolves. Increase the heat, bring to a boil, and then reduce the heat to medium-low and simmer for 10 minutes, without stirring. Reduce the heat to low and keep warm until ready to use. (This can be made 2 weeks ahead and refrigerated. Reheat before using.)

4. Preheat the oven to 350°F, with a rack in the middle of the oven.

5. To make the pancakes, heat a griddle or nonstick frying pan on high heat until a droplet of water will roll in the pan. Reduce the heat to medium-high. Spoon in the batter by tablespoonsful to make pancakes that are about 2½ inches in diameter. Do not do more than 4 at a time. Cook the pancakes until the bottoms are well browned and the top edges are dry, but the centers are still slightly moist. Transfer to a work surface with the uncooked sides up. Place a rounded ½ teaspoonful of filling into the center of each pancake. Fold the pancakes in half to form half-moons. Pinch the edges closed. Make and fill all of the pancakes. Set them in nonstick baking pans (I use a 9 × 12-inch jelly roll pan) and cover with foil. They can now be rewarmed in the oven for 10 to 15 minutes, or they can be refrigerated (up to 1 day ahead) and then reheated before eating. After the pancakes have been heated, spoon a tablespoon of warm syrup over each pancake. Turn them to coat with the syrup. Transfer the pancakes to individual plates or to a large platter. Sprinkle with the pistachio nuts, if desired. Remove the cinnamon stick and pass the remaining syrup.

Caramel Apple Blintzes

ALSO SERVE ON
*Shavuot, Shabbat,
Simkat Torah,
Yom ha-atzma'ut*

DAIRY

NUTRITIONAL
NOTES (PER
SERVING)

169 calories

4g fat (20%)

31mg cholesterol

27g carbohydrates

8g protein

88mg sodium

1g fiber

RDA %

4% vitamin A

7% vitamin C

8% calcium

6% iron

*There is no comparison between these rich-tasting, flavorful dessert
blintzes and the ones that come frozen in the supermarket. The
creamy cheese and sweet apple filling is elegant both for brunch and for
Chanukah dessert. Although low in fat, they are very satisfying.*

MAKES 8 SERVINGS

Blintz Batter

1 large egg

2 tablespoons egg substitute (such as Egg Beaters) or 1 egg white

½ cup skim milk

⅛ teaspoon salt

½ teaspoon canola oil

*½ cup plus 1 tablespoon (60 grams) sifted cake flour, lightly sprinkled
into measuring cup*

Caramelized Apples

*2 large apples (10 ounces), Fuji, Golden Delicious, or a
similar variety*

½ medium lemon

⅔ cup firmly packed light brown sugar

½ teaspoon cinnamon

2 tablespoons orange juice

⅓ cup water

2 teaspoons unsalted butter

Filling

*½ pound nonfat cottage cheese, preferably Light and Lively or
other sweet-tasting cheese*

2 ounces light cream cheese, such as Philadelphia ⅓ Less Fat

Light Jewish
Holiday Desserts

2 tablespoons powdered sugar

¼ teaspoon vanilla extract

1½ teaspoons egg substitute (such as Egg Beaters), or whisked egg

For preparation

1 teaspoon unsalted butter

Decorating Sauce (optional)

3 tablespoons light sour cream

2 tablespoons reserved caramel sauce

1. For the blintz batter, place the egg, egg substitute, milk, salt, and oil in a food processor bowl. Process until well blended. Add the flour all at once. Process for 5 seconds to blend the ingredients. Scrape down the bowl and pulse for 3 more seconds to blend well. Transfer the batter to a storage container. Refrigerate for at least 1 hour, and up to 3 days.

2. To make the blintz wrappers, heat a 6-inch, slope-sided, nonstick frying pan over high heat, until a droplet of water will roll in the pan. Stir the batter, as it will have settled while resting. Add a small ladleful (about 2 tablespoons) of batter to the pan. Immediately, pick the pan up off the burner, and swirl the batter around and around, so that it very thinly coats the bottom of the pan and about ⅛ inch up the sides. Set the pan back on the burner and let the pancake cook for 8 to 10 seconds, only on one side. Flip the pancake out onto a plate (lift an edge with a fork, if it doesn't come out). Repeat with the remaining batter, adjusting the temperature of the burner if the wrappers are browning too much. The wrappers can be stacked one on top of another. They can be used immediately, or can be refrigerated, covered with plastic wrap, for up to 3 days. If you want to freeze them, let them cool, stack with waxed paper between each one, wrap the stack in foil, and freeze for up to 3 months. (Thaw the wrappers in the refrigerator before using.)

3. To caramelize the apples, peel, core, and cut the apples into ¼-inch pieces. Squeeze the lemon into 4 cups of cold water. Add the apples to the lemon-water to prevent browning.

continued

Chanukah

4. Place the brown sugar, cinnamon, orange juice, water, and butter in a large frying pan (I like to use nonstick because cooked sugar is hard to get off of pots). Heat over medium heat, stirring constantly, until the sugar dissolves. Increase the heat to medium-high. When the mixture starts to bubble, add the drained apples and reduce the heat to medium. Stir the mixture to coat the apples with the sugar, and then cover the pan. Turn down the heat so that the mixture is just simmering. Cook for 5 minutes. Stir, cover, and heat for another 5 minutes. Uncover the apples, cook, and stir until the apples are tender and the liquid has thickened lightly, another 3 to 5 minutes. If the apples are to be used immediately, remove them from the liquid with a slotted spoon. Reserve the liquid. If the apples are to be refrigerated, pour the contents of the pan into a storage container. Let cool, and then refrigerate. The apples can be made 1 day ahead. Heat in the microwave to warm them before stuffing the blintzes.

5. When ready to prepare the blintzes, make the filling. Place the cottage cheese in a large (approximately 8 × 8 inches) double layer of cheesecloth. Draw up the sides of the cloth to form a "bag." Twist the top of the bag, and squeeze the cloth to expel the liquid from the cheese. Wipe the liquid off the sides of the bag, twist, and squeeze until no more liquid comes out of the cheese. Transfer the cheese to a processor bowl, and process for 1 minute. Scrape down the bowl, and process for another minute. Add the cream cheese, and pulse-process until the cream cheese is well mixed into the cottage cheese. Add the powdered sugar, vanilla, and egg substitute. Process until smooth.

6. If the apples were made ahead and stored, drain them, reserving the juice. If you are planning on using the optional decorating sauce, mix the sour cream and 2 tablespoons of the reserved sauce. Make a small parchment cone (see directions on pages 169–170) with a tiny hole in the tip. Set aside.

7. To assemble the blintzes, set out 1 blintz wrapper on a work surface, with the browned side up. Spread a rounded tablespoonful of the cheese filling on the blintz, just slightly below the center, into a strip that is about 1 inch wide and about 3 inches long. Spoon 2 tablespoons of the apple filling onto the cheese strip. Fold the bottom of the blintz over the filling, and then fold in the sides. Roll the blintz over to finish making the package. (The blintzes can be frozen at this point. Heat them, covered with foil, in a 350°F oven for 20 minutes and then continue as below.)

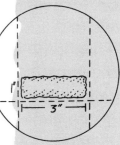

8. Over high heat, melt the butter in a large, nonstick frying pan. When it's sizzling, add 4 to 5 blintzes and turn the heat down to medium. Cook the blintzes until brown, turn, and brown the other side. Transfer the browned blintzes to a plate, and cover with foil. Brown the remaining blintzes. Put all the blintzes back into the pan. Turn the heat to low, cover, and cook for 5 minutes to warm the cheese filling.

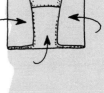

9. For a decorative presentation, spoon a tablespoon of the reserved sauce onto a 6-inch plate. Place a blintz in the center of the plate. Spoon the sour cream mixture into the parchment cone, and make decorations on the sauce—diagonal lines, or squiggles around the perimeter of the plate look nice. Repeat with the remaining 7 plates. Serve immediately.

Bananas Foster

NUTRITIONAL
NOTES (PER
SERVING)

206 calories

3g fat (15%)

8mg cholesterol

39g carbohydrates

1g protein

37mg sodium

2g fiber

RDA %

3% vitamin A

20% vitamin C

2% calcium

4% iron

Here's another flaming dessert to symbolize the miracle of the Temple light. Pair it with some dairy in honor of Judith's bravery. It's not only great for dessert but also makes a wonderful Chanukah breakfast or brunch dish when served with blintzes, crepes, or waffles.

MAKES 4 SERVINGS

1 tablespoon unsalted butter

2 tablespoons orange juice

1 tablespoon fresh lemon juice

½ cup firmly packed brown sugar

½ teaspoon cinnamon

2 tablespoons banana liqueur (optional)

2 tablespoons rum or vodka

4 whole bananas, cut in half lengthwise and then crosswise

1. In a large skillet, combine the butter, juices, brown sugar, and cinnamon. Cook and stir over medium heat until bubbling.

2. Reduce the heat, continue to stir and simmer for 2 minutes. Add the banana liqueur, if using.

3. The best way to ensure that the alcohol will flame is to heat the rum in a small saucepan, ignite it with a long match, and then carefully pour it over the sauce. The flame will shoot up quite high, so make sure that there is nothing in the way that will catch fire. Be careful of your hair, face, and hands, as well. For best effect, turn the lights out so that everyone can see the flame. So that the bananas don't get overcooked, I like to stir them in after the dessert is flambéed, but if you like the flavor of cooked bananas, they can be stirred in before. Serve with nonfat ice cream or yogurt, waffles, crepes, or blintzes.

Custard Cream Puffs

Not all Chanukah desserts need to be fried. After all, there are seven nights of celebration, which allows us to eat many different symbolic foods. Serve dairy-filled cream puffs to honor Judith, a great Jewish heroine. Cream puffs can be casual or elegant depending on how they are served. They can be filled with other fillings, ice cream, or fruit, and served with your own favorite sauce.

MAKES 12 PASTRIES—AVERAGE SERVING 2 PER PERSON

Vanilla Pastry Cream, page 301

Cream Puffs

½ cup water

1½ tablespoons unsalted butter

¼ teaspoon salt

½ teaspoon sugar

½ cup (60 grams) all-purpose flour, lightly sprinkled into measuring cup

2 large eggs

1 tablespoon egg substitute (such as Egg Beaters), or 1 tablespoon egg whisked with ¼ teaspoon water

Cocoa Glaze

¼ cup powdered sugar

1 tablespoon Dutch-processed cocoa, such as Droste

1 tablespoon skim milk

½ teaspoon vanilla extract

continued

ALSO SERVE ON
Shabbat, Shavuot

DAIRY

NUTRITIONAL NOTES
(per serving)

110 calories

3g fat (27%)

53mg cholesterol

17g carbohydrates

3g protein

93mg sodium

0g fiber

RDA %

4% vitamin A

0% vitamin C

6% calcium

3% iron

Chanukah

1. Make the pastry cream and refrigerate it until cold.

2. Preheat the oven to 425°F, with the racks in the middle and lower third of the oven. Line 2 cookie sheets with parchment paper or Teflon liners. Mark 1½-inch circles on the parchment by tapping a floured cookie cutter onto the paper.

3. To make the cream puffs, in a medium saucepan, combine the water, butter, salt, and sugar. Bring to a boil over high heat. Remove from the heat and add the flour all at once. Beat with a wooden spoon until the ingredients form a solid mass. Return the pot to medium-high heat and cook until the dough forms a ball and leaves the sides of the pan, about 30 seconds or less.

4. Transfer the dough to a deep-sided bowl. Add an egg and stir with a wooden spoon, increasing the speed of mixing as the egg gets incorporated into the dough (at first the dough will break up into shiny lumps, but it will smooth out as the egg is incorporated). Repeat with the second egg.

5. The dough can be spooned onto the cookie sheet using 2 teaspoons. Round as much as possible with the spoons and then use a floured finger to finish shaping the dough. To pipe the dough, spoon the batter into a pastry bag that has been fitted with a ¾-inch round (plain) pastry tube. Hold the bag at a 60° angle from the cookie sheet with the tip touching the pan. Squeeze until the batter spreads out around the tip, then raise the tip slightly until the mound is about ½ inch high. Release pressure, and raise the tip. Use a pastry brush dipped in the egg substitute to pat down the "tails" and to glaze the tops of the puffs.

6. Bake for 5 minutes. Switch the position of the cookie sheets, top to bottom. Bake for another 5 minutes. Lower the oven temperature to 350°F. Prop open the oven door with a wooden spoon, and bake the puffs for 20 more minutes. With a toothpick, poke a hole into the bottom of each puff, return to the oven, and let the puffs cook for 5 more minutes. Remove from the oven and let cool on a wire rack. Can be made 1 day ahead or frozen for up to 3 months.

7. Make the cocoa glaze by sifting the powdered sugar and cocoa into a small bowl. Heat the milk in the microwave or on the stove until very hot. Stir it into the cocoa a little at a time. Add the vanilla and continue to stir until smooth.

8. To assemble, fill a pastry bag fitted with a round (plain) ¼-inch tip with the vanilla pastry cream. Poke a hole into the side or bottom of the cream puff (look for a soft spot). Stick in the pastry tip and squeeze until the cream just starts coming back out of the hole. Alternatively, the puffs can be cut in half and the cream can be spooned in.

9. Use a small decorating spatula or a knife to spread the tops of the cream puffs with the chocolate glaze. Fill the cream puffs at least 1 hour in advance. They can be assembled 1 day ahead and stored in a covered container in the refrigerator.

VARIATIONS: Make profiteroles by cutting the cream puffs in half and filling with lowfat frozen yogurt or ice cream. Serve with a sauce of your choosing.

Strawberry Cheese Turnovers

No one will guess that these turnovers are so easily made from packaged white bread. Very sweet, and very popular with children, they're great to do as a Sunday school or class project, or to make with your own children.

MAKES 16 SERVINGS

¼ cup firmly packed light brown sugar

6 tablespoons granulated sugar

½ teaspoon cinnamon

16 slices dense white bread, such as Arnold's Brick Oven Bread

4 teaspoons lowfat tub margarine

¼ pound lowfat cream cheese (preferably Philadelphia ⅓ Less Fat)

2 tablespoons egg substitute (such as Egg Beaters), or whisked egg

½ teaspoon vanilla extract

⅓ cup strawberry jam

continued

DAIRY

NUTRITIONAL NOTES
(per serving)

98 calories

2g fat (20%)

4mg cholesterol

18g carbohydrates

2g protein

106mg sodium

1g fiber

RDA %

1% vitamin A

1% vitamin C

2% calcium

3% iron

Chanukah

1. Preheat the oven to 350°F, with a rack in the middle of the oven. Have a nonstick or parchment-lined cookie sheet handy.

2. On a plate, combine the brown sugar, 4 tablespoons of the granulated sugar, and the cinnamon.

3. Trim off the bread crusts. With a rolling pin, roll the bread as thin as possible. Spread about ¼ teaspoon of the margarine on 1 side of the bread. Place the margarine side of the bread down onto the sugar mixture. Press down to thickly coat the bread with sugar. Set the bread slices on a worktable with the sugared side down.

4. Place the cream cheese, 1 tablespoon of egg substitute, the remaining 2 tablespoons granulated sugar, and the vanilla in a food processor bowl, and process until smooth and well mixed.

5. Spread about 1 teaspoon of cream cheese filling on the lower half of each bread slice, leaving a ¼-inch border on all sides. Brush the border with some of the remaining 1 tablespoon egg substitute. Spoon 1 teaspoon of jam onto the cheese. Fold the bread down over the filling. Push down on the edges and then pinch the edges to seal them well. Place on the cookie sheet. Repeat with remaining bread.

6. Bake 15 to 20 minutes. Let cool, and serve immediately. These can be frozen before baking. (Do not defrost. Bake frozen pastries for 20 to 25 minutes.) Baked pastries should be kept in the refrigerator and brought to room temperature before serving.

VARIATIONS: Use different flavored jams or omit the jams and instead soak dried cherries or raisins in hot water for 5 minutes, drain, and place 3 or 4 in the cheese filling of each turnover.

Oven-Fried *Soofganyot*

Baked Israeli Jelly Donuts

Technically speaking, it is oil that is symbolic for Chanukah, and you may feel odd about serving a dessert that shuns oil. However, soofganyot *themselves are so traditional that baked ones will evoke the feelings and memories that make Chanukah special, even if they are not really fried.*

MAKES 24 SMALL DONUTS

1 cup skim milk

2 tablespoons unsalted butter

¼ cup sugar

1 teaspoon salt

1 large egg

3½ cups (420 grams) all-purpose flour, lightly sprinkled into measuring cup

2 tablespoons instant yeast, such as Fleischmann's Bread Machine Yeast (for other yeasts, please see page 319)

Syrup

2 cups sugar

¾ cup water

Sugar Coating and Filling

¼ cup sugar

1 jar seedless raspberry or grape jam

1. In a medium pot over medium heat, heat the milk and butter until the butter melts. Stir in the sugar and salt. Let cool to 120°F (very warm, but not hot enough to sting your finger).

continued

ALSO SERVE ON
*Shabbat,
Yom ha-atzma'ut*

DAIRY

NUTRITIONAL
NOTES
(per serving; the calories
may be less depending
upon the actual amount of
sugar syrup used)

120 calories

2g fat (13%)

11mg cholesterol

23g carbohydrates

3g protein

107mg sodium

0g fiber

RDA %

1% vitamin A

0% vitamin C

2% calcium

6% iron

Chanukah

2. In a large mixer bowl, whisk the egg. Gradually whisk in the milk mixture. In a separate bowl, mix 2 cups of the flour with the yeast. Add the flour to the egg mixture, and beat it for 2 minutes on medium speed. Stir in the remaining flour to form a soft batter. Cover and let rise for 30 minutes or until doubled in volume.

3. Grease 24 mini-muffin cups (2 pans). Flour your hands, and turn the dough out onto a floured worktable. Roll the dough lightly into a log. Cut off small pieces and form the dough into balls, about 1 inch in diameter. Place 1 ball in each muffin cup. Spray 2 pieces of plastic wrap with cooking spray. Place over the muffin pans and let the dough rise for 30 minutes.

4. Preheat the oven to 375°F, with the rack in the middle of the oven. Bake for 12 to 15 minutes, until the donuts are lightly browned. Turn the donuts out onto a cooling rack.

5. While the dough is baking, prepare the syrup. Combine the sugar and water in a medium pot. Stir, and heat over medium heat until the sugar has dissolved. Increase the heat and boil the syrup for 5 minutes to thicken it. Turn heat to low, and keep the syrup warm.

6. Toss the warm donuts in the sugar syrup. Remove the donuts with a slotted spoon, and roll them in the sugar.

7. Fit a pastry bag with a ¼-inch plain (round) tube. Fill the bag with the jam. Poke a hole in the side of each donut with the pastry tip, squeeze the bag, and fill each donut with jam. Serve as soon as possible. If you want to make them more than 2 hours ahead, delay dipping them in syrup and rolling in sugar until almost ready to serve. Unsugared, they can be frozen for up to 3 months. Reheat them, covered with foil, in a 350°F oven for 15 minutes, then dip in sugar syrup and roll in sugar.

Bimuelos

Fried Donuts in Syrup

ALSO SERVE ON
Shabbat, Yom ha-atzma'ut

PAREVE

Most cultures of the world have some kind of fried dough. Whether they are called bimuelos (*Ladino or Spanish-Jewish*), zalabia (*Egyptian*), zengoula (*Persian*), ponchik (*Polish*), loukumades (*Greek*), or another name, all of them are donuts, the perfect, albeit high-fat, dessert for Chanukah. Unlike soofganyot (*page 127*), these donuts are not made from a rich egg- and-butter dough, but rather from a simple dough of water, yeast, flour, and flavorings. Because the dough is so lean, these donuts only have 2 to 3 grams of fat per donut, when they are fried at the proper temperature and drained on paper towels. If you must fry for Chanukah, this is a lowfat way to go. Be aware, however, that frying changes an oil's composition, so that even though the donuts don't have much fat in them, they might not sit well with you if you are not used to fried foods. As with so many Middle Eastern desserts, bimuelos are dipped in sugar syrup, and like most donuts, they are best when eaten fresh.

MAKES 18 DONUTS

1¼ cups (150 grams) all-purpose flour, lightly sprinkled into
   measuring cup

1½ teaspoons instant yeast, such as Fleischmann's Bread Machine
   Yeast (or see page 319)

2 teaspoons sugar

Pinch of salt

1 cup very warm water (115° to 120°F—not hot enough to
   sting your finger)

Peanut or canola oil (for frying)

continued

NUTRITIONAL
NOTES
(per serving; may vary
depending upon how
much sugar syrup clings,
frying temperature, and
how well drained the
donuts are)

77 calories

2g fat (27%)

0mg cholesterol

14g carbohydrates

1g protein

2mg sodium

0g fiber

RDA %

0% vitamin A

2% vitamin C

1% calcium

3% iron

Chanukah

Sugar Syrup

2½ cups sugar

1 cup water

2 tablespoons orange juice, or 1 teaspoon orange flower water

1 cinnamon stick (optional)

1. Place the flour, yeast, and sugar in a food processor bowl. Process for a few seconds to mix the ingredients together. Mix the salt into the water. Add the warm water to the flour mixture. Process for 5 seconds to make a smooth batter (it will be thin). Cover and let rise for 1 hour.

2. For the syrup, combine the sugar, water, orange juice, and optional cinnamon stick in a medium pot. Heat and stir over medium heat until the sugar dissolves (it won't feel gritty anymore). Increase the heat to high, bring to a boil, reduce the heat, and simmer for 10 minutes (do not stir). Remove the syrup from the heat.

3. Place 3 inches of oil in a deep fryer or large pot and heat to 375°F.

4. Carefully dip a tablespoon into the hot oil, then use the heated spoon to scoop up ½ tablespoon of dough and let it slide into the hot fat. Fry 4 to 6 donuts at a time, depending on the size of the fryer. Cook the donuts for 4 to 5 minutes, until golden brown. Remove and drain on paper towels. While the donuts are still hot, dip them into the sugar syrup. Transfer the donuts to a rack (set over a pan) and let the excess syrup drip off. Repeat with the remaining dough. Eat the donuts as soon as possible.

*C*elebrated on the fifteenth of Shevat (January or February), Tu b'Shevat (Jewish Arbor Day) honors the beginning of fruit formation on trees. Although a minor holiday, there has been much symbolism attached to Tu b'Shevat. Trees may be associated with the Tree of Knowledge in the Garden of Eden, or with the " . . . Tree of Life, which carries divine goodness and blessing into the world," according to Michael Strassfeld in The Jewish Holidays—A Guide and Commentary. Kabbalists in the sixteenth century created a Tu b'Shevat Seder as a means to attain greater spirituality. The ritual involves eating fruits and nuts from three different groups of foods. In the first group are foods that are considered totally edible, having neither pits nor shells—grapes, figs, apples, pears, berries, and quince. This first group symbolizes creation. In the second group are fruits that have pits, but skins that are edible, such as dates, cherries, persimmons, apricots, peaches, and plums. These symbolize formation. The last group symbolizes action and includes foods with inedible outside shells, such as nuts and coconuts. The three groups may also be categorized as follows: edible parts are holy, pits are impure, and shells are protection for the holiness within. Other customs for Tu b'Shevat involve eating fresh and dried fruits and nuts symbolic of Israel, such as almonds, dates, carob, figs, and pomegranates. Drinking a variety of wines and planting trees, both at home and in Israel (through the Jewish National Fund), are also common at Tu b'Shevat.

For Tu b'Shevat, eat the following symbolic foods:

Fruits and nuts indigenous to Israel

Some of each group below, eaten in sequence:

Totally edible: berries, grapes, figs, citrus, pears, apples, star fruit (carambola), quince, and carob

Pits inside: dates, cherries, persimmons, apricots, peaches, and plums

Shells outside: nuts and coconut

Fruit and nut dishes that have at least one from each of the above groups

Dishes with many fruits and nuts—perhaps fifteen (for the fifteenth day of Shevat)

Orange, Apricot, and Walnut Chiffon Cake

This deliciously light cake is a cross between a sponge cake and a true chiffon. It's a great alternative to a standard Jewish sponge cake, as it is never too springy or dry. Although it has slightly more fat than a traditional sponge, it has only one-tenth as much cholesterol. If plain cake does not thrill you, serve it with Winter Fruit Compote (page 135) or with chocolate sauce and pears, oranges, or frozen yogurt.

MAKES 16 SERVINGS

¾ cup (80 grams) sifted cake flour, lightly sprinkled into measuring cup

¾ cup plus 1 tablespoon (100 grams) all-purpose flour, lightly sprinkled into measuring cup

½ teaspoon baking soda

½ teaspoon baking powder

¼ teaspoon salt

1 cup sugar, divided

¼ cup canola oil

1 whole egg, at room temperature

½ cup orange juice, at room temperature

¼ cup frozen orange juice concentrate, thawed, at room temperature

4 large egg whites, at room temperature

Glaze and Garnish

2 tablespoons apricot preserves

1 teaspoon orange juice

2 tablespoons ground walnuts

continued

ALSO SERVE ON
Sukkot,
Yom ha-atzma'ut,
Shabbat

PAREVE

NUTRITIONAL NOTES
(per serving)

140 calories

4g fat (24%)

11mg cholesterol

25g carbohydrates

2g protein

103mg sodium

0g fiber

RDA %

1% vitamin A

17% vitamin C

1% calcium

4% iron

Tu b'Shevat

1. Preheat the oven to 325°F, with a rack in the middle of the oven. Have ready an ungreased angel food or plain-sided tube pan.

2. In a large mixing bowl, stir together both flours, baking soda, baking powder, salt, and ¾ cup of the sugar

3. In another bowl, combine the oil, egg, orange juice, and orange juice concentrate. Add to the flour mixture and beat on medium speed for 1 minute.

4. In a large, clean, grease-free bowl, with clean, grease-free beaters, beat the egg whites until beater marks are just beginning to show and the eggs are very frothy throughout. Gradually add the remaining ¼ cup sugar while continuing to beat. Increase the speed to high, and beat until the egg whites are stiff but not dry. Lightly stir ¼ of the whites into the batter to lighten it. Gently fold in remaining whites.

5. Spoon the batter into the prepared pan. Draw a knife through the batter to break up any large bubbles. Bake for 40 to 50 minutes or until a tester inserted into the center of the cake comes out with no moist crumbs attached.

6. Turn the cake upside down to cool. (Angel food pans have little feet to rest on. If using a tube pan, invert it onto a bottle neck.) When cool, turn it right side up. Cut around the perimeter of the pan and the center tube with a sharp knife. Use a long knife to cut the cake from the bottom of the pan. Push up to remove the sides of the pan. Turn the tube upside down onto a cutting board. Remove the tube from the cake. Place a platter on the bottom of the cake, and using the cutting board and platter to sandwich the cake, turn the cake right side up.

7. To make the glaze, heat the apricot preserves with the juice. Strain out any large lumps. Brush the top of the cake with the preserves. Sprinkle with the walnuts. Can be made 1 day ahead (do not freeze).

Winter Fruit Compote

If kumquats are not to your liking, you can still make this compote, and use the kumquats for flavoring only. This tzimmes not only has an unusual taste but an interesting color as well. The plums "bleed" color into the sauce, creating one of the prettiest pinks I've ever seen in a natural food. The combination of fruits is also a nutritional dynamo. You can eat the compote plain, or you can use it as a filling or topping for cakes.

MAKES 6 SERVINGS

4 cups water, divided

½ pound kumquats (about 25), washed

½ medium lemon

2 cups sugar

1 medium cinnamon stick

4 medium dark purple plums

2 medium pears, preferably Bosc

1. Bring 2 cups of the water to boil in a medium, nonreactive pot. Add the kumquats, and let them blanch for 30 seconds. Drain the kumquats, rinse in cold water, and place back in the pot. Squeeze the lemon into the pot. Add the remaining 2 cups water, the sugar, and cinnamon. Bring the mixture to a simmer, stirring occasionally. Reduce the heat so that the liquid just maintains a simmer, cover the pot, and cook the kumquats for 1 hour.

2. Cut each plum into 16 wedges and remove all stones. Peel, core, and cut the pears into long ¼-inch slices. Slide the fruit into the liquid and stew them for just a few minutes until barely softened. Remove the pot

ALSO SERVE ON
Shabbat,
Yom ha-atzma'ut

PAREVE

NUTRITIONAL
NOTES
(per serving; with a
glazing of sugar syrup)

93 calories

.5g fat (5%)

0mg cholesterol

24g carbohydrates

1g protein

5mg sodium

5g fiber

RDA %

5% vitamin A

45% vitamin C

6% calcium

7% iron

Tu b'Shevat

from the heat, and let the mixture cool with the pot covered. Transfer the mixture to a storage container and place in the refrigerator until cold.

3. Remove the cinnamon stick and serve the fruit with a little syrup, and/or with frozen yogurt, or over ladyfingers (page 42). The juice is very exotic tasting and can be used as a simple syrup for genoise and sponge cakes. It can also be boiled down until thick and used to glaze fresh oranges, grapefruits, pears, or other fruit. The drained fruit is also delicious served with chocolate sauce.

Date, Fig, and Nut Loaf

This moist, fruity, and sweet loaf can be eaten plain, or with whipped cream cheese. It will last for nearly a week, wrapped in foil at room temperature. If you use the pre-chopped dates, which are already sweetened, you might want to reduce the sugar by ¼ cup. .

MAKES 10 SERVINGS

1 cup dried dates, chopped

½ cup dried figs, chopped

1 teaspoon baking soda

1 tablespoon canola oil

¾ cup boiling water

⅔ cup sugar

1 large egg, at room temperature

1⅛ cups (120 grams) sifted cake flour, lightly sprinkled into measuring cup

½ cup chopped walnuts

1. Preheat the oven to 325°F, with a rack in the middle of the oven. Spray-grease and flour a 9 × 5-inch loaf pan.

2. In a large bowl, combine the dates, figs, baking soda, and oil. Pour in the boiling water and let soak for 30 minutes.

3. Stir in the sugar and egg.

4. In another bowl, combine the flour and walnuts. Stir this into the date mixture. Spoon the batter into the prepared pan. Bake for about 1 hour, or until a toothpick inserted into the center of the cake comes out with no moist crumbs attached. Place the pan on a rack to cool completely. Run a knife around the sides of the cake and invert to remove the loaf. Can be made 1 day ahead, or frozen for 3 months.

ALSO SERVE ON
Shabbat, Purim,
Yom ha-atzma'ut

PAREVE

NUTRITIONAL
NOTES
(per serving)

208 calories

5g fat (21%)

40g carbohydrates

18mg cholesterol

3g protein

133mg sodium

2g fiber

RDA %

1% vitamin A

0% vitamin C

1% calcium

4% iron

Tu b'Shevat

Chocolate Fondue with Mixed Fruit

Chocolate Fondue is a delicious and fun way to eat fruit (not to mention chocolate!), especially for fussy kids. It has been lightened considerably, having almost 200 calories and 15 grams of fat less per serving than regular fondue. Use any combination of fruit, but to make it special for Tu b'Shevat, include one from each category: totally edible (apple, orange, strawberry, etc.), pitted fruits (mango, apricot, plums, dates, or papaya), and shelled fruits (bananas, pineapple, coconuts, and nuts).

MAKES 5 SERVINGS

1 teaspoon cornstarch

1 tablespoon plus ⅓ cup skim milk, divided

¼ cup sugar

⅓ cup light corn syrup

⅓ cup Dutch-processed cocoa, such as Droste

2 tablespoons chopped semisweet chocolate, or chips

1 teaspoon vanilla extract

1 large apple

7 ounces pineapple chunks in juice, drained, juice reserved

10 medium strawberries

1¼ large bananas

1. Boil about 2 inches of water in the bottom of a double boiler. Cover and reduce the heat to low.

2. Place the cornstarch in a small bowl. Stir in 1 tablespoon of the milk.

3. Combine the remaining ⅓ cup milk and ¼ cup of sugar (or less, to taste) in a small pot. Heat to boiling over medium heat. Stir in the cornstarch

ALSO SERVE ON
Shabbat—include cubes of sponge cake; Sukkot—use fall fruits; Shavuot—use summer fruits

DAIRY

NUTRITIONAL NOTES
(per serving)

288 calories

3g fat (9.5%)

1mg cholesterol

69g carbohydrates

4g protein

42mg sodium

10g fiber

RDA %

3% vitamin A

276% vitamin C

8% calcium

12% iron

mixture. Simmer, stirring continuously, for 1 minute or until the mixture thickens. Stir in the corn syrup and remove the pot from the heat.

4. Place the cocoa and chocolate chips in the top of the double boiler, but not over the heat yet. Stir in the milk mixture a little at a time until the mixture is mostly smooth. Set the pan over the hot water, cover, and let heat for 1 minute. Uncover the pot and stir the mixture until most of the chocolate is melted. Stir in the vanilla. Strain through a medium-mesh strainer into the fondue pot. (If storing, strain into a container. Leave uncovered until the chocolate is cool, and then cover and refrigerate until ready to serve. Can be made 1 week in advance. When ready to serve, heat 2 inches of water in the bottom of a double boiler. Spoon the chocolate into the top of the double boiler, and heat it over the boiling water until hot.) Set the fondue pot over the flame.

5. Cut the apple into wedges, and then halve the wedges, crosswise. Dip the slices in the reserved pineapple juice to prevent discoloration, and then pat dry. Cut the strawberries in half. Cut the bananas into ¾-inch chunks. If you are cutting up the bananas ahead of time, dip them into the pineapple juice to prevent darkening. Pat dry. Divide the fruit among 5 small plates. Use fondue forks to dip the fruit into the chocolate. Fondue gets hotter as you reach the bottom of the pot, so be careful not to get burned.

Tu b'Shevat

Apple Apricot Brown Betty

ALSO SERVE ON
Shabbat,
Rosh Hashanah,
Sukkot

DAIRY OR PAREVE

NUTRITIONAL NOTES (PER SERVING)

180 calories

5g fat (26%)

0mg cholesterol

32g carbohydrates

2g protein

47mg sodium

4g fiber

RDA %

34% vitamin A

23% vitamin C

3% calcium

6% iron

*C*reated especially for Tu b'Shevat, this brown Betty has one completely edible fruit (apple), one fruit with stones (apricot), and one fruit with an outside shell (almonds). I've lightened it by reducing the butter, and by using crumbs only on the top of the dessert. If you like a crunchier topping, see Deep-Dish Pear-Cherry Gratin on page 52.

MAKES 8 SERVINGS

Filling

16 dried apricots

1 cup boiling water

7 medium apples, preferably greenish Golden Delicious or other sweet, medium-firm variety

1 lemon, juiced

¼ cup firmly packed light brown sugar (or more)

1 teaspoon cinnamon

3 tablespoons cornstarch

Breadcrumb Almond Topping

3 cups coarse, fresh white bread crumbs

2 tablespoons firmly packed light brown sugar

2 tablespoons sliced, blanched almonds, lightly crushed

2 tablespoons canola oil (for dairy, use melted unsalted butter)

1. Preheat the oven to 350°F, with a rack in the middle of the oven. Have ready an 8 × 10-inch Pyrex pan.

2. In a large bowl, soak the apricots in the boiling water for 15 minutes. Drain and return the apricots to the empty bowl.

3. Peel, core, and cut the apples into ¼-inch slices. Mix 6 cups of the sliced apples into the apricots, discarding (or saving for another use) any extra apples. Stir in the lemon juice, brown sugar (if the apricots are very tart, increase the sugar by up to ½ cup more), cinnamon, and cornstarch. Spoon the fruit mixture into the Pyrex pan.

4. In another bowl, toss together the bread crumbs, sugar, and almonds. Sprinkle with the oil and toss again with a fork until the crumbs are lightly coated. Strew the crumbs over the top of the fruit.

5. Bake for 60 minutes, or until the crumbs are golden and the fruit is cooked. Let cool until warm, and serve. If prepared a couple of hours in advance, reheat in a 350°F oven for 15 minutes or until the crumbs get crisp again.

Apple Mango Crisp

ALSO SERVE ON
Rosh Hashanah,
Sukkot, Shabbat

DAIRY OR
PAREVE

NUTRITIONAL
NOTES
(per serving)

180 calories

3.5g fat (17%)

14mg cholesterol

37g carbohydrates

1g protein

24mg sodium

3g fiber

RDA %

29% vitamin A

23% vitamin C

2% calcium

7% iron

If you cook very firm mangoes, they lose their perfumy taste, and become more reminiscent of peaches. Mango lovers might like to use fruit that is riper. The orange flesh makes a beautifully colored dessert, so welcome in the middle of the winter. High in beta-carotene, vitamin C, and fiber, it's nutritious as well as delicious. If you'd like to use fruits from the three groups, add 2 tablespoons of chopped almonds or pecans to the crumb topping. (This will add about 1.5 grams fat per serving.)

MAKES 8 SERVINGS

Apple Mango Filling

1 medium lemon

7 medium apples, preferably greenish Golden Delicious or other sweet, medium-firm to firm variety

2 medium mangoes, ripe but very firm

¼ cup firmly packed light brown sugar

1 teaspoon cinnamon

3 tablespoons cornstarch

Crumb Topping

¾ cup (90 grams) all-purpose flour, lightly sprinkled into measuring cup

⅓ cup firmly packed light brown sugar

¼ teaspoon cinnamon

1 tablespoon canola oil

1 tablespoon unsalted butter (or unsalted pareve margarine), melted

2 teaspoons egg substitute (such as Egg Beaters), or whisked whole egg

Light Jewish
Holiday Desserts

1. Preheat the oven to 350°F, with a rack in the middle of the oven. Have ready an 8 × 12-inch Pyrex or other decorative baking dish.

2. Squeeze the lemon into a large bowl. Peel, core, and cut the apples into ¼-inch slices, and toss in the lemon juice. Peel the mangoes and cut the flesh off the stones in ¼-inch strips. Cut the strips into 2-inch pieces. Add to the apple mixture. Stir in the brown sugar, cinnamon, and cornstarch. Set aside.

3. To prepare the topping, in a medium bowl, mix together the flour, brown sugar, and cinnamon. Mix the oil into the butter, then add it to the flour. Stir with a fork until moistened. Use your fingertips to rub the fats into the flour. Add just enough of the egg substitute to moisten the mixture so that you can squeeze the mixture into crumbs.

4. Stir the fruit, and then spoon it into the baking dish. Sprinkle the crumbs over the top.

5. Bake for 40 to 50 minutes, or until the topping is brown and the fruit is tender. The crumbs will get crisper as they cool. Place on a rack and let the crisp cool until just warm, 30 to 45 minutes. For more elegant service, the fruit can be baked in individual ramekins. The crisp can be made 8 hours ahead. Rewarm at 350°F for about 15 minutes before serving. The fruit can also be covered with foil, and baked ahead, without the crumbs. Bake the crumbs on a cookie sheet at 350°F for 7 to 12 minutes, until browned. Let cool, then sprinkle the crumbs on the warm, cooked fruit. Made this way, the topping will be crunchy. If crumbs are to be made ahead, you could also use the Streusel (Crumb) Topping (page 296), which makes a more tender crumb.

Dried Fruit and Apple Tart

D evotees of dried fruit will love this refreshing tart. Although easy
to prepare, the apple topping is very elegant and festive.

MAKES 10 SERVINGS

One 9-inch tart shell, partially baked (page 290)

Dried Fruit Filling

*One 6-ounce package dried fruit bits (or mixed dried fruit
cut into ¼-inch dice)*

¼ cup orange juice

1 tablespoon firmly packed light brown sugar

2 tablespoons maple syrup

½ medium cinnamon stick

2 whole cloves

Topping

2 medium apples, preferably medium-firm to firm variety

¼ cup orange juice

1½ teaspoons granulated sugar

2 tablespoons apricot jam

1. To make the filling, in a medium pot, combine the dried fruit, orange
juice, brown sugar, maple syrup, and spices. Bring the mixture to a boil.
Lower the heat, cover, and simmer for 10 to 15 minutes, until the fruit is
tender and most of the liquid has been absorbed. Set aside to cool. The
filling can be made 1 week in advance. Store in the refrigerator.

2. Preheat the oven to 350°F, with a rack in the middle of the oven.

3. To make the topping, peel, core, and cut the apples into ⅛-inch slices.
Place the orange juice in a zip-top bag, and add the apples. Seal the bag,

ALSO SERVE ON
*Rosh Hashanah,
Sukkot,
Yom Ha-atzma'ut,
Shabbat*

DAIRY OR
PAREVE

NUTRITIONAL
NOTES
(per serving)

155 calories

6g fat (25%)

10mg cholesterol

29g carbohydrates

2g protein

86mg sodium

2g fiber

RDA %

9% vitamin A

16% vitamin C

3% calcium

8% iron

and shake it so that all of the apples get bathed in the orange juice (this will help to keep them from darkening). Drain the apples, reserving 1 teaspoon orange juice. Pat dry.

4. Press the cool dried fruit into the baked tart shell. Arrange the apples on the dried fruit, perpendicular to the perimeter, in concentric, overlapping circles. Sprinkle the apples with the sugar. Cover the tart with foil and bake for 25 to 35 minutes, or until the apples are tender. Remove the tart from the oven and set on a cooling rack. Remove the foil and let the tart come to room temperature.

5. Mix the reserved teaspoon of orange juice with the apricot jam. Press it through a medium strainer (heat it if it is too thick to be strained). Brush the apricot glaze over the apples. The tart can be served room temperature or may be chilled for up to 8 hours.

Apple-Plum Galette

This pizza-size pastry, with alternating slices of apple and plum, is truly a delight to the eye. The plums "bleed" color onto the apple edges, which become tinged with pink. The effect is wonderful. For the pastry, I use my grandmother's muerbe teig, *a tasty crust that can be rolled very thin.*

MAKES 10 SERVINGS

*½ recipe Sour Cream Muerbe Teig Pastry, page 294,
   refrigerated overnight*

1 medium lemon

*2 large greenish Golden Delicious apples, or
   other medium-firm variety*

2 large purple plums

*2 whole Stella D'oro Almond Toast cookies, or
   ¼ cup lowfat cookie crumbs*

continued

Tu b'Shevat

145

NUTRITIONAL
NOTES
(per serving)

146 calories

5g fat (31%)

2mg cholesterol

24g carbohydrates

2g protein

107mg sodium

1g fiber

R D A %

4% vitamin A

4% vitamin C

0% calcium

6% iron

1 tablespoon sugar

¼ cup apple jelly, or apricot preserves

1. Preheat the oven to 400°F, with a rack in the lower third of the oven.

2. Flour the inside of a jumbo zip-top bag. Place the dough inside the bag, and roll it out into a 10- to 12-inch circle, depending on the size of your pan. Cut the top off the bag. Holding the dough at one edge, invert the plastic onto a greased cookie sheet or pizza pan, peel off the bag, and refrigerate or freeze the pastry while you make the filling.

3. Squeeze the lemon into a large bowl. Peel, core, and cut the apples into ¹⁄₁₆-inch slices, and toss with the lemon juice. Halve the plums, remove the stones, and cut the plums into ¹⁄₁₆-inch pieces. Drain the apples and pat dry.

4. Process the cookies into fine crumbs. Remove the pastry from the refrigerator, and sprinkle the cookie crumbs evenly over it. Starting at the outside edge of the pastry, place an apple slice with the tip not quite perpendicular to the perimeter. Next, place a plum slice slightly overlapping the apple. Continue around the pastry alternating apples and the plums, making concentric, overlapping circles, until you reach the center of the pastry. Make sure that you arrange the fruit so that the edges of the plums (page 21) with the skin on them are visible. The center slices will look like a pinwheel. If the pinwheel is not in the center of the pastry, push the fruit slightly until centered. Sprinkle the sugar over the fruit.

5. Bake for 40 minutes or until the fruit is tender and the crust is browned. Set the pan on a cooling rack.

6. Melt the apple jelly in the microwave until liquidy (if using apricot jam, it will need to be strained). Brush generously over the fruit. Let the pastry cool, and serve within 4 hours. Delicious served with nonfat frozen yogurt.

Apple Date Tart

Apple-orange flavor and crunchy little seeds distinguish this tart. For those not enamored of dates or figs, raisins can be substituted.

MAKES 10 SERVINGS

One 9-inch tart shell, partially baked (page 290)

1 medium lemon

4 medium (440g) Fujis, or other semisweet apples

¼ cup orange juice

⅓ cup chopped dates

¼ cup firmly packed light brown sugar

½ teaspoon cinnamon

3 tablespoons cornstarch

⅓ cup dried figs, stems cut off and fruit diced

1 egg white, whisked with 1 teaspoon water, for glaze

1. Make the tart shell. Roll out the excess dough, cut out Jewish star–shaped cookies, and place them in the freezer.

2. Preheat the oven to 350°F, with a rack in the center (or reduce the temperature if you have just finished baking the tart shell).

3. Squeeze half of the lemon into a large bowl of water. Peel, halve, core, and drop each apple, as it is cut, into the bowl of lemon-water.

4. Drain the apples and grate in a food processor or with a box grater. Transfer to a large bowl and squeeze on the remaining lemon half. Stir in the orange juice, dates, brown sugar, cinnamon, cornstarch, and figs. Spoon the filling into the tart shell.

5. Brush the frozen Jewish-star cookies with the egg white glaze, and arrange them on top of the filling. Bake for 45 to 55 minutes, or until the stars are nicely browned. Cool the tart on a rack. Serve at room temperature. The tart can be made 3 hours ahead. Do not freeze.

ALSO SERVE ON
Rosh Hashanah,
Sukkot, Shabbat,
Yom ha-atzma'ut

DAIRY OR PAREVE

NUTRITIONAL NOTES
(per serving)

222 calories

7g fat (28%)

1mg cholesterol

38g carbohydrates

3g protein

62mg sodium

2g fiber

RDA %

3% vitamin A

9% vitamin C

2% calcium

7% iron

Tu b'Shevat

Pear Tart Frangipane

ALSO SERVE ON
Sukkot,
Yom ha-atzma'ut

DAIRY OR PAREVE

NUTRITIONAL NOTES
(per serving)

171 calories

7.5g fat (37%)

10mg cholesterol

25g carbohydrates

3g protein

93mg sodium

1g fiber

RDA %

5% vitamin A

3% vitamin C

3% calcium

7% iron

*P*ears and almonds were made for each other. Although not as rich as true frangipane, the flavor and texture of this tart are excellent.

MAKES 10 SERVINGS

One 9-inch tart shell, partially baked (page 290)

Frangipane Filling

⅓ cup blanched sliced almonds

3 tablespoons sugar

2 tablespoons (15 grams) all-purpose flour

2 tablespoons applesauce

¼ cup egg substitute (such as Egg Beaters), or 1 large egg, whisked

Pear Topping

2 medium Bosc pears, ripe but firm

1 medium lemon, squeezed into 4 cups cold water

2 teaspoons sugar

2 tablespoons apricot preserves

1. Make and cool the tart shell.

2. Preheat the oven to 350°F, with a rack in the middle of the oven (or lower the temperature if you have just finished baking the tart shell).

3. In a food processor, process the almonds, sugar, and flour until the nuts are finely ground. Add the applesauce and egg substitute, and pulse until combined. Spoon into the cooled partially baked crust.

4. Peel, core, and cut the pears into long slices, ⅛ inch thick. Place the slices into the lemon-water to help keep them from turning brown. Drain and pat dry. Arrange the slices in the pastry so that they are not quite perpendicular to the perimeter and so that they overlap. Make a pinwheel

design in the center with some of the shorter slices. Sprinkle the pears with the sugar. Bake for 25 minutes until the filling is set and the crust is done. Remove the tart to a rack to cool. Strain the apricot preserves and then brush the pears with the glaze. Serve the tart at room temperature or cold. Best eaten within 8 hours.

VARIATION: Purple plums look exquisite in this tart. Use 5 plums, each cut into sixteenths. Place the plums in concentric circles, tip to tip, with the rounded edges parallel to the perimeter.

Tu b'Shevat

Deep-Dish Winter Fruit Pie

ALSO SERVE ON
*Rosh Hashanah,
Sukkot, Shabbat*

**DAIRY OR
PAREVE**

**NUTRITIONAL
NOTES**
(per serving)

267 calories

7g fat (20%)

7mg cholesterol

51g carbohydrates

3g protein

122mg sodium

4g fiber

RDA %

5% vitamin A

14% vitamin C

2% calcium

6% iron

*P*lums and grapes provide a nice blush of color in this family-style pie. By using a pecan crust, you have all three categories of fruits—the ideal combination for Tu b'Shevat. Because it gets scooped out and served in bowls, the serving size is very generous. The crust is quite rich tasting because of the nuts used but still has one third less fat than a standard crust.

MAKES 9 SERVINGS

*Nut Pastry Crust, for an 8 × 10-inch pan, page 292, refrigerated
15 minutes*

Filling

1 cup red seedless grapes

4 medium dark purple plums, very firm

3 large pears, preferably Bosc, firm but ripe

*3 large apples, preferably greenish Golden Delicious, or other
medium-firm to firm variety*

1 medium lemon, squeezed into 8 cups cold water

1 teaspoon cinnamon

½ cup sugar

⅓ cup cornstarch

Glaze

1 large egg white, whisked with 1 teaspoon water

1 teaspoon sugar

1. Preheat the oven to 375°F, with a rack in the middle. Have ready an 8 × 10-inch Pyrex dish, or a decorative baking dish of about the same size.

2. While the pastry is chilling, halve the grapes and place in a large bowl. Cut each plum into 16 wedges, remove the stones, and add the wedges to the grapes.

3. Peel, core, and cut the pears and apples into ¼-inch slices (not wedges). Place in lemon-water. Drain and add to the grapes. Add the cinnamon, sugar, and cornstarch to the fruit. Mix well and then spoon this into the baking pan.

4. To shape the dough, flour the inside of a jumbo zip-top bag. Place the dough in the bag and let the dough rest for about 15 minutes to make it easier to roll. Roll the dough to 1/16 inch thick, and slightly larger than the pan you are using. Cut open the bag. To transfer the dough to the pan, hold the dough on one end firmly to the plastic. Overturn the dough onto the fruit, and then ease it off the plastic. Press the dough to the edges of the pan.

5. For the glaze, brush the crust with the egg wash and sprinkle with the sugar. Make 4 to 5 slits in the crust to allow steam to escape. Cut a piece of foil the same size as the pan. Fold it in half and cut from the folded side, leaving 3 inches along the perimeter of the rectangle. You'll now have a "frame" to shield the edges of the crust to protect against over-browning. Set it aside. Place the dish on a cookie sheet to catch drips.

6. Bake for 30 minutes. If the edges are nicely browned, cover them with the shield that you have made. If the entire crust is brown, cover the whole thing with foil. Continue to cook the pie for another 15 minutes. Remove the pie from the oven and set it on a rack to cool until just warm (about 1 hour). Can be made 8 hours ahead. Store at room temperature, uncovered. To serve, reheat at 350°F for about 15 minutes, or until just warmed through. To serve, spoon some of the crust and fruit into bowls.

Pear Cherry Turnovers

ALSO SERVE ON
Sukkot, Shabbat

DAIRY

NUTRITIONAL NOTES
(per serving)

134 calories

5g fat (34%)

5mg cholesterol

20g carbohydrates

2g protein

108 mg sodium

1g fiber

RDA %

1% vitamin A

1% vitamin C

1% calcium

4% iron

I used to make these turnovers with puff pastry, but with 16 grams of fat, they didn't seem worth it. Now we eat them often. If you would like to include fruits from all three Tu b'Shevat groups, add some nuts or coconut (this will add a little more fat). You can make the turnovers pareve, but they won't be as tasty or as flaky.

MAKES 12 SERVINGS

12 leaves defrosted phyllo dough (see directions below)

2 large Bosc pears, ripe but firm

1 medium lemon, squeezed into 4 cups cold water

1 teaspoon canola oil

1 teaspoon granulated sugar

Cinnamon and nutmeg

2 tablespoons dried cherries

2 tablespoons unsalted butter

5 teaspoons canola oil

5 tablespoons powdered sugar

2 whole lowfat graham crackers, crushed

1. Defrost the package of phyllo overnight in the refrigerator. Remove the dough from the package, but leave it in its inner sleeve. Let it stand at room temperature for 2 hours.

2. Preheat the oven to 425°F, with a rack in the middle of the oven.

3. Peel, core, and cut the pears into long slices, ⅛ inch thick. Drop the slices into the lemon-water to prevent them from darkening. Drain and pat dry. Place in a 9 × 12-inch baking pan. Drizzle on the oil, sprinkle with the granulated sugar and the spices to taste, and then toss the pears to distribute everything evenly. Cover with foil, shiny side down, and bake the pears for 15 to 30 minutes, or until they are tender (time will depend upon ripeness and variety of pear used). Remove from the oven and let the pears cool. When the pears are cool, puree half in the processor. Cut the remaining pears into ⅛-inch chunks. Mix the pureed and chunky pears together. Stir in the dried cherries.

4. Reduce the oven temperature to 375°F.

5. Melt the butter and oil together and set it near the work surface.

6. Tape together 2 pieces of waxed paper so that they are about the same size as the cookie sheet you are using. Cut 3 more pieces of waxed paper, each about 16 inches long. Once the phyllo has been unwrapped, it must be used quickly and kept covered with waxed paper, or it will dry out and crumble like dried leaves. Gather together the pear mixture, powdered sugar in a sprinkler (or a small strainer), grahams, the waxed paper sheets you have assembled, cookie sheet, pastry brush, and long knife.

7. Remove the phyllo from the box and unfold it onto a piece of waxed paper. Remove half of the stack, reroll it, and place back in the plastic sleeve or in a zip-top bag. Refrigerate or refreeze it for another use.

8. Transfer 1 leaf of phyllo (1 sheet) to a work surface. Brush it lightly with the butter mixture and sprinkle with some powdered sugar. Cut the leaf, perpendicular to the long end, into 4 strips. Stack the strips 1 on top of the other. Sprinkle 1 teaspoon of graham crumbs on the lower 3 inches of the dough.

continued

Tu b'Shevat

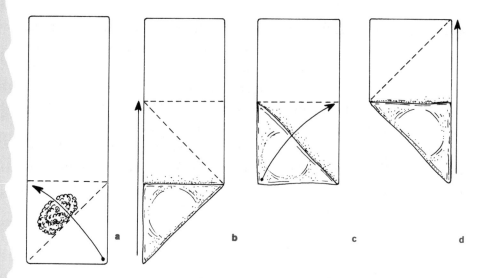

9. Shape the turnovers as follows: Imagine a 3 × 3-inch rectangle at the lower end of the dough with a line through the middle of it that divides the rectangle into 2 triangles. Spoon a tablespoon of the pear filling along that line and into the top triangle. You are now going to fold the dough up, as if it were a flag. To do that, fold 1 corner of the phyllo across the filling so that you can now see the triangle that you have been imagining (a). Next fold the triangle straight up (b). The next fold is diagonal (c), and the next straight up (d). Continue to the end of the dough. If there is a small strip of dough left after all the folds have been made, it can be cut off, or tucked in before the last fold is made. Brush the pastry top with butter, and sprinkle with powdered sugar. Set it on the cookie sheet, and cover with the waxed paper that has been taped together. Repeat steps 8 and 9 with all of the phyllo.

10. Bake the pastries for 12 to 15 minutes or until nicely browned. Remove from the oven and let them cool for at least 30 minutes before serving. They should be served still warm. The pastries can be made 8 hours ahead if left uncovered, at room temperature. Rewarm in a 350°F oven for 10 minutes. Unbaked pastries can also be frozen (bake at 350°F for 10 minutes; raise the heat to 400°F and cook until browned and crispy, another 10 to 15 minutes).

VARIATIONS: Substitute raisins or dates for the cherries. Substitute apples or plums for the pears.

Purim, *observed on the fourteenth of Adar (February or March), and the fifteenth of Adar in cities that were once surrounded by walls, celebrates the triumph of ancient Persian Jews over Haman, the wicked vizier to King Ahasuerus. In the story told in the Scroll of Esther (the Megillah), the King decrees that all subjects must bow down to Haman. Mordecai, a Jew, refuses to do so, which infuriates Haman. He convinces the King that all Jews are disloyal and must die. The date is determined by the casting of lots (purim, in Hebrew). Unbeknownst to the King, his wife,*

Esther, is a Jew and Mordecai's cousin. At a feast that she prepares for the King, Esther reveals her heritage and begs the King to spare her people. Mordecai and Esther convince the King that Haman is his enemy, whereupon Ahasuerus has Haman sent to the gallows instead of Mordecai. The story of Esther and the threat to the Jewish people is probably not historically accurate. Celebrated in a carnival atmosphere with costumes, noise makers, loud merriment, and drunken oblivion (there is a Talmudic suggestion to drink so much wine that one will not know the difference between Mordecai and Haman), it is not supposed to be taken as a literal event. Rather, Purim is a time to relax our inhibitions and laugh at our misfortunes as well as our triumphs.

The traditional Ashkenazi dessert for Purim is hamantashen, a triangular cookie usually filled with poppy or prune filling. According to different theories, the triangular shape of the hamantashen, or "Haman's pockets," is supposed to represent Haman's pockets filled with lots, his tricornered hat, or his ears. The shape may also represent the three patriarchs, Abraham, Isaac, and Jacob, who inspired Queen Esther. The most traditional filling is poppy seed (or *mohn* in Yiddish), perhaps because the Yiddish word is so close to *Homen* (Yiddish for Haman). Sephardic Jews from Israel and other Middle Eastern countries, Italy, and Austria eat cookies called oznai haman, or "Haman's ears." This tradition may have come about from the custom of cutting off a criminal's ears before execution, writes Gloria Kaufer Greene, in *The Jewish Holiday Cookbook.*

Another tradition is to eat foods rich in nuts and seeds to honor Esther, who ate them in order to keep kosher in the "unclean" environment of the court. The Book of Esther also tells us to send gifts (*mishloah minot*) to one another and to the poor. It is most common to send hamantashen and other small cookies or cakes. Celebrate Purim with the following symbolic foods:

Hamantashen

Triangular cakes and cookies

Poppy seed desserts

Desserts with nuts and seeds

Small cakes, bars, and cookies to give away

Prune, Apricot, or Mohn Hamantashen

These are the quintessential Purim cookies. I've cut out just a small quantity of the butter so that they will still taste and feel like the cookies that you know and love. I've also made them smaller, which reduces the fat per cookie. In my classes, most people prefer not to make their own fillings, but I always do, because I like to tailor the sugar to the fruit used.

MAKES 26 COOKIES

1½ cups (180 grams) all-purpose flour, lightly sprinkled into measuring cup

½ cup plus 1 tablespoon (60 grams) sifted cake flour, lightly sprinkled into measuring cup

1 teaspoon baking powder

¼ teaspoon salt

½ cup sugar

7 tablespoons unsalted butter, chilled (vegetable shortening for pareve)

1 teaspoon vanilla extract

1 teaspoon orange juice

1 large egg, cold

One 12-ounce jar prune or other filling, or homemade filling (see Variations)

1. Preheat the oven to 375°F, with racks in the middle and lower third of the oven. Line 2 cookie sheets with parchment paper or nonstick Teflon liners.

continued

ALSO SERVE ON
Yom ha-atzma'ut, Shabbat

DAIRY OR PAREVE

NUTRITIONAL NOTES
(per serving, with bought prune filling)

105 calories

3g fat (28%)

8mg cholesterol

17g carbohydrates

1g protein

43mg sodium

.5g fiber

RDA %

0% vitamin A

0% vitamin C

1% calcium

3% iron

Purim

2. Place the all-purpose flour, cake flour, baking powder, salt, and sugar in a food processor bowl. Process just to mix ingredients together.

3. Cut the butter into ½-inch chunks and place on top of the flour. Pulse-process until the butter is cut into the flour so that the mixture looks like coarse meal.

4. In a bowl, lightly whisk together the vanilla, orange juice, and egg. With the processor running, add the egg mixture through the feed tube. Pulse-process for 10 seconds, 3 times. Dump the dough out onto a board. You should be able to press it into a ball that is neither sticky nor dry. If necessary, add up to 2 tablespoons more cake flour, a little at a time, to make the dough the proper consistency (those who are weighing the flour should use 240 grams).

5. Because this dough has so much sugar in it, it gets stickier as it sits. It is best to use it at once, and to work quickly. Divide the dough into 2 pieces. Flatten each piece, and roll it to a scant ⅛ inch thick. Cut into 2½-inch rounds. Gather the scraps, reroll, and cut as many as possible.

6. Place 1 rounded teaspoon of filling, almost centered, just slightly closer to the top edge than the bottom edge. Fold the edges toward the center to form a triangle, leaving a bit of filling showing.

7. Pinch the edges to seal. Place the cookies ½ inch apart on the cookie sheets. Put 1 cookie sheet on each rack. Bake 6 minutes, switch the position of the top and bottom cookie sheets, and continue to bake for 5 to 6 minutes or until cookies are firm but not brown. Cool completely before eating.

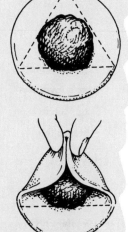

VARIATIONS: Try one of these in place of store-bought filling:

Old-Fashioned Prune Filling

If your prunes are not very moist, you will need to use this recipe.

12 ounces (about 2 cups) dried, pitted prunes

1 cup water

½ teaspoon cinnamon

¼ cup sugar

Combine the prunes, water, cinnamon, and sugar in a medium pot and cook, covered, over medium heat until the prunes can be mashed. Mash with a fork and cook to the desired thickness. Refrigerate until cold.

Quick Prune Filling

12 ounces pitted prunes

2 tablespoons sugar

1 tablespoon boiling water

1 tablespoon orange juice or water

½ teaspoon cinnamon

1. Place all of the ingredients in a food processor bowl, and process until the prunes are pureed. Remove the metal blade, and place the processor bowl in a microwave. Heat on medium-high for 3 minutes.

2. Place the metal blade back in the bowl, and process until the mixture is finely pureed. If necessary, add a little more water.

Apricot Filling

12 ounces (about 2 cups) dried apricots

1 cup water

continued

¼ cup sugar (or more, see Note)

1 tablespoon (or more) orange juice or water

Combine the apricots, water, and sugar in a medium pot and bring to a boil. Cover, reduce the heat, and simmer until apricots can be mashed with a fork, about 30 to 45 minutes. Add the juice to taste and cook to desired thickness. Press the apricots through a food mill to remove the skin. Use when cool, or keep refrigerated until ready to use.

NOTE: Apricots vary considerably in sweetness and moisture content. I have had apricots that needed 2 tablespoons of sugar, and others that were still very tart after adding ⅔ cup of sugar! The length of time and the amount of juice to add will also vary depending on the fruit used. You can puree the apricots in a food processor, but it changes the color, giving them a pale, opaque look, rather than the bright, clear orange that they are when pressed through a food mill.

Mohn Filling

1 cup poppy seeds

½ cup boiling water

½ cup water

½ cup honey

2 teaspoons fresh lemon juice

½ teaspoon cinnamon

1 large egg

1. Soak the seeds in the boiling water until cool, or overnight.

2. Grind the drained seeds in a coffee or spice grinder, as finely as possible. A mortar and pestle can also be used. Combine the seeds, water, honey, lemon juice, and cinnamon in a small pot, stirring frequently, and cook over medium heat until the filling is thick.

3. Remove from heat, cool, and then stir in the egg. Refrigerate until ready to use.

Yeast Hamantashen

My kids are so used to cookie hamantashen that when I make them with yeast, they ask what's wrong with them. If your family is like this, you might want to stick with the cookie type. For some families, however, hamantashen are supposed to be made from yeast dough. These have about half the fat of traditional ones but are delicious just the same. The trick to making sure they don't split open during baking is to make a very moist dough.

MAKES 20 PASTRIES

1 large egg

1 tablespoon orange juice

¼ cup sugar

¼ teaspoon salt

2 tablespoons unsalted butter or unsalted pareve margarine, melted

½ cup very warm water (115° to 120°F—not hot enough to sting your finger)

2⅛ cups (265 grams) bread flour, lightly sprinkled into measuring cup

1½ teaspoons instant yeast, such as Fleischmann's Bread Machine Yeast (for other yeasts, see page 319)

1 large egg white, whisked with 1 teaspoon water, for glazing

12-ounce jar store-bought filling, or homemade (see pages 159–160)

1. If using homemade fillings, make them before you begin the dough, or while the dough is rising.

2. In a large mixer bowl, lightly whisk the egg with the orange juice, sugar, salt, and butter. Gradually whisk in the warm water. Add 1½ cups of the flour and the yeast, and beat together on low speed. By hand or

ALSO SERVE ON
Shabbat, Yom ha-atzma'ut

PAREVE OR DAIRY

NUTRITIONAL NOTES
(per serving)

113 calories

1.5g fat (13%)

12mg cholesterol

21g carbohydrates

2g protein

53mg sodium

1g fiber

RDA %

1% vitamin A

1% vitamin C

0% calcium

5% iron

Purim

with a dough hook, knead the dough for 7 to 10 minutes, adding the remaining flour as necessary to keep the dough from sticking too much (you can knead the dough by hand if necessary). The dough will be very soft and elastic.

3. Lightly coat the dough with oil, place back in the mixer bowl or in another deep bowl, cover with plastic wrap, and let rise at room temperature for about 1 hour or until doubled in volume. To test, flour your finger and gently poke into the dough. If the indentation remains, the dough has risen enough.

4. Punch down the dough, knead it a few times, and then roll it out on a floured board to about 1/16 inch thick. Cover, and let the dough rest for a few minutes. Cut the dough into 3-inch rounds using a sharp cookie cutter.

5. Place a slightly rounded measuring teaspoonful of filling in the center of the top half of the round, leaving about 1/4 inch at the top without any filling on it. Use the diagram on page 158 to fold the cookies into triangles, but leave less filling showing than for hamantashen made without yeast. Make sure to pinch the edges to seal them very well, or they may open during baking.

6. Set the pastries on cookie sheets that have been lined with parchment paper or nonstick Teflon liners. Spray plastic wrap with cooking spray, and cover the cookies. Let them rise for 30 minutes. While they are rising, preheat the oven to 350°F, with a rack in the middle of the oven.

7. Brush the cookies with the egg white/water glaze. Bake the cookies for 15 to 20 minutes until lightly browned. Slide the parchment paper onto cooling racks, and let the cookies cool completely before eating.

Phyllo Triangles

A combination of Ashkenazi and Sephardic traditions, these pastries are a delight for adults and kids alike. Mohn (poppy) or prune is the traditional Ashkenazi filling for Purim, but the pastries are equally delicious when filled with dates, figs, or a nut mixture. Use your imagination to create them the way you like.

MAKES 24 PASTRIES

9 leaves defrosted phyllo dough (see directions below)

2 tablespoons unsalted butter (or unsalted pareve margarine)

1 tablespoon canola oil

1 cup powdered sugar

6 ounces prune, poppy, or date store-bought filling, or ½ recipe
Old-Fashioned Prune Filling, page 159, or ½ recipe Mohn
Filling, page 160, or doubled recipe Date Filling, page 177

1. Defrost the package of phyllo overnight in the refrigerator. Remove the dough from the package, but leave it in its inner sleeve. Let it stand at room temperature for 2 hours.

2. Preheat the oven to 375°F, with a rack in the middle of the oven. Melt the butter and oil together and set it near the work surface.

3. Tape together 2 pieces of waxed paper so that they are about the same size as the cookie sheet you are using. Cut 3 more pieces of waxed paper, each about 16 inches long. Once the phyllo has been unwrapped, it must be used quickly and kept covered with waxed paper, or it will dry out and crumble like dried leaves. Before opening the plastic sleeve, gather together powdered sugar in a sprinkler (or a small strainer), all of the fillings, the waxed paper sheets you have assembled, cookie sheet, pastry brush, and a long knife.

continued

ALSO SERVE ON
*Yom ha-atzma'ut,
Shabbat, Sukkot*

DAIRY OR
PAREVE

NUTRITIONAL
NOTES
(per serving)

60 calories

2g fat (25%)

2mg cholesterol

11g carbohydrates

.5g protein

47mg sodium

0g fiber

RDA %

0% vitamin A

0% vitamin C

0% calcium

1% iron

Purim

4. Remove the phyllo from the sleeve and unfold it onto a work surface. Take off about half of the stack, reroll it, and place it back in the plastic sleeve or in a zip-top bag. Refrigerate or refreeze it for another use.

5. Cut the stack of phyllo leaves, perpendicular to the long end, into eight 2-inch strips. Place the stack on a piece of waxed paper and cover with another piece of waxed paper. Set 3 strips of dough on the work surface. Brush each piece lightly with the butter mixture. Sprinkle with powdered sugar. Stack the strips one on top of the other.

6. To make the triangles, imagine a rectangle at the lower end of the dough with a line through the middle of it, which divides the rectangle into 2 triangles. Spoon a rounded half-teaspoonful of filling along that line and into the top triangle. You are now going to fold the dough up, as if it were a flag. To do that, fold 1 corner of the phyllo across the filling so that you can see the triangle that you have been imagining. Now fold the triangle straight up. The next fold is diagonal, and the next straight up (see diagram on page 154). Continue to the end of the dough. If there is a small strip of dough left after all the folds have been made, it can be cut off or tucked in before the last fold is made.

7. Brush the pastry top with the butter mixture, and sprinkle with powdered sugar. Set it on the cookie sheet, and cover with the waxed paper that has been taped together. Repeat with all of the dough.

8. Bake the pastries for 15 to 20 minutes or until nicely browned. Remove from the oven and let them cool before serving. Pastries can be made 8 hours ahead if left uncovered, at room temperature. Unbaked pastries can also be frozen (bake at 350°F for 10 minutes; raise heat to 400°F and bake until browned and crispy, another 10 to 15 minutes).

Bulemas Dulces

Sephardic Sweet Pastry Rings

Bulemas *are usually filled with cheese, either savory or sweet, and served for one of the dairy holidays. For Purim, however, they are often filled with dried fruit or nut fillings, such as the one given here.* Bulemas *dough is similar to phyllo, but it contains a tiny bit of yeast. Because it is not rolled as thin as phyllo, it is not as flaky and crispy.*

MAKES 18 PASTRIES

¾ cup very warm water (115° to 120°F—not warm enough
    to sting your finger)

½ teaspoon salt

3 tablespoons canola oil, divided

1½ cups (180 grams) all-purpose flour, lightly sprinkled into
    measuring cup

½ cup plus 1 tablespoon (60 grams) sifted cake flour,
    lightly sprinkled into measuring cup

½ teaspoon instant yeast, such as Fleischmann's Bread Machine Yeast
    (for other yeast, see page 319)

Raisin Nut Filling

4 slices pareve bread with crusts removed (enough to make
    1 cup fresh bread crumbs)

1 teaspoon cinnamon

½ cup sliced almonds

½ cup raisins (dates are a nice alternative)

¼ cup sweet marmalade (I like Smuckers' low-sugar)

1 large egg white

Powdered sugar

continued

ALSO SERVE ON
*Shabbat,
Yom ha-atzma'ut*

PAREVE

NUTRITIONAL
NOTES
(per serving)

104 calories

3g fat (25%)

0mg cholesterol

18g carbohydrates

2g protein

72mg sodium

1g fiber

RDA %

0% vitamin A

0% vitamin C

1% calcium

5% iron

Purim

1. Mix the water, salt, and 2 tablespoons of oil in a mixer bowl. In another bowl, mix 1¼ cups of all-purpose flour with the cake flour and yeast. Dump this into the water, and then mix to make a dough. Add more all-purpose flour as necessary to make a soft, but not sticky, dough. Knead by hand or with a dough hook until the dough is elastic, 5 to 10 minutes.

2. Pour the remaining tablespoon of oil into a bowl. Cut the dough into 18 balls, and place them in the bowl, turning to coat each with oil. Cover the dough, and let it rest for 15 minutes.

3. Preheat the oven to 375°F, with a rack in the middle of the oven. Line a cookie sheet with parchment paper.

4. Make the filling by processing the bread, cinnamon, almonds, raisins, marmalade, and 1 tablespoon of egg white to an almost smooth paste.

5. With a rolling pin, roll 1 ball at a time into a 7 ¥ 3-inch rectangle (the dough will be as thin as you can get it by rolling). Cut off any raggedy edges. Brush the dough with oil. Place the filling along 1 long edge, in a ¼-inch line, using about 3 teaspoons of filling. Roll the dough into a jelly roll, tucking in the ends as you roll. Coil the rolls up, or form them into rings.

6. Whisk the remaining egg white with ½ teaspoon water. Brush the tops of the cookies with the egg white, and sprinkle them with powdered sugar. Bake for 25 to 30 minutes, until lightly browned and crispy. Pastries can be eaten warm or cool. If made ahead, they will need to be re-crisped by baking them at 350°F for 5 to 10 minutes.

Pecan Oatmeal Lace Cookies

By adding oatmeal and milk to this traditional recipe, I've been able to cut out half of the fat. To compensate for the loss of buttery flavor, maple syrup has been substituted for corn syrup and the pecans have been toasted. Also known as "snaps," they can be eaten as wafers, sandwiched together with melted chocolate, or rolled, curved, or shaped and used as a container for filling and/or fruit.

MAKES SIXTY 2¼-INCH COOKIES

½ cup pecans

2 tablespoons unsalted butter (or unsalted pareve margarine)

2 tablespoons canola oil

½ cup maple syrup

½ cup sugar

1 teaspoon vanilla extract

3 tablespoons skim milk (or pareve nonfat soymilk)

½ cup old-fashioned oats

½ cup plus 1 tablespoon (60 grams) sifted cake flour,
    lightly sprinkled into measuring cup

¼ cup regular or pareve chocolate, chopped (optional)

1. Preheat the oven to 350°F. Line 2 baking sheets with parchment paper. Place the pecans on 1 sheet, and toast in the oven for 5 minutes. Transfer the pecans to a processor bowl.

2. Place the butter, oil, maple syrup, and sugar in a small pot. Cook over medium heat, stirring often, until the butter melts and the mixture just starts to simmer. Remove from heat and stir in the vanilla and milk.

3. Add the oats and cake flour to the pecans in the processor bowl. Process in 5-second bursts (about 15 seconds total), until the oats and

ALSO SERVE ON
Purim, Shabbat,
Yom ha-atzma'ut

DAIRY OR
PAREVE

NUTRITIONAL
NOTES
(Per single cookie)

36 calories

2g fat (41%)

2mg cholesterol

5.3g carbohydrates

.3g protein

16mg sodium

0g fiber

RDA %

1% vitamin A

0% vitamin C

2% calcium

2% iron

nuts are finely chopped. Add the butter mixture. Pulse a few times to mix batter together. Let cool and thicken for 10 minutes.

4. Spoon the batter by slightly rounded measuring-teaspoonfuls, 2 inches apart, onto the prepared sheets. Bake in the middle of the oven for 8 to 10 minutes, until cookies are lightly browned, switching the position of the sheets, top to bottom, after half of the baking time. Slide the parchment onto a cooling rack and let cookies cool completely.

5. Melt the chocolate in the top of a double boiler over hot water, or in a microwave on medium power (heat for 1 minute, stir, and heat in 30-seconds bursts until melted). Make a small paper decorating cone (see page 169) and spoon the chocolate into it. Snip the end and pipe chocolate lines, a checkerboard, or other decoration onto the cookies. The cookies can also be sandwiched together with chocolate (this will double the fat content).

6. Alternatively, if you wish to shape the cookies, spoon the uncooked batter onto individual pieces of parchment paper. Bake, and then form while the cookies are still warm and pliable. For best results do not bake more than 2 cookies at a time, or they will harden before you have time to work with them. To re-soften hard cookies, place them back in the oven for a minute and then shape. Cookies are prettiest when molded in brioche molds or mini-tart pans in which the bottom is narrower than the top. They can also be draped over the bottom of cups or bowls, molded in round-bottomed pans, or rolled around wooden spoons, dowels, horn molds, etc. Fill the shapes immediately before serving if you want them crunchy, 15 minutes before for slightly softened, but no more than 25 minutes before, or they will be too soft.

7. The cookies can be prepared up to 1 week ahead (store in an airtight container at room temperature). Do not freeze.

How to make paper decorating cones using precut parchment rounds

1. A very small decorating cone can be made using a precut, 10-inch parchment paper circle. Fold the paper in half, in half again, and in half one more time.

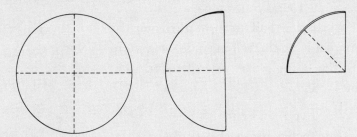

2. Place a piece of tape on the outside seam, and a small piece of tape on the inside seam. Squeeze the sides of the cone, gently, to open up the paper into a cone that can now be filled.

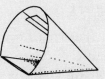

3. Fill the cone no more than half full. To use, fold down the two sides of the top of the cone toward the center so that the top is now triangle-shaped.

4. Fold the top of the bag down several times until the paper is touching the filling.

5. Snip off a tiny bit of the tip so that the filling can come out of the cone. Make sure to maintain pressure at the top of the cone, so that the filling will flow out of the cone without air bubbles.

Making a paper cone using parchment triangles

1. Cut a piece of parchment paper into a square that is twice as long as the length of the cone you desire. (If you have a standard roll of parchment paper, the largest size you can cut is a 13-inch square. A 10-inch square will make a 5-inch cone, the same size as the round cone on page 169.) Fold the parchment paper in half to form a triangle. Set the triangle on a table, with the long side away from you. The points of the triangle have been lettered to make the directions easier.

2. Fold point C toward you, and curl it under, on top of point A, so that you can still read the letter C.

3. Put your fingers inside the cone, and holding points A and C between your fingers and thumb, turn your hand up so that the cone is on your hand. Turn your hand around so that your thumb is facing you.

4. With your other hand, bring point B around toward your thumb, pulling the parchment down so that the seam is flat, and the tip of the cone is closed. Slide your thumb over so that you are now holding all three points between your thumb and fingers. Tape the seam closed.

5. Remove your hand from inside the cone, and turn it so that the closed tip is down. Turn the triangular top of the cone down, toward the outside of the cone. Place a small piece of tape on the upper part of the inside seam and down over the triangular part that you have just folded down. This should keep the cone from coming undone. Fill and fold the cone as per the instructions for the small cone, above.

Menenas or Ma-amoul

Middle Eastern Filled Cookies

For menenas, *you can use* Adjweh *dough (see page 177) or this one,* *which is slightly less crunchy and a little more tender.* Menenas *have a different shape from* adjweh, *which changes the date/dough proportions and therefore changes the taste and texture of the cookie.*

MAKES 30 COOKIES

> 1⅛ cups (120 grams) sifted cake flour, lightly sprinkled into measuring cup
>
> 1 cup (120 grams) all-purpose flour, lightly sprinkled into measuring cup
>
> ½ cup unsalted butter or unsalted pareve margarine, cold and cut into ½-inch chunks
>
> 3 tablespoons corn syrup
>
> 3 tablespoons orange juice
>
> Doubled recipe Date Filling, page 177, made without water
>
> Powdered sugar

1. Place both flours in a processor bowl. Scatter the butter on top of the flour. Pulse-process until the butter is cut into the flour to resemble coarse meal.

2. Pour the corn syrup into the processor. Pulse-process to mix it in. Add the orange juice, and process until the dough forms a ball. It should be very soft and moist.

3. Remove the dough from the processor, wrap in plastic wrap, and set aside, at room temperature, for 1 hour.

4. While the dough is resting, make the date filling.

continued

ALSO SERVE ON
Chanukah, Shabbat, Yom ha-atzma'ut, life-cycle events, Onegs

DAIRY OR PAREVE

NUTRITIONAL NOTES
(per cookie)

80 calories

3g fat (36%)

9mg cholesterol

12g carbohydrates

1g protein

3mg sodium

1g fiber

RDA %

3% vitamin A

2% vitamin C

0% calcium

4% iron

Purim

5. Preheat the oven to 350°F, with the racks in the upper and lower thirds of the oven. Line 2 cookie sheets with parchment paper or nonstick Teflon liners (or grease the sheets).

6. Divide the dough into 30 balls. Press your thumb into the center of each ball to form a cavity. Form the dough into a little "pot" with the sides being about 1/16 inch thick. Fill each about three-quarters full, with a level half-teaspoonful of filling. Press the dough to seal in the filling. For *ma-amoul*, shape the dough into a gumdrop shape. Using fork tines, make a vertical design in the top of each ball. For *menenas*, shape the cookies to resemble Brazil nuts (in the shell). Pinch the top edges to make a little well that will catch the powdered sugar. Set them on the parchment paper, and bake for 18 to 22 minutes, until lightly browned. Slide the parchment onto cooling racks. When the cookies are cool, sprinkle them liberally with powdered sugar. Store in airtight containers.

Lemon Poppy Buttermilk Mini-Loaves

Perfect for Purim mishloah minot (gifts), this classic Jewish dessert has two-thirds less fat and three-quarters less cholesterol than its traditional counterpart. For the perfect texture, make the cake at least four hours in advance. If you like a bitter edge to your cakes, add 1/2 teaspoon of lemon extract and/or one teaspoon of grated lemon zest.

MAKES FOUR 3 ¥ 5-INCH MINI-LOAVES OR ONE 12-CUP BUNDT CAKE

Lemon Glaze and Soak

1 cup 10x powdered sugar

5 tablespoons fresh lemon juice (about 2 lemons),
    at room temperature

2 teaspoons water

Cake

¼ cup unsalted butter, at cool room temperature (68° to 70°F)

1 cup firmly packed light brown sugar

1 large egg, at room temperature

3 large egg whites, at room temperature

2¾ cups plus 1 tablespoon (300 grams) sifted cake flour,
    lightly sprinkled into measuring cup

½ teaspoon baking soda

½ teaspoon baking powder

½ teaspoon salt

¼ cup poppy seeds

1 cup nonfat or lowfat buttermilk, at room temperature

2 tablespoons fresh lemon juice (about ½ lemon),
    at room temperature

¼ cup pear baby food (less than a 3-ounce jar), at room temperature

1. Preheat the oven to 325°F, with a rack in the middle of the oven. Spray-grease and flour four 3 ¥ 5-inch loaf pans or 1 Bundt pan.

2. In a small bowl, make the glaze by mixing together the powdered sugar, lemon juice, and water. Cover with plastic wrap and set aside.

3. To make the cake, in a large mixer bowl, beat the butter on medium speed until creamy. Add the brown sugar, and beat for 2 minutes.

4. In another bowl, whisk together the egg and egg whites. On medium speed, beat the eggs into the butter mixture a little at a time. Beat on medium-high until the mixture is smooth, thick, and fluffy, about 5 minutes.

5. In another bowl, sift together the flour, baking soda, baking powder, and salt. Stir in the poppy seeds.

continued

NUTRITIONAL
NOTES
(per serving;
1-inch piece of a small
cake or ¹/₂₀ of the Bundt
cake)

144 calories

4g fat (21%)

16mg cholesterol

26g carbohydrates

3g protein

144mg sodium

1g fiber

RDA %

2% vitamin A

2% vitamin C

6% calcium

8% iron

Purim

6. In another bowl, mix together the buttermilk, lemon juice, and baby food. On low, in 3 additions, alternately stir the flour and buttermilk mixtures into the batter, mixing only until no flour is visible.

7. Divide the batter among the pans. Rap them on the counter to remove any large bubbles. Bake for 30 to 40 minutes for loaf pans, and 35 to 45 minutes for a Bundt pan, or until a tester inserted into the center of the cake comes out with no moist crumbs attached. Remove from the oven and set the pans on a cooling rack. Immediately use a thin skewer to poke about 2 dozen holes into each of the cakes (8 dozen in the tube pan), making sure the skewer goes all the way to the bottom. Spoon 3 table-spoons of glaze over each mini-loaf (the whole thing over a tube pan). Cool completely before removing from the pans.

8. Cakes can be wrapped in foil and stored at room temperature for 4 days, or frozen for up to 3 months. (Defrost in foil at room temperature. Individual slices defrost nicely in the microwave.)

VARIATIONS: Orange juice makes a great substitute for the lemon juice. The poppy seeds can be omitted or replaced with finely chopped nuts.

Travados

Sephardic Half-Moon Cookies

ALSO SERVE ON
*Chanukah, Shabbat,
Yom ha-atzma'ut*

PAREVE

Light Jewish
Holiday Desserts

These Rhodean cookies are enjoyed throughout the Sephardic world, although they have many different names. For example, in the Balkans, they are called roscas di alhasu (Haman's ears), and in Morocco they are called kabulzel. Most recipes include wine, either sweet or dry, red or white. Although all are stuffed with nuts, there is great variation in the amount of sugar and oil used. To lighten them, I have added corn syrup for half of the fat and have substituted graham *cracker crumbs for part of the nut filling. Because of the added sweetness from the corn syrup, I use a dry white wine. Cookies made with white wine are also a more pleasing color.*

MAKES 25 COOKIES

1¼ cups (130 grams) sifted cake flour, lightly sprinkled into measuring cup

1 cup (120 grams) all-purpose flour, lightly sprinkled into measuring cup

¼ teaspoon baking soda

Dash of salt

¼ cup canola oil

½ cup dry white wine

¼ cup corn syrup

Syrup

½ cup sugar

½ cup water

2 teaspoons cinnamon

2 tablespoons honey

Filling

2 whole lowfat graham crackers

½ cup walnuts

2 tablespoons marmalade (we prefer sweet marmalade)

¼ teaspoon cinnamon

1. Preheat the oven to 350°F, with a rack in the middle of the oven. Line a cookie sheet with parchment paper or a nonstick Teflon liner, or spray it with cooking spray.

2. In a medium mixer bowl, stir together both flours, baking soda, and salt. Add the oil, wine, and corn syrup, and mix on low until the dough

Purim

comes together. Press the dough into a ball. Cover it with plastic wrap, and let it rest for 1 hour. If the dough is sticky after resting, sprinkle it with 1 teaspoon of flour.

3. In a medium pot, combine the sugar, water, and cinnamon. Heat over medium heat until the sugar dissolves. Bring the mixture to a boil, reduce the heat, and simmer for 10 minutes. Stir in the honey, and remove the pot from the heat.

4. To make the filling, place the grahams in a processor bowl, and process to fine crumbs. Add the nuts, marmalade, and cinnamon. Process until the nuts are chopped medium-fine.

5. Divide the dough into 25 balls. Flatten and press each ball into a 2-inch circle, a scant ⅛ inch thick. Place a rounded half-teaspoonful of filling in the middle of each piece of dough. Fold the dough over the filling to form a half-moon. Pinch the edges or use a fork to press the edges until well sealed. Bend each moon, just slightly, into a crescent.

6. Place the cookies on the baking sheet and bake 18 to 22 minutes, or until lightly browned. Just before the cookies come from the oven, reheat the syrup. Dip the hot cookies into the syrup. Cool before eating. These cookies lose a lot of flavor if frozen.

Apricot Rugelach
(page 80)
and Sticky Buns
(mini variation)
(page 87)

Prune and Apricot
Hamantashen *(page 157)*
and Raisin Mandel
Bread *(page 272)*
and Mocha Chip
Mandel Bread *(page 274)*

Apple-Plum Galette *(page 145)*

Chocolate Babka *(page 68)*

Blueberry Lemon Phyllo Napoleons *(page 252)*

Mandarin Orange Cheesecake *(page 109)*

Raspberry
Charlotte

(page 189)

Summer
Pudding
Miniatures

(page 243)

Apple Honey
Strudel *(page 26)*

Marble Pound
Cake *(page 265)*

Fresh
Strawberry
Torte

(page 187)

Lemon
Pistachio
Roulade

(page 71)

Adjweh

Middle Eastern Filled Crescents

The dough for these crescent-shaped cookies can also be used for menenas or ma-amoul, *similar cookies with a different shape. This version uses fine semolina (smead) which can be bought in Middle Eastern groceries (do not use pasta flour). It provides an interesting crunch to these cookies. Fillings for adjweh are usually dates, nuts, or a combination of the two. Because the cookies contain a generous amount of butter, I have chosen to include just a date filling. A portion of the fat has been eliminated by using corn syrup in the cookies.*

MAKES 20 COOKIES

Date Filling

4 ounces whole pitted dates (about ½ cup, packed)

¼ teaspoon cinnamon

1 teaspoon orange juice

1 to 6 teaspoons water

Pastry Dough

5 tablespoons unsalted butter, or unsalted pareve margarine, softened

2 tablespoons corn syrup

⅔ cup (70 grams) sifted cake flour, lightly sprinkled into measuring cup

⅔ cup (80 grams) all-purpose flour, lightly sprinkled into measuring cup

¼ cup fine semolina flour (smead—if unavailable, substitute more all-purpose flour)

¼ teaspoon salt

2 tablespoons orange juice

Powdered sugar

continued

ALSO SERVE ON
Chanukah, Yom ha-atzma'ut, Shabbat, Simkat Torah (don't bend into crescents), life-cycle events, Onegs

DAIRY OR PAREVE

NUTRITIONAL NOTES
(per cookie)

81 calories

3g fat (33%)

8mg cholesterol

12g carbohydrates

1g protein

58mg sodium

1g fiber

RDA %

2% vitamin A

2% vitamin C

2% calcium

4% iron

Purim

1. If the dates are very soft, they can be processed without cooking them. Place them in the processor, add the cinnamon, and process until they form a ball. Add the orange juice, and pulse-process to incorporate the juice (if you continually process instead of pulse-process, the paste gets very soft and changes to an unpleasant color). Add the water, 1 teaspoon at a time, and pulse-process until a soft, spreadable paste forms. If you have miscalculated the moistness of your dates, and feel they need to be softer, remove the metal blade and set the processor bowl in a microwave. Heat on medium-high for 2 minutes. Pulse-process again to smooth out the paste. Set aside. If you have very dry dates to begin with, cook them in a pot with the cinnamon and a few tablespoons of water. Simmer until the dates are soft, and then mash or process them with a little orange juice.

2. For the dough, beat the butter in a large mixer bowl. Beat in the corn syrup. In another bowl, mix both flours, semolina, and salt. On low, beat the flour mixture into the butter. When the flour has little lumps in it, add the orange juice. Continue mixing until a soft dough is formed. Press it into a ball, wrap in plastic, and let it stand at room temperature for 1 hour. It will firm as it rests. If it's sticky after resting, dust it lightly with flour.

3. Preheat the oven to 350°F, with a rack in the middle of the oven. Line a cookie sheet with parchment paper or a nonstick Teflon liner.

4. Divide the dough into 20 balls. Work with half of the balls at one time, and cover the others with plastic wrap to prevent them from drying out. Press the balls flat into 2½-inch rounds. Spread the date filling on the bottom ⅔ of each round, leaving ¼ inch at the perimeter of each without filling. Roll the dough up jelly roll style. Seal the ends and then roll the dough back and forth to better seal it and to elongate it slightly. Shape each piece into a crescent. Bake for 18 to 22 minutes, until browned. While the cookies are hot, roll them in powdered sugar. The cookies can be kept in an airtight container for a few days. They can be frozen, but the date filling loses quite a bit of flavor.

Maronchinos

Sephardic Chewy Almond Cookies

Traditionally these cookies are served for Passover, Purim, and for the Yom Kippur break-the-fast. In order to halve the fat content of the cookies, however, I have substituted graham cracker crumbs for half of the almonds, making them unsuitable for Passover. If you can forgive the brown color of the cookies, you'll be pleased to find that these lowfat maronchinos are very similar to their high-fat cousins.

MAKES 26 COOKIES

7 whole lowfat graham crackers

1 cup blanched almonds

¼ teaspoon ground cardamom

1 cup sugar

2 large egg whites, at room temperature

½ teaspoon almond extract

2 teaspoons water

1. Preheat the oven to 325°F, with a rack in the middle of the oven. Line a cookie sheet with parchment paper or a nonstick Teflon liner.

2. Place the graham crackers in a processor bowl and process until finely ground. Measure out 1 cup. Discard or save any extra graham crumbs, and place the cupful back in the processor.

3. Add the almonds, cardamom, and sugar to the work bowl. Pulse-process until the almonds are finely ground. Add the egg whites, almond extract, and water to the processor. Pulse-process until well mixed.

4. Spoon the batter onto the cookie sheets by rounded teaspoonful, leaving 2 inches between cookies. Bake the cookies for 7 minutes. Switch the cookie sheet on the upper rack to the lower, and vice versa. Continue

ALSO SERVE ON
Yom Kippur break-the-fast, Shabbat, Yom ha-atzma'ut, Onegs

PAREVE

NUTRITIONAL NOTES
(per cookie)

86 calories

2.5g fat (26%)

0mg cholesterol

15g carbohydrates

2g protein

40mg sodium

1g fiber

RDA %

0% vitamin A

0% vitamin C

1% calcium

2% iron

Purim

179

baking for 8 to 10 minutes until the cookies are cooked through but still very soft. Remove from the oven and slide the parchment onto cooling racks. Store cookies in an airtight tin at room temperature for several days, or freeze for up to 3 months.

Iraqi Date Balls

These confections are served throughout North Africa. Because all of the fat comes from nuts, they're pretty healthy even when made the traditional way. It's easy to pop down several of these at one sitting, though, so I've reduced the fat by more than half by eliminating three quarters of the nuts, replacing some with cookie crumbs. For mishloah minot (Purim gifts), place them in paper mini-muffin liners or candy cups.

MAKES 20 BALLS

3 tablespoons plus ½ cup walnuts

1 whole Stella D'oro almond cookie, or 1 slice stale white bread

One 8-ounce box whole pitted dates

1 to 3 teaspoons orange juice

¼ teaspoon cinnamon and/or cardamom (optional)

1. Place 3 tablespoons of the walnuts and the cookie in the processor. Process until finely ground. Transfer to a small bowl and set aside.

2. Process the dates for 10 to 20 seconds until they form a ball. Add 1 to 3 teaspoons of orange juice, processing after adding each teaspoonful, using just enough to make the dates less gluey but still firm. If using any spices, pulse them in. Add the remaining ½ cup walnuts, and pulse-process until the nuts are coarsely chopped. Wet your hands. Roll the date paste into 20 small balls—about ¾ inch in diameter. Roll the balls in the reserved walnut–cookie crumb mixture to coat them well. Date balls can be refrigerated for up to 1 week, or frozen for up to 3 months.

ALSO SERVE ON
Yom ha-atzma'ut,
Shabbat, life-cycle
events, Onegs

PAREVE

NUTRITIONAL
NOTES
(per ball)

50 calories

2g fat (34%)

0mg cholesterol

8g carbohydrates

1g protein

0mg sodium

1g fiber

RDA %

0% vitamin A

1% vitamin C

0% calcium

1% iron

Pesach *(or Passover) commemorates the*

liberation of the Israelites from bondage in

Egypt. Beginning on the fifteenth of Nisan

(March or April), the holiday continues for seven

or eight days, depending on where one lives.

The holiday is also known as Hag ha Matzot

(the holiday of unleavened bread), or Hag ha-Aviv

(the holiday of spring). The name Passover is taken

directly from the Exodus story. In order to force the

Pharaoh to let the Jewish people leave, ten plagues

descended upon the Egyptians. The final and

decisive plague was the killing of the firstborn

children. It is written that God "passed over" the Israelites' homes and spared them from the plague, whereupon the Pharaoh agreed to let them go. When word came from Moses to leave, the Israelites hurried forth with no time to allow their bread to rise. To symbolize the hurried departure of the Israelites, we eat unleavened bread (matzo). The holiday is celebrated in the spring for those in the Northern Hemisphere, but even those in the Southern Hemisphere can view the holiday as a symbolic spring, when the hope and rebirth of liberation follows the long dark winter of slavery.

Passover actually marks the beginning of Judaism as a religion, because it established a Covenant between the Israelites as a group and their God. "And I will take you to be My people . . . And you shall know that I, the Lord, am your God who freed you from the burdens of the Egyptians" (Exodus 6:7). The observance of Passover, therefore, is not just a commemoration of a historic event, but an affirmation that we are part of this history and that our Covenant exists today. As commanded in the Torah, we relive the story of the Exodus by reading the Hagaddah and participating in the Seder meal (Seder means "order") in which all of the foods eaten have symbolic meaning. For a week we eat matzo and refrain from eating and owning *hametz* (leavened foods).

Passover Dietary Guidelines

Dietary laws and preparations for Passover vary widely within the Jewish community. Strictly observant Jews will remove all trace of *hametz* (literally bread but used to mean anything that is not kosher for Passover) from their homes, replace their dishes, silver, pots and pans; cover counters; clean oven and sink; use only equipment that is special for Passover; and eat only foods deemed acceptable by their rabbinic governing bodies. Less observant Jews may celebrate by eating matzo for just one night. For the great majority, observance will fall within these two opposite poles. Dietary guidelines are complex. Sephardim (Jews from Mediterranean and Arabic countries) eat rice and beans, while Ashkenazim (Jews of Germanic and Eastern European descent) do not, and consider these foods *kitnyot* (foods that could rise). The guidelines that follow are excerpted from the Rabbinical Assembly Pesach Guide, the authority for Conservative congregations (*Rabbinical Assembly on Jewish Law and Standards,* Rabbi Mayer Rabinowitz, December 12, 1984). Reform Jews are instructed to make informed choice, and Orthodox Jews will follow slightly different guidelines. It's best to contact your own *shul* or rabbi for rules.

When baking, avoid the following foods:

- Wheat Flour (except matzo) and any foods containing flour, such as cookies or cakes
- Leavening agents such as yeast, baking powder, or sourdoughs

Ashkenasic authorities also forbid the following:

- All grains—except matzo and matzo products
- Cornstarch—a derivative of corn
- Corn syrup—and any foods containing corn syrup
- Legumes—beans and bean products
- Cream of tartar—because it is made during alcohol distillation

Some foods require a "kosher for Passover" label if purchased during Passover, but not if purchased before Passover. Kosher for Passover products are usually labeled right on the package and may have the name of the rabbi who has certified the product. The kosher symbol will usually have a "P" next to it. For example, the Orthodox

Pesach
(Passover)

183

Union's symbol for "kosher for Passover" would be ⓤₚ. Anything purchased before Passover must be unopened. The following lists will help you determine what is required.

Requires No Label Ever

> *Fresh fruits and vegetables*
>
> *Eggs*

Requires Label Whenever Purchased

> *Vanilla and other extracts (because they are made with grain alcohol)*
>
> *Candy*
>
> *Yogurt (Dannon lowfat vanilla, plain, and lemon are kosher for Passover, even if the label only says kosher)*
>
> *Soda*
>
> *Alcoholic beverages*
>
> *Ice cream*
>
> *Dried fruit*
>
> *Matzo and matzo products*
>
> *Canned or bottled juice*
>
> *Oils*
>
> *Vinegar*

Requires Label Only If Purchased During Passover

> *Salt (only non-iodized permissible)*
>
> *Spices*
>
> *Frozen fruits and juices (without additives permissible)*
>
> *Milk*
>
> *Butter*

Baking soda (should not be used as leavening)

Nuts

Cocoa

Cream cheese and cottage cheese (generally, nonfat products are not kosher for Passover—Breakstone's Reduced-Fat Sour Cream is kosher for Passover)

Tea

Coffee (must not contain additives)

Sugar

Honey

Preparing for Passover

Baking requires a certain amount of equipment, some of which must be purchased especially for Passover, and some of which may be kashered. Rules vary and you might want to consult your own rabbi. "The process of kashering utensils depends on how the utensils are used. . . . Utensils used for cooking are kashered by boiling, those used for broiling are kashered by fire and heat and those used for cold food are kashered by rinsing" (Rabbinical Assembly Pesach Guide). Because baking pans cannot withstand the temperature necessary for kashering, these will have to be bought especially for Passover. Plastic tools, pastry brushes, rubber scrapers, and thermometers will also have to be bought for Passover. Other things such as measuring cups, bowls, metal spatulas, and metal beaters can probably be kashered. Strainers and sifters are controversial, so contact your rabbi about these.

To kasher the sink, clean it thoroughly. For a metal sink, pour in boiling water. For a porcelain sink, a rack or dish basin must be used.

The dishwasher should not be used for 24 hours, and then should run empty through a full cycle, with detergent. Thoroughly wipe down the outside and inside parts that do not get clean during the cycle. Measuring cups, glassware, and other equipment that is used for cold food can then be run through a cycle and kashered.

To kasher the oven and range, clean thoroughly and then heat on the highest setting for at least ½ hour. Microwave ovens should be cleaned, and then a cup of water should be placed inside. The microwave should be turned on and kept on until the water evaporates. If the microwave has a browning element, it cannot be kashered.

Clean the refrigerator and the freezer thoroughly, removing all *hametz*. Line shelves with butcher paper. If freezing food prior to Passover, don't forget to kasher the freezer beforehand.

Metal pots and pans can be cleaned and then immersed in boiling water.

Fresh Strawberry Torte

This light and moist torte is topped with a decorative pattern of fresh strawberries. The texture and flavor are so good that you won't believe it's a Passover cake. Beautiful to look at, it's sure to make an impression.

PAREVE OR DAIRY

NUTRITIONAL NOTES
(per serving)

172 calories

3g fat (13%)

24mg cholesterol

35g carbohydrates

3g protein

39mg sodium

1g fiber

RDA %

2% vitamin A

22% vitamin C

1% calcium

8% iron

MAKES 15 SERVINGS

Passover Genoise

2 large eggs

6 large egg whites

1 cup sugar

1 teaspoon Passover vanilla extract (optional)

½ cup matzo cake meal

½ cup potato starch

2 tablespoons Passover oil (or melted butter for dairy)

Strawberry Syrup, Topping, and Glaze

1½ pounds fresh strawberries

2 tablespoons sugar

2 teaspoons fresh lemon juice, divided

2 tablespoons Passover strawberry preserves, strained

1. Preheat the oven to 375°F, with a rack in the middle of the oven. Grease a 9 × 12-inch rectangular pan and line it with parchment paper or a nonstick Teflon liner.

2. Bring about 2 inches of water to boil in the bottom of a double boiler. Reduce the heat so the water is simmering. Place the eggs and egg whites in the top of the double boiler or in a metal mixer bowl (not over the heat). With a wire whisk, lightly whisk the eggs. Gradually whisk in the

Pesach
(Passover)

187

sugar. Place the eggs over the simmering water and whisk until the eggs are just barely warm (about 110°F).

3. Remove from the heat and beat the eggs with an electric mixer, on high, until they have doubled in volume (they will not be as thick as when using only whole eggs). Beat in the vanilla extract, if using.

4. In a bowl, sift together the matzo cake meal and potato starch. Sprinkle 2 tablespoons of the matzo meal mixture over the eggs and fold together with a slotted spoon or rubber scraper. Repeat until all of the matzo has been incorporated.

5. Place the oil in a medium microwavable bowl. Microwave for 30 seconds on medium or until the oil is warm.

6. Stir 2 cups of batter into the oil until blended. Fold this gently back into the remaining batter. Pour the batter into the pan and carefully spread it to the edge. DO NOT tap the pan to remove bubbles.

7. Bake the cake until lightly browned and springy, about 12 to 15 minutes. Remove from the oven and let cool on a rack. Place a cakeboard or serving platter on top of the pan and invert. Leave the cake with the bottom side up. (The cake can be made 1 day ahead or frozen for up to 3 months. If storing, wrap tightly in foil. Defrost in foil at room temperature for 2 hours.)

8. Wash and hull 2 cups of the strawberries. Quarter them and place in a small pot with the sugar and lemon juice. Mash the berries and let them macerate for 15 minutes. Heat over medium heat to dissolve the sugar. Let it cool. Spoon the mashed berries onto the cake.

9. Wash and hull the remaining berries. Slice half of them vertically into petal-shaped slices, and slice the other half horizontally into rounds. Place the berries, overlapping one another, in alternating rows of round and petal-shaped berries. Brush the berries with the preserves. Cover and store in the refrigerator for at least 3 hours and up to 8 hours. Do not freeze the cake with the berries on top.

Raspberry Charlotte

The Bavarian or mousse filling of a typical charlotte is usually made with loads of egg yolks and lots of whipped cream. In this version, lowfat sour cream fills in for the egg yolks, and egg whites replace the whipped cream. The meringue used is a variation of Alice Medrich's *Safe Meringue* from Chocolate and the Art of Low-Fat Desserts. The result is a light, airy dessert with a full-bodied raspberry flavor and only 3 grams of fat per serving.

MAKES 12 SERVINGS

Mock Powdered Sugar

2 tablespoons sugar

Pinch of potato starch

Passover Ladyfingers

3 large eggs, at room temperature

7 large egg whites, at room temperature

¾ cup sugar, divided

1 tablespoon orange juice

¾ cup matzo cake meal

6 tablespoons potato starch

Pinch of salt

Raspberry Mousse

1 cup fresh raspberries

¼ cup sugar

4 tablespoons water, divided

continued

DAIRY

NUTRITIONAL NOTES (PER SERVING)

243 calories

3g fat (11.5%)

53mg cholesterol

49g carbohydrates

6g protein

63mg sodium

2g fiber

RDA %

4% vitamin A

17% vitamin C

4% calcium

10% iron

MAKE 1 DAY AHEAD

Pesach (Passover)

¾ *cup reduced-fat sour cream, preferably Breakstone's*

1½ *teaspoons Kolatin kosher gelatin, see page 317*

Marshmallow Meringue

2 *large egg whites*

½ *cup sugar*

2 *tablespoons water*

Soaking Syrup

¼ *cup reserved raspberry puree*

1 *tablespoon sugar*

Garnish

1 *pint raspberries*

¼ *cup seedless raspberry jam, or currant jelly mixed with 1 teaspoon water (optional)*

1. Preheat the oven to 400°F, with racks in the middle and lower third of the oven. Line 2 cookie sheets with parchment paper. On each piece of parchment, as close to the edge of the paper as you can, draw an 8-inch circle (or use a precut parchment round). Next to each circle, draw 2 parallel 12-inch lines, 3 inches apart. Turn both pieces of parchment over, so that the drawn lines are facing down. Alternatively, you can use reusable Teflon liners which have been cut to the desired size.

2. Make mock powdered sugar by placing the sugar and potato starch in a coffee mill. Grind until finely pulverized. Set aside (if you do not have a mill that is kashered for Passover, make the ladyfingers without the sugar topping).

3. To make the ladyfingers, place 2 of the eggs in a large mixer bowl. Separate the other egg, and add the yolk to the mixer bowl, and the white to the other egg whites.

4. Beat the egg yolk mixture on medium speed, gradually adding 6 tablespoons of sugar. Increase the speed to high, and beat the egg yolks until thick and pale colored, 2 to 5 minutes. Add the orange juice and beat a few seconds just to blend.

5. Beat the egg whites until they are very foamy throughout and beater marks are just beginning to show. Continue to beat while gradually

adding the remaining 6 tablespoons of sugar. Increase the mixer speed to high, and beat the whites until stiff but not dry.

6. In another bowl, stir together the matzo cake meal, potato starch, and salt. Sprinkle ⅓ over the yolks. Spoon ⅓ of the whites on top, and fold together. Repeat twice more, until all of the ingredients are well folded together.

7. Fit a pastry bag with a ⅝- to ¾-inch pastry tube (if you don't have this for Passover, use a disposable plastic decorating bag, and cut a hole in the bottom that will measure ⅝ inch). Spoon the batter into the bag, and pipe out the ladyfingers between the lines so that they are about ⅝ inch wide, 3 inches long, and about ½ inch high. They should be piped very close together—almost touching, so that when they come from the oven, they will be attached. To pipe the circles, start at the outside of each drawn circle, and pipe in a spiral until you reach the center. This should also be about ½ inch thick. The spirals should be touching so that the piece will be completely solid when baked. Use a fine-mesh strainer to broadcast the mock powdered sugar over the batter. Do not try to spoon it over, as it is too heavy and will fall in thick clumps.

8. Bake for 4 minutes and then switch the upper cookie sheet to the lower rack and vice versa. Continue baking for 4 to 6 minutes until the fingers are lightly browned and no beads of moisture can be seen on the outside of the cookies. Slide the parchment paper (with the fingers still on them) onto cooling racks and let cool. Turn the paper over so that it is on top, and peel it off the cakes. Ladyfingers can be made 1 day ahead, or can be frozen for up to 3 months (defrost at room temperature for about an hour before using).

9. Before making the mousse, use scissors to trim the cake circles by ¼ inch all around (thus reducing the cakes to 7¾-inch rounds).

10. Spray the inside of an 8-inch springform pan with cooking spray. The springform can be set directly onto a serving platter, or you can leave the bottom of the pan in, and set an 8-inch cakeboard into the bottom of the pan. Line the ring with the ladyfingers, rounded side out, and set 1 of the disks, rounded side down, into the bottom of the pan.

11. To make the raspberry mousse, in a small nonreactive pot, combine the raspberries, sugar, and 2 tablespoons of the water. Heat over medium heat to dissolve the sugar and soften the berries. Press the berries through a food mill, and if any seeds remain in the puree, strain them out.

continued

Pesach
(Passover)

12. Place the sour cream in a large bowl. Stir in ¾ cup puree, and reserve the remaining puree.

13. Place the gelatin in a microwavable bowl. Mix in the remaining 2 tablespoons water. Let it soften for 5 minutes, and then heat it in the microwave, on high, for about 30 seconds, or until the gelatin is completely melted. Stir the hot gelatin into the sour cream a little at a time.

14. Set the bowl in a larger bowl filled with ice water. Stir the raspberry mixture every 5 minutes to keep it smooth. When it gets very thick and will "mound" rather than "run," remove it from the ice.

15. To make the marshmallow meringue, fill a large skillet with 1 inch of water. Bring the water to a simmer. In a small metal bowl, whisk the egg whites with the sugar and water. Have a rubber scraper, instant-read thermometer, a timer, another mixing bowl, and a beater near the stove.

16. Place the bowl with the egg white mixture into the simmering water, and rapidly stir with the rubber scraper for 20 seconds. Remove the bowl from the simmering water and check the temperature. If the eggs are not yet at 160°F, heat them for 10 seconds more. Remove the bowl from the water, dip the thermometer into the boiling water, and then retest. The temperature needs to be at 160°F to kill salmonella but not much higher, or the eggs will overcook. The time that it takes depends upon the type of bowl and pot that are being used—I've had it take from 20 to 80 seconds.

17. As soon as the eggs reach 160°F, transfer them to a cool bowl, and beat at medium-high speed until the egg whites are firm and cool. They will look like shaving cream and stand in stiff peaks when the beater is raised from them.

18. When the raspberry mixture is ready, fold in the meringue.

19. For the soaking syrup, mix the reserved puree and sugar in a small microwavable bowl. Heat in the microwave on medium for 30 seconds. Stir to dissolve the sugar. Repeat if the sugar has not dissolved. Brush the syrup on the bottom cake and halfway up the ladyfingers. Spoon half of the mousse into the pan. Place the remaining cake circle, rounded side down, on top of the mousse. Brush it with some of the soaking syrup. Spoon on the rest of the mousse. Cover and refrigerate overnight. At this point the mousse can be frozen for up to 3 months (defrost overnight in

the refrigerator). Before serving, place the garnish berries on top of the charlotte. (They can be arranged in circles or haphazardly strewn.) If you'd like the berries to shine a little, melt the jam-water mixture in a small saucepan and then brush this onto the berries. Remove the spring-form ring, and serve.

Mixed Fruit Trifle

This layered dessert of English origin usually contains sponge cake, jam, alcohol, and some kind of custard. Most trifles also have fruit, whipped cream, and almonds. As with so many other desserts, the variations are endless. A typical trifle serving might have 30 grams of fat and 300 milligrams of cholesterol (due to the large quantity of egg yolks used). To trim down this recipe, I use a low-cholesterol Passover sponge cake and a thin custard made with only one egg. If you feel deprived without whipped cream topping, pipe a ring of rosettes at the top. To complete the customary presentation, make the trifle in a large glass bowl or in individual goblets that will show off the layers.

MAKES 10 SERVINGS

1 recipe Passover Ladyfingers batter, page 189

Soaking Syrup

½ *cup water*

¼ *cup sugar*

2 *tablespoons blackberry Passover wine, Passover sherry, or raspberry or orange juice*

continued

DAIRY

NUTRITIONAL NOTES
(per serving; add 4 grams of fat for whipped cream if using)

203 calories

2g fat (9%)

24mg cholesterol

44g carbohydrates

3g protein

44mg sodium

4g fiber

RDA %

4% vitamin A

48% vitamin C

8% calcium

4% iron

Pesach
(Passover)

Soft-Set Vanilla Custard

1 large egg, at room temperature

½ cup sugar, divided

1 teaspoon potato starch

2 cups 1% milk

½ large vanilla bean, split in half lengthwise (or 1 teaspoon Passover vanilla extract)

¼ cup reduced-fat sour cream, preferably Breakstone's

For Assembly

2 cups strawberries

2 cups raspberries

2 cups blueberries

2 small pears, very ripe

½ cup Passover raspberry or strawberry jam

Garnish (optional)

½ cup whipping cream

1 tablespoon sugar

¼ teaspoon Passover vanilla extract

1. Preheat the oven to 400°F, with a rack in the middle of the oven. Place a piece of parchment paper, or a nonstick Teflon liner, in a 10 × 15-inch jelly roll pan.

2. Make the ladyfinger batter, but instead of piping it, spread it in the prepared jelly roll pan. Bake for 8 to 10 minutes until lightly browned and springy. Cool the pan on a cooling rack. Cut the cake off the sides of the pan and then flip the cake out of the pan onto a cutting surface. Remove the parchment or nonstick liner. Leave the cake inverted.

3. Make the soaking syrup by combining the water, sugar, and wine in a small pot. Stir and cook over medium heat until the sugar dissolves. Set aside.

4. For the custard, place the egg into a large bowl. Whisk in ¼ cup of the sugar and the potato starch. Place the milk, remaining ¼ cup sugar, and

vanilla bean in a small pot (if using extract do not add it now). Heat and stir over medium heat until the sugar dissolves. Increase the heat to medium-high, and bring the milk to a boil. Whisk the milk into the egg, drop by drop, until the egg is warmed, and then add the remaining milk in a steady stream. Pour the mixture back into the pot, and bring it to a boil for 1 minute. The mixture will be thin but will coat the back of a spoon. Strain the custard through a medium-mesh strainer. Scrape out the vanilla seeds, add them to the custard (add vanilla extract, if using), and discard the bean. Place the sour cream in a large bowl and add the custard little by little, mixing until smooth. Let the custard cool while you prepare the fruit.

5. Wash, peel, seed, and cut the fruit, as appropriate, into bite-size pieces.

6. Using a pastry brush, dab the soaking syrup onto the cake. Spread the jam over the cake. Cut the cake into 1-inch pieces.

7. Place a layer of the cake in the bottom of a 2- to 3-quart glass trifle or salad bowl (or use individual crystal goblets). Spoon on half of the custard. Cover with half of the fruit. Repeat layering, ending with a decorative array of fruit. Cover with plastic wrap and refrigerate for 3 to 24 hours.

8. If you must have whipped cream, make the optional garnish 15 minutes before serving time. Mix the cream with the sugar and vanilla. Refrigerate for 15 minutes, along with the bowl and beaters. Beat at high speed until soft peaks form. Scrape down the bowl, and finish beating the cream to stiff peaks. Pipe the whipped cream decoratively around the perimeter of the bowl or however you desire.

Lemon Berry Roulade

DAIRY

**NUTRITIONAL
NOTES**
(per serving)

150 calories

2g fat (10%)

43mg cholesterol

29g carbohydrates

5g protein

50mg sodium

1.5g fiber

RDA %

2% vitamin A

17% vitamin C

6% calcium

7% iron

*C*ustards and puddings made with potato starch can be gluey. To counterbalance this, I use just a little potato starch, and then add drained yogurt to provide some thickness and body to the filling. The yogurt continues to weep a little after the roulade is assembled, which moistens the sponge cake. Make sure that you use lowfat yogurt, as nonfat yogurt contains too much moisture (and is not kosher for Passover). The Passover sponge sheet is a terrific foundation cake that you can use with your own favorite fillings or frostings.

MAKES 14 SERVINGS

Passover Lemon Filling

1 cup lowfat lemon yogurt (Dannon is kosher for Passover—their regular yogurt is lowfat)

1 large egg yolk

2 tablespoons potato starch

1 cup 2% milk

⅔ to ¾ cup sugar

½ cup fresh lemon juice (2 to 3 lemons)

2 tablespoons orange juice

Zest from 1 lemon

Passover Sponge Sheet

2 large eggs, at room temperature

½ cup sugar

½ teaspoon Passover vanilla extract (optional)

1 teaspoon water

5 large egg whites, at room temperature

Light Jewish
Holiday Desserts

½ cup matzo cake meal

¼ cup potato starch

2 cups fresh raspberries or blueberries, or a combination

1. To make the lemon filling, place the yogurt in a double layer of cheese-cloth or a doubled coffee filter. Set this over a bowl, and place in the refrigerator for several hours to drain off some of the liquid.

2. Preheat the oven to 400°F, with racks in the middle and bottom of the oven. Line 2 jelly roll pans with parchment paper or nonstick Teflon liners. Grease lightly, and sprinkle with matzo cake meal. Set out a sheet of waxed paper, at least 6 inches longer than the jelly roll pan, and sprinkle it lightly with matzo cake meal.

3. To make the sponge sheet, place the eggs in a large mixer bowl. Beat on medium speed, gradually adding ¼ cup of the sugar. Increase the speed to high, and beat until thick and pale colored, about 5 minutes. Add the vanilla and water, and beat a few seconds just to blend.

4. In another mixer bowl, beat the egg whites until they are very foamy throughout and beater marks are just beginning to show. Continue to beat, while gradually adding the remaining ¼ cup of sugar. Increase the mixer speed to high, and beat the egg whites until stiff but not dry.

5. Stir together the matzo cake meal and potato starch. Sift ⅓ over the eggs. Spoon ⅓ of the whites on top, and fold together. Repeat twice more, until all of the ingredients are well folded together.

6. Remove 1 cup of batter, and spread it in one of the pans so that it is about ½ inch thick (it will cover only a small portion of the pan). Spread the remaining batter into the second pan. Set the completely filled pan in the middle of the oven, and the other pan in the bottom of the oven. Bake for 9 to 12 minutes until the cake in the upper pan is browned and springy. Remove both pans from the oven, and let them cool on a cooling rack. Turn the oven off. After 5 minutes, break the smaller piece of sponge cake into chunks, place them back in the pan, and set in the turned-off oven. Leave them in the oven for 20 minutes to 1 hour, or until they are almost completely hard. Process the chunks to fine crumbs. Place in a storage container until ready to use. *continued*

continued

Pesach
(Passover)

7. Meanwhile, run a knife around the edge of the remaining cake. Turn it upside down onto the waxed paper so that there are 3 inches of waxed paper free at one short end. Fold that edge over the cake, and roll up the cake into a jelly roll. Set aside to cool (can be made 2 days before assembly).

8. To continue with the filling, place the egg yolk in a medium mixer bowl. Whisk it lightly, cover with plastic wrap, and set aside.

9. In a medium, nonreactive pot, place the potato starch. Gradually add the milk, stirring after each addition, until smooth. Stir in the sugar to taste. Place the pot over medium heat and cook and stir until the sugar dissolves. Raise the heat to medium-high and bring the mixture to a boil, stirring constantly in a figure eight or "s" pattern (this will ensure that the filling on the bottom of the pan does not scorch). Cook and stir for 1 minute. Stirring constantly, add the pudding to the egg yolk, drop by drop, until the egg is hot, and then add the pudding in a constant stream. Return the mixture to the pot. Place over medium-low heat. Cook and stir until the mixture just starts to boil (to cook the yolk and destroy the enzyme in the yolk that can cause the sauce to thin). Stir in the lemon juice, orange juice, and zest. Strain the filling through a fine-mesh strainer into a storage container. Press a piece of parchment paper directly onto the top of the filling (this will prevent a skin from forming). Let the pudding cool until warm.

10. Place the yogurt in a large bowl. Press and stir with a wooden spoon to smooth it out. Stir-fold in the pudding. Cover the filling and place in the refrigerator until cool (can be made 3 days ahead).

11. When ready to assemble the roulade, unroll the cake (leave it on the waxed paper). Spread a ¼-inch layer of filling over the cake. Wash and pat the berries dry. Scatter them over the filling, reserving 4 berries for the top. Roll up the cake. Spread a very thin layer of the filling on the outside of the roll. Press the reserved crumbs over the cake. Dip the bottoms of the reserved berries into some of the filling, and stick the berries down the center of the cake roll. Refrigerate the cake for at least 4 hours and up to 24 hours before serving. Store in the refrigerator, and serve the cake cold. Do not freeze.

Chocolate Sundae Roulade

I originally made this roulade with bananas but soon discovered that the banana taste overwhelmed everything else if the cake was made ahead. As I always try to make my desserts at least one day ahead, I abandoned the bananas and opted for pineapple instead.

The results were even better than I had hoped for. The pineapple adds just the right amount of tang, and moistens the cake as well. When the occasion allows, try the cake with Light Whipped Cream, page 299, instead of the marshmallow meringue.

MAKES 12 TO 14 SERVINGS

2 large eggs, at room temperature

½ cup sugar, divided

½ teaspoon Passover vanilla extract (optional)

1 teaspoon water

5 large egg whites, at room temperature

½ cup matzo cake meal

¼ cup Passover cocoa powder (preferably Dutch-processed)

Marshmallow Meringue

2 large egg whites

½ cup sugar

1 tablespoon water

Filling

One 12-ounce jar cherry preserves

2 tablespoons water, divided

1 small can of crushed pineapple in juice, well drained

2 tablespoons walnuts, chopped medium-fine

PAREVE

NUTRITIONAL NOTES
(per serving; based on 12)

196 calories

2g fat (7%)

30mg cholesterol

44g carbohydrates

4g protein

53mg sodium

1g fiber

RDA %

1% vitamin A

7% vitamin C

1% calcium

5% iron

Pesach (Passover)

Glaze

1 tablespoon water

2 tablespoons (1 ounce) pareve semisweet chocolate chips

1. Preheat the oven to 400°F, with a rack in the middle of the oven. Line a jelly roll pan with parchment paper or a nonstick Teflon liner. Spray with Passover cooking spray, and sprinkle with matzo cake meal.

2. Place the eggs in a large mixer bowl. Beat on medium speed, gradually adding ¼ cup of the sugar. Increase the speed to high, and beat the eggs until thick and pale colored, 2 to 5 minutes. Add the vanilla and water, and beat for a few seconds just to blend.

3. In a clean, grease-free bowl, using clean, grease-free, and dry beaters, beat the egg whites until they are very foamy throughout and you can just begin to see beater tracks. Continue to beat, while gradually adding the remaining ¼ cup sugar. Increase the mixer speed to high, and beat the whites until stiff but not dry.

4. Sift together the matzo cake meal and cocoa. Sift ⅓ over the egg mixture. Spoon ⅓ of the egg whites on top, and fold together. Repeat twice more, until all of the ingredients are well folded together. Spread the batter evenly in the prepared pan. Bake for 9 to 12 minutes until springy. Cool for 5 minutes on a rack. Loosen the edges with a knife, and invert the pan onto a piece of waxed paper, leaving 3 inches of paper at one short end. Fold that paper over the short edge of the cake, and roll the cake up. Let the cake cool.

5. To make the marshmallow meringue, fill a large skillet with 1 inch of water. Bring the water to a simmer. In a small metal bowl, whisk the egg whites with the sugar and water. Have a rubber scraper, instant-read thermometer, a timer, another mixing bowl, and a beater near the stove.

6. Place the bowl with the egg whites into the simmering water, and rapidly stir with the rubber scraper for 20 seconds. Remove the bowl from the simmering water and check the temperature. If the eggs are not yet at 160°F, heat them for 10 seconds more. Remove the bowl from the water, dip the thermometer into the boiling water, and then retest. The temperature needs to be at 160°F to kill salmonella, but not much

higher, or the eggs will overcook. The time that it takes depends upon the type of bowl and pot that are being used—I've had it take from 20 to 80 seconds.

7. As soon as the eggs reach 160°F, transfer them to a cool bowl, and beat at medium-high speed until the egg whites are firm and cool. They will look like shaving cream and stand in stiff peaks when the beater is raised from them.

8. To make the filling, mix the preserves and 1 tablespoon of the water in a microwavable bowl or pot. Microwave on high, or heat over medium heat on the stove until the jam melts. Strain, reserving both the liquid and solids. Make a soaking syrup by mixing 2 tablespoons of the liquid jam with the remaining 1 tablespoon water. Discard the remaining liquid jam.

9. Unroll the cake. Prick it all over with a skewer, and then brush the soaking syrup over the cake. Strew the cherry pieces and pineapple over the cake. Spread a ¼-inch layer of meringue over the fruit. Sprinkle with the nuts. Roll the cake up.

10. For the glaze, place the water in a small microwavable bowl. Heat it on high for 30 seconds. Place the chocolate in another bowl, and pour the water over the chocolate. Microwave the chocolate on medium for 30 seconds. Stir until smooth. Repeat if the chocolate is not completely melted. The chocolate can be painted on the outside of the roll, or you can emboss the roll with fork tine marks, or you can drizzle the chocolate over the roll. With the remaining meringue, frost the ends of the roll, and pipe a decorative strip down the center of the cake (I like a stem and leaf effect made by piping elongated connected shells). Refrigerate the cake until ready to serve. May be made 1 day ahead. Do not freeze.

Applesauce Spice Cake

DAIRY

NUTRITIONAL
NOTES
(per serving)

109 calories

4g fat (34%)—

5.8g if using real

cream cheese

28mg cholesterol

15g carbohydrates

3.5g protein

50mg sodium

0g fiber

RDA %

2% vitamin A

0% vitamin C

2% calcium

3% iron

*T*hese spicy little squares are even tastier the day after they are
baked. They're great for after-school snacks, dairy Seder, to bring
to Temple, or for company. The cake can even be left whole, and
decorated for birthdays or other special events.

MAKES 24 SERVINGS

¾ cup walnuts, divided

½ cup firmly packed light brown sugar

2 teaspoons cinnamon

½ teaspoon dried ginger

½ teaspoon ground nutmeg

¼ teaspoon ground cloves

¼ cup matzo cake meal

3 large eggs, at room temperature

⅓ cup applesauce, at room temperature

¼ cup raisins

6 large egg whites, at room temperature

½ cup granulated sugar

Cream Cheese Frosting

8 ounces lowfat cream cheese (preferably Philadelphia ⅓ Less Fat—
for strictly kosher, use full-fat cream cheese)

2 tablespoons firmly packed light brown sugar

½ teaspoon Passover vanilla extract

1 teaspoon apple juice

1. Preheat the oven to 350°F, with a rack in the bottom third of the oven.
Line a 9 × 13-inch cake pan with parchment paper. Spray-grease with
Passover cooking spray, and sprinkle with matzo cake meal.

2. Place ½ cup of the walnuts, brown sugar, cinnamon, ginger, nutmeg, cloves, and matzo cake meal in a processor bowl, and process until the nuts are finely ground. Add the eggs and applesauce, and process until blended. Transfer the mixture to a large bowl, and stir in the raisins. Coarsely chop the remaining ¼ cup nuts, and stir into the mixture.

3. In another bowl, beat the egg whites on medium-high speed until beater marks begin to show. Continue to beat, while gradually adding the sugar. Increase the speed, and beat until whites are very stiff. Stir 1 cup of the whites into the nut mixture to lighten it. Fold in the remaining whites, in 3 additions. Spoon the batter into the prepared pan, and bake for 30 to 40 minutes, until a toothpick inserted into the center of the cake comes out with no moist crumbs attached. Cool pan on a rack. Turn the cake out of pan and remove the parchment paper. If you want to cut the cake into squares for serving, reinvert it onto a cutting board. If you want to present the cake whole, reinvert it onto a serving platter.

4. Place the cream cheese in a small mixer bowl. Beat until creamy. Mix the brown sugar, vanilla, and apple juice. Add to the cream cheese, and beat until smooth. The frosting can either be piped or spread onto the cake (piping looks nice if the cake is to remain whole). To cut neat squares, trim ¼ inch off all sides, and then cut the cake into squares, wiping the blade off between each cut. Keep the cake refrigerated, but allow it to come to room temperature before serving. Can be made 1 day ahead. Can be frozen without the frosting.

Pesach
(Passover)

Chocolate Nut Seafoam Layer Cake

PAREVE

NUTRITIONAL
NOTES
(per serving)

236 calories

6g fat (21%)

54mg cholesterol

43g carbohydrates

6g protein

62mg sodium

1g fiber

RDA %

1% vitamin A

0% vitamin C

2% calcium

6% iron

*T*his is a variation of my Chocolate Noisette Layer Cake that is featured on the cover of my book Passover Desserts. That cake is high in fat due to the enormous quantity of nuts and chocolate used. It may be true that fat from nuts is not bad for us, but just in case the experts are mistaken, I've designed this cake with three-quarters less fat.

MAKES 10 SERVINGS

Chocolate Nut Layer Cake

⅓ cup walnuts or pecans

¼ cup matzo cake meal

1 tablespoon pareve Passover semisweet chocolate, or chips

¼ cup Passover cocoa (preferably Dutch-processed)

3 large eggs

3 large egg whites (2 should be at room temperature)

1 cup plus 2 tablespoons granulated sugar, divided

Seafoam Frosting

4 large egg whites

1 cup firmly packed light brown sugar

2 tablespoons water

Filling and Garnish

2 tablespoons pareve Passover chocolate chips

3 tablespoons walnuts or pecans

1. Preheat the oven to 350°F, with a rack in the middle of the oven. Place parchment paper or nonstick Teflon liners into the bottom of two 8-inch round cake pans. Do not grease the pans.

2. Place the nuts, matzo cake meal, chocolate, and cocoa in the bowl of a food processor. Pulse-process until the nuts are finely ground, about 30 seconds. It's okay if some of the chocolate is still in small pieces.

3. Heat 2 inches of water in the bottom of a double boiler.

4. Combine the eggs and 1 egg white in a metal mixer bowl, or in the top of the double boiler (not over the heat yet). Whisk in 1 cup of the granulated sugar. Set the bowl over the double boiler, and whisk the mixture for about 2 minutes, until it is warm (about 110°F). Remove the bowl from the heat, and beat the eggs for about 5 minutes, until they are very thick and tripled in volume. Fold in the chocolate-nut mixture, ⅓ at a time.

5. Place the remaining 2 egg whites in a clean, grease-free bowl. With clean, grease-free beaters, beat the whites on medium-high speed until they are very foamy throughout, and beater marks are just beginning to show. Beat in the remaining 2 tablespoons of granulated sugar. Increase the speed to high, and beat the whites until stiff but not dry. Fold the whites into the batter, half at a time. Divide the mixture between the 2 pans. Bake the cakes for 20 to 25 minutes, until there are no beads of moisture on the surface of the cakes. Remove from the oven and let the pans cool on a rack. Run a knife around the outside of each cake, and then invert the pans to remove the cakes. Remove the parchment paper, set a 6-inch cakeboard onto the bottom of each cake, and reinvert the cakes so that they are right side up.

6. To make the frosting, fill a large skillet with 1 inch of water. Bring the water to a simmer. In a small metal bowl, whisk the egg whites with the brown sugar and water. Have a rubber scraper, instant-read thermometer, a timer, another mixing bowl, and a beater near the stove.

7. Place the bowl with the egg whites into the simmering water, and rapidly stir with the rubber scraper for 20 seconds. Remove the bowl

from the simmering water and check the temperature. If the eggs are not yet at 160°F, heat them for 10 seconds more. Remove the bowl from the water, dip the thermometer into the boiling water, and then retest. The temperature needs to be at 160°F to kill salmonella but not much higher, or the eggs will overcook. The time that it takes depends upon the type of bowl and pot that are being used—I've had it take from 20 to 80 seconds.

8. As soon as the eggs reach 160°F, transfer them to a cool bowl, and beat at medium-high speed until the egg whites are firm and cool. They will look like shaving cream and stand in stiff peaks when the beater is raised from them. Set aside.

9. For the filling, coarsely chop the chocolate and the walnuts. Mix together. Spread a ½-inch layer of the frosting on one of the cakes. Sprinkle on 2 tablespoons of the chocolate-nut mixture. Top with the second cake layer.

10. Spread about ½ inch of the frosting evenly on the top and a thin layer on the sides of the cake. Finely chop the remaining chocolate and nuts. Lift the cake up (on its board) and holding the cakeboard on your palm, pat the chocolate-nut mixture on the sides of the cake (do it over a pan so that you can reuse what falls off). Place the remaining frosting in a pastry bag with a fluted (shell) tip, and pipe a row of shells around the border of the cake.

11. The cake can be made 1 day ahead. If freezing, sprinkle the chocolate-nut mixture on the top of the cake, as it is not as pretty once frozen, and it needs a garnish to hide the appearance.

Passover *Tish Pishti*

Soaked Nut Cake

This Turkish Sephardic cake is an almost puddinglike dessert. Popular throughout the year, there are versions containing mounds of nuts, some with flour, and others like this one, with matzo cake meal. Most are high in cholesterol, due to the large quantity of eggs used. To lighten this cake, I've cut out 4 egg yolks, and reduced the nuts by half. The matzo cake meal helps maintain body, and the extra egg whites keep the cake moist and fluffy. Because the syrup is mostly juice, it is not overly sweet. Soaked cake is not to everyone's liking; however, if you are a "dunker," you'll probably enjoy it.

MAKES 24 SERVINGS

¾ cup sliced almonds or walnuts, divided

¾ cup matzo cake meal

1 cup sugar

1 teaspoon orange zest

2 teaspoons cinnamon

4 large eggs, at room temperature

6 large egg whites, at room temperature

Orange Soaking Syrup

3 cups orange juice

1¼ cups sugar

2½ tablespoons sliced almonds (choose whole, nice-looking slices)

PAREVE

NUTRITIONAL
NOTES
(per serving)

150 calories

4g fat (22%)

30mg cholesterol

27g carbohydrates

3.5g protein

24mg sodium

1g fiber

RDA %

2% vitamin A

26% vitamin C

2% calcium

4% iron

Pesach
(Passover)

continued

1. Preheat the oven to 350°F, with a rack in the bottom third of the oven. Place parchment paper or a nonstick Teflon liner in a 9 × 13-inch baking pan. Grease the pan and sprinkle with matzo cake meal.

2. Place ½ cup of the nuts, the matzo cake meal, ½ cup of the sugar, the zest, and cinnamon in a food processor bowl. Process for 10 to 20 seconds to grind the nuts. Add the whole eggs, and process to blend. Transfer the mixture to a large bowl and stir in the remaining ¼ cup nuts.

3. In a large mixer bowl, beat the egg whites on medium-high speed until beater tracks show. Continue beating while gradually adding the remaining ½ cup sugar. Increase the speed to high, and beat the whites until very stiff. Gently stir 1 cup of the whites into the batter to lighten the mixture. Fold in the remaining whites in 3 additions. Spoon the batter into the prepared pan. Bake for 40 to 45 minutes. Cool on a rack. Turn the cake out of the pan, and cut it into 24 pieces. Place back in the pan.

4. Make the syrup by combining the orange juice and sugar in a medium pot. Heat and stir over medium heat until the sugar dissolves, and then bring the mixture to a boil. Pour half of the hot syrup over the cake. Let the cake soak for 10 minutes, and then turn the pieces over. In the center of each piece, arrange 3 almond slices in a fleur de lis pattern. Pour the remaining syrup over the cake, and if necessary, use a pastry brush to make sure that the nuts are glazed. Cover the cake with foil, and let it soak and mellow for several hours or overnight. Do not freeze.

A different soaking method is to cut the hot cake into pieces and pour chilled syrup over the hot cake. The hot cake seems to absorb more of the syrup, making it softer throughout. Because Passover *Tish Pishti* does not contain flour, I prefer that the cake not be quite so soft.

Filling

2 pounds nonfat cottage cheese (if strictly kosher, use regular)

12 ounces light cream cheese, preferably Philadelphia ⅓ Less Fat
    (if strictly kosher, use regular)

¼ cup reduced-fat sour cream, such as Breakstone's

1¼ cups sugar

2 large eggs, at room temperature

1 large egg white, at room temperature

1 tablespoon orange juice

Blueberry Topping

4 cups fresh blueberries

½ cup water

⅓ cup sugar

½ teaspoon cinnamon

1 tablespoon orange juice

1 tablespoon potato starch

2 tablespoons water

1. If using the crumb crust, preheat the oven to 350°F, with a rack in the lower third of the oven. Wrap a 10-inch springform pan with heavy-duty foil, so that the foil comes up over the top of the pan (heavy-duty foil is wider and so will wrap around the whole pan without a seam). Crimp the foil at the top of the pan. Boil water in a teakettle, reduce the heat, and keep it warm. Have ready a baking dish at least 12 × 12 inches.

2. For the crumb crust, process the mandel bread until finely crushed. Transfer the crumbs to a small mixing bowl. Stir in the oil, and work it into the crumbs with your fingers. Stir in the egg white, and use your fingers to squeeze the crumbs into clumps. Firmly press the clumps into the bottom of the prepared pan.

3. If using the sponge sheet, preheat the oven to 400°F, with racks in the middle and bottom of the oven. Prepare the pans as follows: Place a pre-cut 10-inch parchment circle in a jelly roll pan. Line another jelly roll pan with parchment, make the batter, and spoon all but 1 cup of batter

Berry Cheesecake

We like to eat cheesecake year-round, and Passover is no exception. Those who are strictly kosher will have to substitute regular cottage cheese and full-fat cream cheese, because the lowfat products contain starches that are not kosher for Passover (lowfat sour cream is fine). You can use either a crumb crust or sponge cake for the base. Sponge cake is a nice change from the traditional crumb crust and it's lower in fat, but the crumb crust is quicker to make. If you're not fond of blueberries, try the strawberry variation, or use fresh fruit glazed with jam. You can also use any of the other cheesecake recipes in the book, substituting the Passover Sponge Sheet or the Passover Crumb Crust for the crust listed. Those who aren't kosher or who are planning a dairy Seder will find the cheesecake light enough for dessert even after the heavy Seder meal. It's also great for company or special occasions during Passover week. Dividing the cake into 20 slices may sound like the pieces will be too small, but each will be about 1 inch wide and 5 inches long—quite sufficient for a rich dessert.

MAKES 20 SERVINGS

Passover Crumb Crust (alternatively, use Passover Sponge Sheet, page 196)

9 pieces Goodman's Passover Almond Mandel Bread
    (or other packaged Passover mandel bread)

2 teaspoons Passover oil

1 tablespoon egg white (whisk and it will be easier to measure)

continued

DA

NUTRI
NO
(per serving
sponge cake
grams

203 c

(245 if usi

prod

5g fat (

9g if usin

proc

34mg ch

29g carb

11g p

227mg

1g f

R D

4% vit

7% vit

8% ca

4%

MA
DAY

Pes
(Pass

into a pastry bag fitted with a ¾-inch plain tip. Pipe concentric circles or a spiral to fill the 10-inch round (there will be excess batter). Spoon the remaining 1 cup of batter onto the other jelly roll pan, and spread it about ½ inch thick (it will only fill part of the sheet). Bake and cool as directed in step 6, page 197. Put the cake round into the bottom of the prepared springform pan. Turn the oven down to 350°F. Move the top oven rack down to the lower third of the oven.

4. To make the filling, place the cottage cheese in a large double-layer piece of cheesecloth. Fold the cheesecloth into a "bag," twist the top, and squeeze to remove as much liquid from the cheese as possible. Wipe off the moisture on the outside of the bag, and continue squeezing and wiping until no more liquid comes out of the bag. Transfer the cheese to the processor bowl and process for 1 minute. Scrape down the bowl, and process for at least 2 more minutes or until completely smooth. Cut the cream cheese into 6 lumps and add them to the processor. Pulse-process until the cheeses are well blended. Scrape down the sides of the bowl, add the sour cream, and process until mixed. Add the sugar and process for 1 minute to fully incorporate. Whisk together the eggs, egg white, and orange juice. Add to the processor bowl, and process for a few seconds to blend. Scrape down the bowl sides and process a few more seconds.

5. Pour the batter into the prepared pan. Put the cheesecake pan into the larger pan and place it in the oven. Pour boiling water into the larger pan so that it comes halfway up the sides of the cheesecake pan. Be careful not to splash water into the cheesecake. Bake for 55 to 65 minutes, until the cheesecake is set, but a toothpick inserted into the center of the cake will still come out with a little moist cheese attached. For firmer cheesecake, cook an additional 5 minutes, but cover the pan with foil if cooking more than 60 minutes. Remove the cheesecake from the oven, lift the pan out of the water-bath, and let the cheesecake cool on a wire rack.

6. For the blueberry topping, combine 2 cups of the blueberries, the water, sugar, cinnamon, and orange juice in a small pot. Bring it to a boil over medium-high heat. Reduce the heat and simmer for 5 minutes.

7. Place the potato starch in a small bowl. Stir in the water, a little at a time. Add the potato starch to the pot, bring back to a simmer, and cook,

stirring, for 1 minute. Remove from the heat and stir in the remaining berries. Let the berries cool slightly and then pour onto the cheesecake. When the topping is completely cool, cover the pan with foil and refrigerate the cheesecake overnight.

8. The next day, run a knife around the perimeter of the cheesecake, and remove the springform sides. To cut nice slices, clean the knife off between cuts with a damp cloth. Cheesecake can be made 2 days ahead, or frozen, without the topping.

Strawberry Topping

6 cups fresh strawberries

⅔ cup sugar

2 tablespoons fresh lemon juice (1 lemon or less)

1 tablespoon potato starch

1. Mash 3 cups of berries in a medium (3-quart) pot. Slice the remaining berries and add to the pot. Stir in the sugar and lemon juice. Let macerate for 5 minutes.

2. Place the potato starch in a small bowl. Stir in 2 tablespoons of the strawberry liquid.

3. Heat the berries over high heat until boiling. Add the potato starch mixture. Turn the heat to medium-low, and cook until the liquid clears (it will be whitish and cloudy, and as it cooks will get clearer and redder). Let it cool to lukewarm before pouring over the cheesecake.

MULTIBERRY VARIATION: You can make a spectacular-looking cheesecake by placing a 6-inch round baking pan in the middle of the cooked and cooled cheesecake, spooning the blueberry filling around the sides, and when it is set, removing the pan and filling the center with the strawberry filling (if you have a "checkerboard" mold, it will give you 3 rings of berries, which is even nicer). When the springform sides are removed you see all the layers: the crust, white sides, and the blue and red on top.

Fudgy Coconut Macaroons

ALSO SERVE ON
Purim, Shabbat,
Yom ha-atzma'ut

PAREVE

NUTRITIONAL NOTES
(per serving)

53 calories

1.5g fat (24%)

0mg cholesterol

10g carbohydrates

1g protein

8mg sodium

1g fiber

RDA %

0% vitamin A

0% vitamin C

0% calcium

1% iron

Coconut is one of those ingredients that has a tendency either to fluff or pack when it is measured in cups. Because of this, the moistness of the cookies will change every time you make them, unless the coconut is weighed and remains constant. I like these macaroons on the underdone side so that they are slightly fudgy in the middle. The timing is crucial, and you will have to experiment to see how long to cook them in your oven. If using sweetened coconut, see the variation at the end of the recipe. I have a similar recipe in my book *Passover Desserts*, but these are more fudgy, and easier to make than those. Both have the same amount of fat, if you make the cookies the same size. Macaroons can be made with or without potato starch or matzo cake meal. Those made with neither will be moist and soft, but it will be easier to either under- or overbake them. Those with potato starch will be slightly firmer, and those with matzo cake meal will be slightly chewier, my personal preference.

MAKES 32 COOKIES

9 ounces unsweetened coconut (about 3½ cups, lightly packed)

¼ cup Passover cocoa (preferably Dutch-processed)

1 cup sugar

2 tablespoons matzo cake meal, or potato starch (optional)

4 large egg whites, at room temperature

½ teaspoon Passover vanilla extract or water

¼ cup honey

Light Jewish
Holiday Desserts

1. Preheat the oven to 325°F, with the racks in the middle and lower third of the oven. Place parchment paper or nonstick Teflon liners on 2 cookie sheets.

2. Put the coconut, cocoa, sugar, and matzo meal (if using) in a food processor bowl. Pulse-process until the coconut is finely ground, about 10 to 20 seconds. Add the egg whites, vanilla, and honey. Process until everything is well mixed, 10 to 20 seconds.

3. Spoon the mixture onto the cookie sheets by well-rounded teaspoonsful, leaving 1 inch between cookies. Moisten hands, and shape the mounds into pyramids. Bake the cookies for 6 minutes. Switch the position of the cookie sheets, top to bottom, and continue to cook for 6 to 8 minutes, or just until they are dull and there are no beads of moisture showing on the cookies. Slide the parchment onto cooling racks, and let the cookies cool before eating. Cookies become moister and sweeter when frozen. Cookies can be made 1 day ahead, or frozen for 3 months.

VARIATION: Sweetened coconut is sweeter and much moister than unsweetened coconut, so the recipe needs to be modified. Use these ingredients and the same technique as above:

> 10 ounces sweetened coconut (3½ cups)
>
> ¼ cup Passover cocoa (Dutch-processed if possible)
>
> 3 tablespoons sugar
>
> 3 tablespoons matzo cake meal, or potato starch (optional)
>
> 3 large egg whites, at room temperature
>
> ½ teaspoon Passover vanilla extract, or water
>
> ¼ cup honey

Chocolate Chip and Nut Meringue Kisses

ALSO SERVE ON
*Purim, Shabbat,
Onegs,
Yom ha-atzma'ut,
life-cycle events*

PAREVE OR
DAIRY

NUTRITIONAL
NOTES
(per serving)

43 calories

2g fat (37%)

0mg cholesterol

7g carbohydrates

1g protein

5mg sodium

1g fiber

RDA %

0% vitamin A

0% vitamin C

0% calcium

0% iron

These kisses are a little less sweet than usual, which makes them very popular with adults. Because of the chocolate chips, they're appealing to kids too. They're great after a Seder because they're not very filling, but the nuts and chocolate chips make them quite satisfying. They can also be whipped up in a flash for after-school treats or unexpected company.

MAKES TWENTY-FOUR 1½-INCH COOKIES

2 large egg whites, at room temperature
½ cup sugar
¼ teaspoon Passover vanilla extract (optional)
⅓ cup walnuts or pecans, coarsely chopped
½ cup (85 grams) Passover chocolate chips (pareve or dairy)

1. Preheat the oven to 400°F, with a rack in the middle of the oven (if you cannot fit 2 cookie sheets on 1 rack, set the racks in the lower and upper thirds of the oven). Line 2 cookie sheets with parchment paper or nonstick Teflon liners.

2. In a large, clean, and grease-free mixer bowl, beat the egg whites on high speed until very foamy throughout, and beater marks are just becoming visible. Gradually add the sugar as you continue to beat. Beat until soft peaks form and the whites are marshmallowy, about 5 minutes. Toward the end of the beating, add the vanilla. Fold in the nuts and chocolate chips. Spoon the meringue onto the cookie sheets by well-rounded teaspoonsful to make 1½-inch mounds. Reduce the oven to 250°F, and bake for 1 hour until the meringues are firm. If using 2 oven

racks, switch the position of the upper and lower cookie sheets halfway through baking. Slide the parchment paper onto cooling racks and let the cookies cool on the paper. The cookies will keep for 3 to 4 days in dry weather but get chewier as they sit. Do not freeze.

VARIATION: Fold in ¼ cup cocoa powder along with the chocolate chips and nuts.

Chocolate Cookie Sandwiches

These fudgy wafers sandwiched with jam are nice for snacks, lunches, and dessert buffets. They're very quick to make—perfect for the busy Passover season.

MAKES 21 SANDWICH COOKIES

½ cup pecans, chopped

¾ cup sugar

⅓ cup Passover cocoa (preferably Dutch-processed)

2 tablespoons matzo cake meal

2 tablespoons potato starch

3 large egg whites, at room temperature

½ teaspoon Passover vanilla extract, or water

1 teaspoon water

½ cup Passover jam (we like sweet orange marmalade or raspberry)

1. Preheat the oven to 400°F, with a rack in the middle of the oven. Line 2 cookie sheets with parchment paper or nonstick Teflon liners. Spray with cooking spray.

2. Place the pecans, sugar, cocoa, matzo cake meal, and potato starch in a food processor bowl. Process until the pecans are finely ground, about 25

PAREVE

NUTRITIONAL NOTES
(per serving)

86 calories

2g fat (20%)

0mg cholesterol

17g carbohydrates

1g protein

12mg sodium

1g fiber

RDA %

0% vitamin A

1% vitamin C

0% calcium

2% iron

Pesach
(Passover)

217

seconds. Add the egg whites, vanilla, and water. Process until well blended. Drop the batter by rounded measuring teaspoonsful onto the prepared sheets.

3. Bake for 7 to 8 minutes, until just barely set.

4. Slide the parchment paper or liners onto a cooling rack, and let the cookies cool (if using greased sheets only, let the cookies set for 1 minute and then remove them from the baking sheet to prevent them from continuing to cook).

5. Spread a very thin layer of the jam (don't use any chunks of fruit) on half of the cookies. Press the plain cookies to the jelly-covered ones to make sandwiches. Cookies can be made 1 day ahead. They can be frozen but get tacky on the outside.

Apple Pear Crisp

DAIRY OR
PAREVE

This down-home dessert can be served family-style, or in individual ramekins. It's got lots of fiber and is light and refreshing after a big holiday celebration such as Pesach.

MAKES 8 GENEROUS SERVINGS

Passover Streusel

⅓ cup matzo cake meal

⅓ cup potato starch

⅓ cup firmly packed light brown sugar

½ teaspoon cinnamon

2 tablespoons unsalted butter, or unsalted pareve Passover margarine

2 teaspoons Passover oil

½ large egg white (whisk for easier measuring)

Apple Pear Filling

4 medium apples, preferably a mix of semitart and tart varieties

4 medium pears, preferably Bartlett

1 medium lemon, squeezed into 8 cups cold water

3 to 4 tablespoons firmly packed light or dark brown sugar
(or more to taste)

¼ teaspoon nutmeg

½ teaspoon cinnamon

1 to 2 tablespoons potato starch

NUTRITIONAL
NOTES
(per serving)

210 calories

5g fat (20%)

8mg cholesterol

49g carbohydrates

2g protein

11mg sodium

4g fiber

RDA %

3% vitamin A

14% vitamin C

3% calcium

14% iron

1. Preheat the oven to 350°F, with a rack in the middle of the oven. Place parchment paper or a nonstick Teflon liner on a cookie sheet.

2. To make the streusel, in a medium bowl, mix together the matzo cake meal, potato starch, brown sugar, and cinnamon.

3. Melt the butter and oil in a pot or in the microwave. Add to the matzo meal mixture and mix with a fork until moistened. Add 1 tablespoon of the egg white to the matzo mixture, and stir with a fork to moisten. Use your fingertips and then palms to form the mixture into small crumbs no larger than a pea. Break up any larger crumbs. Dump the crumbs onto the baking sheet and spread into an even layer, 1 crumb thick. Bake for 8 minutes. Turn the crumbs over with a pancake turner or spatula, and continue to bake for 2 to 4 minutes until the crumbs are nicely browned. Remove from the oven and cool on a rack. Can be made 1 week ahead and stored in an airtight container at room temperature, or frozen for up to 3 months.

4. Peel, core, and cut the apples and pears into ¼-inch slices, dropping them into the lemon-water as they're cut to keep them from turning brown. When all are prepared, drain and pat them dry. There should be 10 to 11 cups of fruit.

5. In a mixing bowl, combine the fruit with the brown sugar (to taste), nutmeg, cinnamon, and potato starch. The amount of potato starch to use will depend on how thick you like your fillings, and the mix of apples that you use. As there is no bottom crust to get soggy, crisps do not actually need any thickener at all. In addition, potato starch can be pretty gluey, so I prefer to make a fairly thin sauce, and use only 1 tablespoon of

Pesach
(Passover)

thickener. Spoon fruit into a 9 × 12-inch nonstick pan. Cover with aluminum foil, and bake in the middle of the oven until the apples are almost tender, about 50 minutes.

6. Place half of the streusel in the processor, and pulse-process until the crumbs are coarsely ground. Sprinkle the chunky streusel over the fruit, and then sprinkle on the finer crumbs. Continue to bake, uncovered, until the apples are tender, 5 to 10 minutes longer.

7. Remove the fruit from the oven and let it cool until just barely warm, about 20 minutes. The fruit can be made 1 day ahead, but do not top with the crumbs. Reheat the fruit in a 350°F oven for 10 minutes, top with the crumbs, and continue baking for 10 minutes, or until just warm. For extra-crispy crumbs, sprinkle them on the fruit just before serving. For a prettier presentation, spoon the warm fruit into individual ramekins, sprinkle with crumbs, and if dairy is okay, serve with a dollop of Light Whipped Cream (see page 299).

Sweet Apple *Chremslach*

Matzo Meal Pancakes

Chremslach, *or grimslach, dates back two thousand years. A variation of a Roman dish called* vermiculos, *it was composed of chunks of dough, deep-fried and served with honey. The Jews of the Middle Ages must have eaten it regularly, as it is mentioned in several books of Jewish law written at the time, according to Patti Shosteck's* A Lexicon of Jewish Cooking.

MAKES 4 TO 6 SERVINGS

2 large eggs

½ cup egg substitute (such as Egg Beaters), or 4 large egg whites

1 cup skim milk, or water

1 teaspoon cinnamon

2 teaspoons sugar

1 cup matzo meal

¼ cup walnuts, finely chopped

2 small apples, peeled, cored, and finely chopped

1. In a medium bowl, whisk together the eggs, egg substitute, milk, cinnamon, and sugar. Gradually, stir in the matzo meal, and then the nuts and apples. Cover and refrigerate for 10 minutes.

2. Very lightly oil a large, nonstick frying pan, and heat it over high heat until hot. Reduce the heat to medium-high. Spoon in the batter by well-rounded tablespoonsful. Cook until the undersides are nicely browned (less than 1 minute). Turn the pancakes, and cook on the other side until browned. Turn down the heat to low, and let the pancakes cook about 30 seconds longer, to make sure that the interior is cooked. Place the pancakes on a cookie sheet, and set in a warm oven while you make the remaining pancakes. Serve with warmed honey or maple syrup.

DAIRY OR PAREVE

NUTRITIONAL NOTES
(per serving)

188 calories

4.5g fat (22%)

61mg cholesterol

30g carbohydrates

7g protein

67mg sodium

2g fiber

RDA %

4% vitamin A

5% vitamin C

7% calcium

10% iron

Pesach
(Passover)

221

Baked Nutmeg Pears with Chocolate Sauce

ALSO SERVE ON
Sukkot, Shabbat

DAIRY

NUTRITIONAL NOTES
(per serving)

130 calories

4g fat (26%)

2mg cholesterol

25g carbohydrates

2g protein

11mg sodium

3g fiber

RDA %

1% vitamin A

5% vitamin C

4% calcium

4% iron

These lightly caramelized pears don't need stirring or turning, as they would if caramelized in a pan. They hold together beautifully, and are easy to test for doneness. Nutmeg pears can be eaten warm or cold, can be used to top cakes, or can be chopped for pastry fillings.

MAKES 8 SERVINGS

Passover Chocolate Sauce

⅓ cup sugar

3 tablespoons water

⅔ cup 2% milk

2 tablespoons chopped Passover semisweet chocolate,
    or chocolate chips

⅓ cup Passover cocoa powder, preferably Dutch-processed

Baked Pears

2 medium lemons, squeezed into 8 cups cold water

4 medium pears (preferably Bosc), ripe but firm

4 teaspoons Passover oil

4 teaspoons sugar

¼ teaspoon freshly grated nutmeg

1. For the sauce, combine the sugar and water in a small pot. Heat and stir over medium heat until the mixture begins to simmer. Lower the heat to medium-low, swirl the pot occasionally, but do not stir, and cook for 8 to 10 minutes, until the syrup is thickened and just glazes the bottom of the pot. Stir in the milk. Bring the mixture to a boil over medium-high heat.

2. Place the chocolate and cocoa in a processor bowl. Process until the chocolate is finely grated. With the machine running, pour the boiling milk through the feed tube. Process for about 30 seconds. Let the mixture rest for a minute. Use a rubber scraper along the sides of the bowl to scrape up any unmelted chocolate and to stir it into the hot liquid. Strain the mixture through a medium-mesh strainer into a storage container. Cover and refrigerate at least 6 hours until cold and thickened (can be stored for up to 2 weeks).

3. Preheat the oven to 425°F, with a rack in the middle of the oven.

4. One at a time, peel, core, and cut the pears in half lengthwise, and place in the lemon-water.

5. Remove the pears from the water and pat dry. Brush them with oil and place in a single layer in a Pyrex or nonstick pan. Sprinkle the pears with the sugar and grate fresh nutmeg (to taste) over them. Cover with foil and bake for 15 to 30 minutes depending on the ripeness of the pears and the variety used. Pears are done when a knife can be easily inserted into the flesh. Remove from the oven, take off the foil, and let the pears cool.

Alternatively, the pears can be cut decoratively into fans. Starting in the center of each pear, make a long cut that begins ⅛ inch from the stem and goes through the pear to the other end. The next cut will be parallel to the first about ⅛ inch away. Continue cutting like this to each side of the pear. When done the pear will be sliced into ⅛ inch pieces but they will all be attached at the stem end (see diagram 11.1). Place the pear back into the lemony water so that the slices won't end up with brown centers, prepare, and bake the pears the same as above.

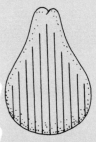

6. To serve, sauce the plates, and place pears on the sauce, pressing lightly to fan the slices. They can also be placed on top of a dessert. Use a knife to fan the slices.

This can be prepared 2 days ahead. Store in the refrigerator.

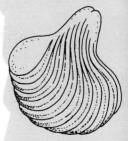

Yom ha-atzma'ut, celebrated on the fifth of Iyyar (April or May), commemorates Israeli independence, won in 1948. If it falls on a Friday or Saturday, celebrations will take place on the preceding Thursday. Although there is liturgical ritual to observe, Yom ha-atzma'ut is mostly a day of partying, parades, picnics, and cookouts.

There are no specific desserts for the holiday—Israelis usually have barbecues and eat watermelon and other picnic items. We, in the Diaspora, can celebrate the holiday by eating typically Jewish desserts, desserts made with Israeli or biblical products, foods shaped like the Israeli flag, or sweets suitable for picnics.

The following lists will help:

Picnic foods

Chocolate Chip and Nut Meringue Kisses

Butter Cookie Dreidels (shape them like flags instead)

Fudgy Coconut Macaroons

Pecan Oatmeal Lace Cookies

Phyllo Triangles

Recipes using Israeli or Biblical produce

Apple Date Tart

Apple Mousse Layer Cake

Apple-Plum Galette

Date, Fig, and Nut Loaf

Dried Fruit and Apple Tart

Honey Coffee Chiffon Cake

Honey Spice Thumbprints

Key Lime Pie

Lemon Mousse Charlotte

Lemon Pistachio Roulade

Little Lemon Tarts

Mandarin Orange Cheesecake

Maple Baked Apples

Orange Apricot Chiffon Cake

Orange Crepe Scrolls

Pear Tart Frangipane

Winter Fruit Compote

Traditional Ashkenazi recipes

Almond Bundt Cake

Apple Bundt Cake

Apple Cherry Strudel

Apple Date Bundt Cake

Apple Honey Strudel

Babka

Bread Pudding

Caramel Apple Blintzes

Hamantashen

Lekach *(Honey Cake)*

Lemon Poppy Buttermilk Mini-Loaves

Low-Cholesterol Sponge Cake

Kuchen

Mandel Bread

Marble Cheesecake

Marble Pound Cake

Peach Melba Varenikes

New York–Style Rice Pudding

Rugelach

Sticky Buns

Yom ha-atzma'ut

Traditional Sephardic recipes

Adjweh

Baklava

Bimuelos

Bulemas Dulces

Couscous Pudding

Iraqi Date Balls

Kadaif *or* Konafa

Menenas *or* Ma-amoul

Maronchinos

Reshicas

Travados

Shavuot is celebrated on the sixth and seventh days of Sivan (only the sixth in Israel), usually occurring in May or June. It translates as "weeks," so named because the holiday comes after the seven weeks of counting the Omer (the counting of the days between the first offering of grain on the second night of Passover and the last offering on Shavuot). Biblical references regard it as the end of the grain harvest and the beginning of a new agricultural season, so the festival has also been called Hag ha'Katzir (Festival of the Harvest) or Hag ha'Bikurim

(Festival of the First Fruits). Farmers would bring their first fruits, whenever ripe, during the period between Shavuot and Sukkot. After the destruction of the temple, in A.D. 70, the agricultural rites could not be observed, and Shavuot gradually became linked to the Revelation at Sinai, or the giving of the Torah to the Jewish people.

Symbolic foods eaten for Shavuot can be linked to the holiday's agricultural roots or to its religious components. The obvious choices for agricultural significance would be first fruits of the season. In Israel these would include figs, grapes, honey, and pomegranates. In the United States these might include peaches, berries, cherries, and melons. Cheese and dairy products are usually eaten, and there are many possible explanations for this tradition. It is implied in the Song of Songs (4:11) that the words of the Torah are as sweet as honey and as nourishing as milk. Another explanation is that when the Israelites received the laws of kashrut at Sinai, they realized that their pots were not kosher, and so chose to eat only dairy. Mystics note that the numerical value of milk is forty, the number of days that Moses waited for the Torah. Milk desserts may also be eaten because they are white, a traditional symbol of purity. Desserts to symbolize these facets of the holiday might include cheesecakes and puddings. Sephardic peoples often eat rice pudding. Other white foods, such as cakes iced with snow-white frosting, could be eaten to symbolize the purity of the Torah. There are several theories about the use of rose water and spices on Shavuot. One is that when the Israelites received the law they fainted with fear and had to be revived with fragrant spices, writes Michael Strassfeld in *The Jewish Holidays*. Another is that the world filled with fragrance when the law was received.

Shavuot should be celebrated with the following symbolic foods:

First fruits of the season (May–June)

Cheese and dairy products

Honey

White foods

Spices and rose water

Spiced Peach Shortcakes

After tasting these light and luscious shortcakes you will never want to go back to the high-fat version. The filling is very sweet, complementing the slight tang of buttermilk in the biscuits. Using very ripe summer peaches, just a touch of spice, and lightened whipped cream, they are delightful for Shavuot.

MAKES 8 SERVINGS

Shortcakes

¾ cup (90 grams) all-purpose flour, lightly sprinkled into
    measuring cup

1⅔ cups (175 grams) sifted cake flour, lightly sprinkled into
    measuring cup

¼ cup plus 1 teaspoon granulated sugar

1½ teaspoons baking powder

1½ teaspoons baking soda

¼ teaspoon salt

1 tablespoon shortening, chilled and cut into quarters

1 tablespoon unsalted butter, chilled and cut into quarters

¾ cup nonfat or lowfat buttermilk

½ teaspoon vanilla extract

1 tablespoon skim milk

Peach Filling

3 medium lemons

12 medium peaches, very ripe

⅔ cup granulated sugar

⅓ cup firmly packed brown sugar

½ teaspoon cinnamon

¼ teaspoon nutmeg

1 recipe Light Whipped Cream, page 299 (topping)

continued

ALSO SERVE ON
Shabbat

DAIRY

NUTRITIONAL NOTES
(per serving, with 2 tablespoons of whipped topping)

282 calories

6g fat (16%)

72g carbohydrates

14mg cholesterol

4g protein

372mg sodium

2g fiber

RDA%

13% vitamin A

45% vitamin C

9% calcium

10% iron

Shavuot

1. Preheat the oven to 425°F, with a rack in the middle of the oven. Spray-grease an insulated cookie sheet. If you don't have one, nest 2 cookie sheets together.

2. To make the shortcakes, in a medium bowl, sift together both flours, ¼ cup granulated sugar, baking powder, baking soda, and salt. Using a pastry blender or 2 knives, cut the shortening and butter into the flour until the fat particles are the size of lentils.

3. In another bowl, mix the buttermilk and vanilla. Make a well in the dry ingredients and pour in all but about 1 tablespoon of buttermilk. Stir with a fork to moisten the ingredients.

4. Gently toss the dough to form a rough mass. If it will not come together, add the remaining buttermilk. Turn the dough out onto a floured board and pat it down to about ¾ inch thick. Cut into four 3-inch rounds. Brush the tops of the shortcakes with the skim milk and sprinkle lightly with the remaining 1 teaspoon sugar. Transfer to the prepared cookie sheet.

5. Bake 10 to 12 minutes until puffed and golden. Transfer to a rack and cool slightly. (Can be made 1 day ahead. To rewarm, wrap with foil and heat at 350°F for 10 minutes. Shortcakes can also be frozen for 3 months—reheat in the same manner, adding 5 minutes to the time.)

6. While the shortcakes are cooking, make the filling. Squeeze the lemons into a large bowl. Peel the peaches (with a knife or by plunging them into boiling water for 1 to 2 minutes). Cut in half, remove the pits, and cut each half into 8 wedges. Toss with the lemon juice. Add both sugars, cinnamon, and nutmeg and let macerate for 15 minutes. Place 1½ cups of peaches with some juice into a processor, and puree completely. Add to the remaining peaches and set aside until ready to serve. Can be made 1 day ahead. Cover and refrigerate, but allow to come to room temperature before serving.

7. To serve, reheat the biscuits as per instructions in step 5. Cut each one horizontally, in half. On each of 8 plates, spoon several tablespoons of sauce. Set a shortcake half on each plate. Arrange peach wedges on each shortcake in a spoke pattern, spoon on some more sauce, top with a rounded tablespoon of whipped cream, and serve.

Cherry Vanilla Trifle Cups

Unlike the Mixed Fruit Trifle on page 193, this one uses a thick custard. Served in wineglasses that show off the different layers, these are elegant and beautiful. Fresh cherries provide a tremendous burst of flavor, as well as a nice texture.

MAKES 6 SERVINGS

Vanilla Pastry Cream, page 301, cold

Sponge Cake Sheet

1⅛ cups (120 grams) sifted cake flour, lightly sprinkled into measuring cup

1 teaspoon baking powder

⅛ teaspoon salt

3 large eggs, at room temperature, separated

⅓ cup plus 3 tablespoons sugar, divided

1 teaspoon vanilla extract

2 tablespoons warm water

Soaking Syrup

2 tablespoons sugar

¼ cup water

1 tablespoon kirsch (cherry) liqueur, or cherry juice

¼ cup cherry preserves

36 fresh cherries, washed, pitted, and halved (reserve 6 whole cherries with stems attached)

1. Preheat the oven to 375°F, with a rack in the middle of the oven. Cut parchment paper to fit a 10 x 15-inch jelly roll pan.

2. Sift together the cake flour, baking powder, and salt. Set aside. *continued*

ALSO SERVE ON
Shabbat, Chanukah
(use canned cherries
or another fruit)

DAIRY

NUTRITIONAL
NOTES
(per serving; ⅔ of the
sponge cake is used)

270 calories

3g fat (11%)

94mg cholesterol

53g carbohydrates

7g protein

143mg sodium

1g fiber

RDA %

7% vitamin A

3% vitamin C

16% calcium

9% iron

Shavuot

233

3. In a clean grease-free bowl, combine the egg whites. Beat on medium-high until the eggs are very foamy and thickened. Slowly add 3 tablespoons of the sugar, continuing to beat on high until the egg whites form stiff, but not dry, peaks.

4. In another bowl, beat the egg yolks with the remaining ⅓ cup sugar on medium-high speed for 2 to 5 minutes, until the yolks are pale yellow and very thick. Lower the speed and beat in the vanilla and water.

5. Spoon ⅓ of the egg whites onto the egg yolks. Sift on ⅓ of the flour, and fold gently together. Repeat twice more, gently folding ingredients together.

6. Spoon the batter into the prepared pan. Spread it in an even layer to cover the pan. Bake in the middle of the oven for 8 to 10 minutes or until golden brown and springy. Remove pan from the oven and set on a cooling rack.

7. To make the soaking syrup, combine the water and sugar in a small pot. Cook over medium heat until the sugar dissolves, about 2 minutes. Remove from the heat and add the kirsch. Set aside (can be refrigerated for 2 weeks).

8. To assemble, you will need 6 wineglasses. They will contain 3 layers each of custard, cake, and cherries. The size of the cake rounds will be determined by the diameter and slope of the sides of your wineglasses. To measure, use a set of round cookie cutters. Set a small cookie cutter into the wineglass for the first layer of cake. Use the size that will fit about ½ inch from the bottom of the glass. For the next size, use the cutter that will fit in the middle of the glass, and for the last round, use the cutter that will fit near the top of the glass. (My glasses are 3 inches in diameter and 3 inches high, excluding the stem. I use 1¾-inch, 2¼-inch, and 2½-inch cutters.)

9. To make the trifles, spoon a rounded teaspoonful of custard into the bottom of the glass. Brush the nonsticky side of the smallest cake round with the soaking syrup. Spread a thin layer of cherry jam on the other side. Set it on top of the custard. Place 4 cherry halves on top of the cake, around the perimeter of the glass. Top the cherries with 2 rounded teaspoons of custard. Repeat the layering, ending with a layer of cake. Each successive layer will need a little more custard and a few more cherries, as the glass will be getting wider as it gets taller. Each glass will use about ⅓ cup custard and about 5 cherries. For the top, spoon a teaspoonful of custard in the center of the last cake layer, and center a stemmed cherry on top of the custard. If making ahead, leave the last teaspoon of custard and the cherry off the trifles. Cover with plastic wrap until ready to serve. When ready to serve, garnish with the custard and cherry.

VARIATION: Berries are also delicious in this dessert.

Cherry Sour Cream Cheesecake

*W*hen Shavuot falls late in the season, or for summer Shabbat
dessert, fresh cherries make an exquisite topping for cheesecake.
Extra sour cream is added to complement their sweetness. Out of
season, canned or frozen cherries can be used. This tangy cheesecake is
the least creamy one that I make, as it contains the least amount of
cream cheese. Of course, you can mix and match any of the cheesecakes
with any of the toppings, so you should be able to satisfy your family's
preferences. If you want to cut down the fat even more (by 2 to 3 grams
per serving), try using a sponge cake or Almondbread Crumb Crust
(see variations at the end of recipe).

MAKES 12 TO 14 SERVINGS

ALSO SERVE ON
Shabbat

DAIRY

continued

Shavuot

235

NUTRITIONAL
NOTES
(per serving; based on 12
pieces–because the
cottage cheese gets
squeezed dry, the actual
numbers may be lower)

261 calories

6g fat (22%)

46mg cholesterol

38g carbohydrates

13g protein

427mg sodium

0g fiber

RDA %

8% vitamin A

7% vitamin C

7% calcium

6% iron

MAKE 1 DAY AHEAD

1 recipe Graham Cracker Crust for 8-inch springform pan, page 295

Sour Cream Filling

32 ounces lowfat cottage cheese, preferably a sweet-tasting brand such as Light and Lively

4 ounces reduced-fat cream cheese, such as Philadelphia ⅓ Less Fat

½ cup reduced-fat sour cream, preferably Breakstone's

1 cup sugar

2 large eggs, at room temperature

1 large egg white, at room temperature

2 teaspoons vanilla extract

Fresh Cherry Topping

¼ teaspoon gelatin (either Kolatin kosher, or for nonkosher use regular)

1 teaspoon kirsch (cherry liqueur), or water

¼ cup currant jelly

½ pound fresh dark cherries, pitted and halved

1. Preheat the oven to 350°F, with a rack in the middle of the oven. Wrap an 8-inch springform pan with heavy-duty foil, so that the foil comes up over the top of the pan (heavy-duty foil is wider so no seam is needed). Crimp the foil at the top of the pan. Boil water in a teakettle, reduce the heat, and keep it warm. Have ready a baking dish, at least 10 × 10 inches.

2. Press the graham cracker crumbs firmly into the bottom of the spring-form pan.

3. To make the filling, place the cottage cheese in a large, double-layer piece of cheesecloth. Fold the cheesecloth into a "bag," twist the top, and squeeze to remove as much liquid from the cheese as possible. Wipe off the moisture on the outside of the bag, and continue squeezing and wip-ing until no more liquid comes out of the bag. Transfer the cheese to the processor bowl and process for 1 minute. Scrape down the bowl, and process for at least 2 more minutes or until completely smooth. Cut the cream cheese into 6 lumps and add to the processor. Pulse-process until the cheeses are well blended. Scrape down the sides of the bowl, add the

sour cream, and process until mixed. Add the sugar and process for 1 minute to fully incorporate. In another bowl, whisk together the eggs, egg white, and vanilla. Add to the processor bowl, and process for a few seconds to blend. Scrape down the bowl sides and process a few more seconds. Pour the batter into the prepared pan. Put the cheesecake in the larger pan and place it in the oven. Pour boiling water into the larger pan so that it comes halfway up the sides of the cheesecake pan. Be careful not to splash water into the cheesecake.

4. Bake for 55 to 65 minutes, until the cheesecake is set but a toothpick inserted into the center of the cake will still come out with a little moist cheese attached. For firmer cheesecake, cook an additional 5 minutes, but cover the pan with foil if cooking more than 60 minutes. Remove the cheesecake from the oven, lift the pan out of the water-bath, and let the cheesecake cool on a wire rack. Cover the cheesecake with foil, and refrigerate overnight.

5. To make the fresh cherry topping, 1 to 2 hours before serving, mix the gelatin and kirsch, and let stand for 5 minutes. Place the jelly in a small, microwavable bowl, add the gelatin mixture, and microwave until the mixture is melted and bubbling. Brush the cheesecake with the jelly mixture. Arrange the cherries in concentric circles to cover the top of the cheesecake. Brush the cherries with more of the currant glaze. Refrigerate until the glaze is set (about 1 hour). If using canned or frozen (defrosted) cherries, drain well and pat dry. Leave the cherries whole, as they are softer than fresh berries. Make the glaze and use, as above.

6. Run a knife around the perimeter of the cheesecake to remove the springform sides. If you don't like the way the sides look (the jelly will probably have run down the sides somewhat), they can be coated with graham cracker crumbs. The cheesecake, without the cherries, can be made 2 days ahead, or frozen for 3 months. Put the cherries on a few hours before serving, as they tend to weep after being cut.

VARIATIONS: Instead of the Graham Cracker Crumb Crust, substitute Almondbread Crumb Crust (page 238), or Sponge Cake Sheet (page 233). For directions on using the sponge cake as a base for cheesecake, see page 209.

Shavuot

237

Marble Cheesecake

ALSO SERVE ON
Shabbat, Chanukah,
Yom ha-atzma'ut

DAIRY

NUTRITIONAL
NOTES
(per serving–because the
cottage cheese gets
squeezed dry, the actual
numbers may be lower)

204 calories

4g fat (18%)

42mg cholesterol

27g carbohydrates

16g protein

69mg sodium

0g fiber

RDA %

4% vitamin A

0% vitamin C

12% calcium

4% iron

MAKE 1 DAY AHEAD

Light Jewish
Holiday Desserts

My original chocolate almond cheesecake had 35 grams of fat and 600 calories per serving—a dessert we didn't eat too often, and now have no need for. My family actually prefers this rich-tasting yet light version, and with only 4 grams of fat per serving we can eat it more often.

MAKES 16 SERVINGS

Almondbread Crumb Crust

12 whole Stella D'oro Almond Toast Cookies

2½ teaspoons egg substitute (such as Egg Beaters), or egg white

Filling

¼ cup chopped semisweet chocolate, or chocolate chips

3 pounds nonfat cottage cheese, preferably a sweet-tasting brand such as Light and Lively

½ pound reduced-fat cream cheese, preferably Philadelphia ⅓ Less Fat, at room temperature

1¾ cups sugar

3 large eggs, at room temperature

1½ teaspoons almond extract

¼ cup Dutch-processed cocoa, preferably Droste

1. Preheat the oven to 350°F, with a rack in the lower third of the oven. Boil water in a teakettle, reduce the heat, and keep warm. Have a baking pan, at least 10 × 10 inches, ready. Wrap the outside of a 9-inch spring-form pan with heavy-duty foil (it's wider than the regular foil, so it will come up and over the sides of the pan with no seams). Crimp the foil around the pan top so that the pan is watertight.

2. To make the crust, process the cookies until finely ground. Measure out 1½ cups of crumbs and place in a small bowl. Stir in 1½ teaspoons of the egg substitute. Use your fingertips to distribute the egg substitute throughout the mixture. If the crumbs will not hold together, add the remaining egg substitute, ½ teaspoon at a time until they will just hold together. Press the crumbs into the bottom of the springform. Transfer the remaining crumbs to a storage container and reserve for the next day. Wipe out the processor bowl.

3. To make the filling, melt the chocolate over hot water, or in the microwave on medium power for 1 to 2 minutes. Set aside to cool.

4. Place the cottage cheese in a large, double-layer piece of cheesecloth. Fold the cheesecloth into a "bag," twist the top, and squeeze to remove as much liquid from the cheese as possible. Wipe off the moisture on the outside of the bag, and continue squeezing and wiping until no more liquid comes out of the bag. Transfer the cheese to the processor bowl and process for 1 minute. Scrape down the bowl and process for at least 2 more minutes or until completely smooth.

5. Add the cream cheese to the processor. Pulse-process until the cheeses are well blended. Add the sugar and process for 1 minute to fully incorporate the sugar. In a small bowl, whisk together the eggs and almond extract. Add to the processor bowl, and process for a few seconds to blend. Scrape down the bowl sides and process a few more seconds.

6. Measure out 1 cup of batter. Add the melted chocolate and the cocoa to the batter in the processor. Pulse-process several times to blend the ingredients. Pour half of the chocolate batter into the prepared springform pan. Drizzle in half of the almond batter and then the remaining chocolate batter. Drizzle in the rest of the almond batter in a haphazard pattern. Using a small knife, draw through the batter to create a marble effect. Put the cheesecake in the larger pan and place it in the oven. Pour boiling water into the larger pan so that it comes halfway up the sides of the cheesecake pan, being careful not to splash water into the cheesecake.

7. Bake for 55 to 65 minutes, until the cheesecake is set, but a toothpick inserted into the center of the cake will still come out with moist cheese

Shavuot

attached. For firmer cheesecake, cook an additional 5 minutes, but cover the pan with foil if the total time is more than 60 minutes. Remove the cheesecake from the oven, remove it from the water-bath, and let it cool on a wire rack. Cover the cake with foil, and chill overnight.

8. Run a knife around the outside edge of the cheesecake, and then remove the springform sides. Press the reserved crumbs on the sides of the cheesecake. To cut nice slices, clean the knife off between cuts with a damp cloth. The cake can be made 2 days ahead or frozen for up to 3 months.

VARIATIONS

Chocolate and Coffee Marble: Delete the almond extract and add 1 teaspoon of finely ground instant coffee to the white batter. One teaspoon of coffee liqueur, such as Kahlúa, can also be added.

Chocolate and Vanilla Marble: Substitute vanilla extract for the almond extract.

Chocolate Orange Marble: Delete the almond extract and substitute 1 tablespoon of orange liqueur, such as Grand Marnier.

Chocolate Rum: Delete the almond extract and substitute 1 teaspoon vanilla and 1 tablespoon rum.

New York-Style Rice Pudding

For years I tried to make rice pudding that tasted like the pudding I grew up with in New York City. I was never successful in achieving the perfect texture until risotto became popular in the '90s. It was then that I realized that arborio rice was the key to making the perfect rice pudding. I no longer enjoy regular New York–style rice pudding, because it is generally made with cream, and too rich for me. Thankfully, however, I can now make a light version that we love.

MAKES 8 TO 10 SERVINGS

1 cup arborio rice

2 cups water

1½-inch piece of vanilla bean

¼ teaspoon salt

5 cups 2% milk

⅔ cup sugar

¾ cup raisins

Nutmeg and cinnamon

1. Place the rice, water, vanilla bean, and salt in a 3-quart pot. Bring to a boil, cover, reduce the heat, and simmer for 20 minutes (be sure to use a large enough pot, as arborio rice is very starchy and bubbles up a lot).

2. Meanwhile, place the milk and sugar in another medium pot, and bring it to a boil over medium-high heat. Cover, reduce the heat to low, and keep warm until the rice is done cooking.

3. Add the milk mixture to the cooked rice. Stir gently to break up any lumps. Place over medium-high heat, and bring it to a simmer. Adjust the heat to keep the mixture at a slow simmer. Cook, uncovered, for about 30 minutes, stirring occasionally. During the last 5 minutes of

ALSO SERVE ON
Chanukah, Shabbat, Yom ha-atzma'ut

DAIRY

NUTRITIONAL NOTES
(per serving; based on 10 servings)

211 calories

2g fat (10%)

9mg cholesterol

43g carbohydrates

6g protein

120mg sodium

0g fiber

RDA %

5% vitamin A

2% vitamin C

15% calcium

1% iron

Shavuot

241

cooking, the mixture will thicken dramatically. Stir in the raisins (if they are not soft and plump to begin with, add them about 5 minutes earlier).

4. Spoon the pudding into a storage container, let it cool briefly, and then cover and refrigerate until completely cool (about 6 hours). If the pudding is too thick, or too gluey, stir in enough milk to loosen it, and to create just a small bit of creamy sauce. Before serving, grate some fresh nutmeg over the pudding, and lightly sprinkle it with cinnamon. It should keep for a week in the refrigerator (ours is always gone by day 2).

Couscous Pudding

*T*his is not everyone's idea of dessert, but it is a traditional Sephardic dish, and it really is delicious. We actually prefer to eat it for breakfast. Those who like rice pudding will probably enjoy it, and it can be ready to eat in under 10 minutes. You can make it less fattening by also using skim milk for the small bit that gets spooned over the pudding. To further symbolize Shavuot, try it topped with diced peaches or berries of the season.

MAKES 4 SERVINGS

1 tablespoon sugar

1⅓ cups skim milk

1-inch piece of vanilla bean, or ½ teaspoon vanilla extract

¼ cup raisins or chopped dates

¾ cup couscous (uncooked)

½ cup 2% milk

Cinnamon

Powdered sugar

1 tablespoon sliced almonds (roasted at 350°F until light brown) or cashews, lightly crushed

ALSO SERVE ON
Chanukah,
Yom ha-atzma'ut

DAIRY

NUTRITIONAL NOTES
(per serving)

231 calories

2g fat (8%)

2mg cholesterol

43g carbohydrates

9g protein

60mg sodium

2g fiber

Light Jewish
Holiday Desserts

1. Combine the sugar, skim milk, vanilla bean, and raisins in a medium pot (if using vanilla extract, add it when you add the couscous). Bring the mixture to a boil. Stir in the couscous. Remove the pot from the heat, and cover it. Let the couscous stand for 5 minutes.

2. While the couscous is resting, heat the 2% milk in the microwave, or in a small saucepan over medium heat.

3. Fluff the couscous with a fork. It should be moister than entrée couscous but not soupy. Divide the pudding among 4 dessert bowls. Sprinkle each with cinnamon, powdered sugar, and almonds. Spoon about 2 tablespoons of warm milk around each mound of couscous, and serve immediately.

VARIATION: This is not traditional, but my kids love to have some mini-chocolate chips sprinkled on top (¼ teaspoon per serving adds 1 gram of fat).

Summer Pudding Miniatures

A dessert for true berry lovers only, summer pudding is a mass of sweetened berries, covered in drenched, juice-soaked bread. Usually, there are two pitfalls in making summer pudding: It can be difficult to cut the bread so that it fits properly in the bottom of the mold (usually a charlotte mold), and the pudding tends to fall apart rapidly once it is cut, making presentation a little less than desired. To solve these problems, I make individual puddings. The bread for the bottoms gets cut into small rounds using the ramekin in which the pudding gets molded. These mini-puddings get unmolded onto dessert plates and served immediately, without any cutting. The result is a dessert that is simple to make, pleasant to look at, and a delight to eat. Be sure to make the pudding one day before serving. *continued*

MAKES 6 SERVINGS

ALSO SERVE ON
Shabbat

DAIRY OR PAREVE

Shavuot

NUTRITIONAL
NOTES
(per serving; reflects only
actual amount of bread
used—values will vary
depending on the type of
bread used)

232 calories

2g fat (7%)

1mg cholesterol

52g carbohydrates

4g protein

181mg sodium

6g fiber

R D A %

1% vitamin A

180% vitamin C

6% calcium

9% iron

MAKE 1 DAY AHEAD

8 cups mixed berries, mostly raspberries and blackberries

⅔ cup sugar

2 tablespoons fresh lemon juice (about ½ lemon)

*15 slices old-fashioned white bread, or challah, crusts removed
(amount needed will vary depending upon the size and
shape of the slices)*

*1 recipe Light Whipped Cream (page 299; optional
for dairy dessert)*

1. I usually use 4 cups raspberries, 2 cups blackberries, and 2 cups strawberries (strawberries are not traditional), but any combination will work. Wash the berries well and place them in a large pot along with the sugar and lemon juice. Cook over medium heat until the berries are warmed through and juicy. Do not boil. Remove from the heat and let cool.

2. Use the bottom of a 1-cup ramekin as a guide to cut out 12 rounds of bread.

3. Line six 1-cup ramekins with plastic wrap, leaving a 2-inch overhang. Set a round of bread in each ramekin.

4. Cut the remaining bread into rectangles 1 inch wide and as high as the ramekin sides. Arrange the bread rectangles around the sides of the ramekins, overlapping them slightly. Press against the bread so that it won't fall away from the sides.

5. Divide the berries and juice among the ramekins, filling them right up to the top. Place a bread round on the top of each ramekin. Fold the plastic wrap over the top to enclose the pudding. Place the ramekins on a tray with sides (just in case the juice spills out). On top of each ramekin, place a plate, bowl, or lid that is just slightly smaller than the ramekin diameter. On top of this place a 1- or 2-pound can or weight (I use a spaghetti jar). Set the tray in the refrigerator overnight.

6. The next day, take the pudding from the refrigerator. Remove the weights and lift up the plastic wrap. Set a dessert plate on top of each ramekin, and invert. Remove ramekins and plastic wrap.

7. Serve immediately. For a dairy dessert, garnish with Light Whipped Cream Topping.

Apricot Blueberry Ginger Crisp

Gingersnaps can have a very assertive or a more muted flavor, depending on the brand used. I particularly like them with tart and strong-tasting fruits, such as apricots or rhubarb. Apricots are sometimes extremely tart. Therefore, you should cut them into small cubes, so that a mouthful of fruit will have a good balance of tart and sweet. If a more tender crumb is desired, substitute cake flour for half of the all-purpose flour.

MAKES 8 SERVINGS

Gingersnap Crumbs

24 whole lowfat gingersnaps

½ cup plus 1 tablespoon (70 grams) all-purpose flour,
lightly sprinkled into measuring cup

¼ cup firmly packed light brown sugar

2 tablespoons unsalted butter, melted

1 tablespoon canola oil

1 tablespoon egg substitute (such as Egg Beaters), or egg white

Filling

1 pint blueberries (2 cups)

16 firm, but ripe, apricots, washed, stoned, and
cut into ¼-inch chunks

1 medium lemon, juiced

¾ cup firmly packed light brown sugar

1 teaspoon cinnamon

3 tablespoons cornstarch

continued

ALSO SERVE ON
Shabbat

DAIRY OR PAREVE (SEE VARIATIONS)

NUTRITIONAL NOTES
(per serving)

289 calories

6g fat (18.5%)

8mg cholesterol

58g carbohydrates

2g protein

154mg sodium

3g fiber

RDA %

37% vitamin A

21% vitamin C

5% calcium

11% iron

Shavuot

1. Preheat the oven to 350°F, with a rack in the middle of the oven. Have ready a baking sheet and an 8 x 10-inch Pyrex pan.

2. Place the gingersnaps in a food processor, and pulse until fine crumbs form. Measure out ¾ cup crumbs, and place in a medium bowl. Stir in the flour and brown sugar. Add the butter and oil to the flour, and mix with a fork until moistened. Add the egg substitute and continue to mix and press with the fork, until the mixture forms raisin-size crumbs. Break up any larger crumbs. Dump the crumbs onto the baking sheet and spread into an even layer, 1 crumb thick. Bake for 8 minutes. Turn the crumbs over with a pancake turner or spatula, and continue to bake for 2 to 4 minutes, until the crumbs are nicely browned. Remove from the oven and cool on a rack. Do not turn off the oven if you plan to continue with the recipe now. (The crumbs can be made 1 week ahead and stored in an airtight container at room temperature, or frozen for up to 3 months. If the crumbs soften, recrisp in the oven for 5 minutes at 350°F.)

3. To make the filling, place the blueberries, apricots, lemon juice, brown sugar, cinnamon, and cornstarch in the Pyrex pan. Cover with foil and let stand for 15 minutes.

4. Bake for 40 to 60 minutes or until the fruit is tender. Place on a cooling rack, remove the foil, and let cool to warm.

5. Sprinkle with the crumbs and serve (for softer crumbs, sprinkle them on 5 to 10 minutes before serving). For more elegant service, spoon the warmed fruit into individual ramekins, sprinkle on the crumbs, and serve. If the fruit has been made ahead, rewarm at 350°F and then top with the crumbs.

VARIATIONS

Apple-Mango: Replace the apricots with 2 large mangoes (peel, cut fruit off stone in ¼-inch chunks) and add ¼ teaspoon allspice.

Pareve: Pareve gingersnaps are difficult to find, but you can use graham crackers and add ¼ teaspoon each of ground ginger and ground cloves. Use unsalted pareve margarine instead of butter.

Papaya (or Peach) Blueberry Pandowdy

Pandowdy is a New England dessert in which the top crust of the pastry is half-baked on top of the fruit, pushed down into the fruit juices, and then baked until it pops back up to the top and recrisps. It's an unusual-looking dessert in that it appears that maybe you've had an accident with the crust. The results will be worth the comments, as the crust is really delicious after it has soaked up the juices. Although apple pandowdy is traditional, I think it's best with fruits that are very juicy, such as berries and peaches.

MAKES 9 SERVINGS

1 recipe either Tart Pastry Dough (page 290) or Nut Pastry Crust (page 292) for 8 × 10-inch rectangle

Filling

3 whole papayas

1 whole lemon, juiced

1 pint blueberries, washed

1¼ cups sugar

½ teaspoon nutmeg

1 tablespoon cornstarch

1. Prepare the pastry. Have ready an 8 × 10-inch Pyrex pan.

2. Peel, seed, and cut the papayas into 1-inch squares. Toss with the lemon juice. Mix the blueberries, sugar, nutmeg, and cornstarch. Spoon into the Pyrex dish.

continued

ALSO SERVE ON
Shabbat

DAIRY OR PAREVE

NUTRITIONAL NOTES
(per serving)

268 calories

6g fat (18%)

14mg cholesterol

55g carbohydrates

2g protein

100mg sodium

2g fiber

RDA %

8% vitamin A

92% vitamin C

3% calcium

5% iron

Shavuot

3. Cut open one short end and one long end of a jumbo zip-top bag. Flour the inside of the bag. Place the dough inside, and roll it to slightly smaller than 8 × 10 inches (scant ⅛ inch thick). Flip the dough over several times during the rolling process, lifting the plastic and generously sprinkling the dough with flour. Set the dough rectangle on top of the fruit. Refrigerate for 15 minutes.

4. Preheat the oven to 375°F, with a rack in the middle of the oven. Bake for 25 minutes.

5. Cut the pastry into 9 squares and press them down into the pan juices. Bake for another 20 to 25 minutes, or until the crust resurfaces, and is crisp. Cool for 30 to 45 minutes before eating. Can be made a couple of hours ahead of time (before serving, reheat in a 350°F oven to warm the fruit and crisp the topping).

VARIATIONS: Instead of papaya, use mangoes (3; firm but ripe), or peaches (10; firm but ripe).

Peach Raspberry Potpies

ALSO SERVE ON
Shabbat

DAIRY

*T*hese *scrumptious individual potpies showcase fresh summer fruits. The raspberries disintegrate to form a delicious sauce for the peaches. Garnish with lowfat frozen yogurt or Light Whipped Cream (page 299) to round out this Shavuot dessert.*

MAKES 8 SERVINGS

12 medium peaches, ripe but firm

2 medium lemons

1 pint raspberries

¾ to 1¼ cups sugar

3 tablespoons cornstarch

1 recipe Nut Pastry Crust, for eight 4-inch rounds (page 292)

1. Preheat the oven to 375°F, with a rack in the middle of the oven.

2. Peel the peaches (with a knife or by plunging them into boiling water for 1 to 2 minutes), remove the pits, and cut into ¼-inch chunks. Place 8 cups of the peaches into a large bowl (discard or save any remaining). Squeeze the lemons over the peaches as you cut them, so that they do not turn brown. Add the raspberries. Use your judgment to decide how much sugar to use—less if the fruit is fairly sweet or you like your desserts on the tart side, and more if the fruit is tart or you like sweeter desserts. Stir in the cornstarch and let the mixture macerate for 15 minutes. Spoon the fruit into eight 1-cup ramekins (with a 3-inch diameter).

3. In a floured jumbo zip-top bag, roll the dough into a round about 12 inches in diameter and about ¹⁄₁₆ inch thick. Cut open the bag and cut the dough into eight 4-inch rounds (I use a Tupperware container as a cutter). Use a small cookie cutter or the back of a decorating tip to cut out a ½-inch circle in the center of each round.

4. Cover each filled ramekin with a pastry round, pressing the edges firmly to the ramekin.

5. Bake for 30 to 40 minutes until the pastry is cooked through and brown. Remove and set on a rack to cool for at least 1 hour. Can be made 8 hours ahead. Store at room temperature. To serve, reheat at 350°F for 15 minutes. The fruit should be just warm. If desired, dollop a heaping teaspoon of Light Whipped Cream or a small scoop of lowfat yogurt onto the crust.

NUTRITIONAL NOTES
(per serving)

321 calories

8.5g fat (23%)

9mg cholesterol

62g carbohydrates

3g protein

96mg sodium

4g fiber

RDA %

14% vitamin A

57% vitamin C

3% calcium

7% iron

Shavuot

Strawberry Blueberry Sour Cream Tart

DAIRY

NUTRITIONAL
NOTES
(per serving)

206 calories

8g fat (36%)

21mg cholesterol

31g carbohydrates

3g protein

148mg sodium

2g fiber

RDA %

7% vitamin A

58% vitamin C

1% calcium

5% iron

This red, white, and blue tart is also perfect for the Fourth of July! The slight tartness of the filling complements the sweet crust, and the berries provide flavor, texture, and great eye appeal.

MAKES 8 SERVINGS

One 9-inch tart shell, page 290

Strawberry Filling

1 pound fresh strawberries

2 tablespoons sugar

2 teaspoons cornstarch

1 teaspoon fresh lemon juice

1 teaspoon water

Whipped Sour Cream Topping

1 large egg white

2 tablespoons sugar

1 teaspoon water

2 to 3 tablespoons reduced-fat sour cream, preferably Breakstone's

¼ teaspoon vanilla extract

1 pint blueberries (2 cups)

1. Make and bake the tart shell.

2. To make the filling, wash and hull 6 ounces of strawberries (about 1½ cups). Quarter them and place in a food processor with the sugar, cornstarch, lemon juice, and water. Pulse-process until well pureed, scraping the bowl down as necessary. Transfer to a small pot and cook over high

heat until the mixture comes to a boil. Boil for 1 minute. Remove and refrigerate until cold.

3. For the sour cream topping, fill a large skillet with 1 inch of water. Bring the water to a simmer. In a small metal bowl, whisk the egg white with the sugar and water. Have a rubber scraper, instant-read thermometer, a timer, another mixing bowl, and a beater near the stove. Place the bowl with the egg white mixture into the simmering water, and rapidly stir the mixture with the rubber scraper for 20 seconds. Remove the bowl from the simmering water and check the temperature. The temperature needs to be at 160°F to kill salmonella, but not much higher, or the eggs will overcook. The time that it takes depends upon the type of bowl and pot that are being used—I've had it take from 20 to 80 seconds using different types of pots and bowls. If the eggs are not yet hot enough, heat them for 10 seconds more. Remove the bowl from the water, dip the thermometer into the boiling water and then retest. Repeat the process if necessary. As soon as the eggs reach 160°F, transfer them to a cool bowl, and beat at medium-high speed until the mixture looks like shaving cream and stands in stiff peaks when the beater is raised from it.

4. In a large bowl, mix together the sour cream and vanilla extract. Fold in the egg white mixture.

5. Up to 3 hours before serving, vertically slice the remaining strawberries into ⅛-inch slices. Wash the blueberries. Spoon the cooked strawberry filling into the tart and spread evenly. There will just be enough to cover the bottom of the tart. Spoon ½ cup of the sour cream topping into the tart and lightly spread it so that it does not mix with the strawberry filling. For the decorations make concentric rings of alternating berries beginning with a row of strawberry slices standing upright along the perimeter of the tart. Make 2 rows of blueberries with a third row on top of the first 2, then another row of strawberries standing upright, and another ring of blueberries. Overlap strawberries to make a bud in the center of the tart.

Shavuot

Blueberry Lemon Phyllo Tiles or Napoleons

DAIRY

NUTRITIONAL NOTES
(per serving)

226 calories
....
4g fat (17%)
....
43mg cholesterol
....
44g carbohydrates
....
4g protein
....
124mg sodium
....
2g fiber

RDA %

4% vitamin A
....
29% vitamin C
....
7% calcium
....
5% iron

These wonderful pastries were originally created as napoleons. However, I hate desserts that look great but fall apart when they are cut into. Made as tiles, with the pastry only on the bottom, these are not only great to look at but neat to eat as well. For those less fussy about crumbling desserts, a napoleon variation is included. The lightly flavored lemon filling gets its color from orange juice concentrate rather than from egg yolks, a trick I learned from Have Your Cake and Eat It, Too by Susan G. Purdy.

MAKES 11 SERVINGS

Double recipe of Lemon Filling, page 300
2 tablespoons reduced-fat sour cream, preferably Breakstone's

Phyllo Tiles
6 sheets defrosted phyllo dough (see directions next page)
1 tablespoon unsalted butter
2 teaspoons canola oil
⅓ cup powdered sugar
¾ cup lowfat graham cracker crumbs
(about 6 whole crackers, crushed)

Topping
1 pint blueberries (2 cups)
Powdered sugar (optional)

1. Make the Lemon Filling, cool slightly, and then stir in the sour cream. Refrigerate until cold, about 6 hours. Can be made 3 days in advance.

2. Before the phyllo dough can be handled, it must be placed in the refrigerator overnight and left (in the unopened box) at room temperature for 2 hours.

3. Preheat the oven to 375°F, with racks in the upper and lower thirds of the oven. Line 2 cookie sheets with parchment paper or nonstick Teflon liners, or use 2 nonstick pans.

4. While the dough is defrosting, gather all of the supplies needed—pastry brush, spatula, waxed paper, cutting board, large knife, and dish towel.

5. Melt the butter and oil together (I do this in the microwave in a covered container on high for 1 or 2 minutes).

6. When ready to make the pastries, open the package of phyllo and take it out of the plastic sleeve. Remove 6 sheets, place on waxed paper, and cover with more waxed paper. Roll up the remaining phyllo, place in a jumbo zip-top bag, and refreeze for use another time. When working with the phyllo, always keep the unused sheets covered with waxed paper. If you do not do this, the pastry will crumble like dried leaves.

7. Pick up 1 sheet of phyllo and slide it onto a surface on which you can cut. Brush a light, even coat of the butter mixture over the pastry, making sure to brush the edges of the dough. Using a strainer or sprinkler, dust the pastry with powdered sugar, using about 2 teaspoons per sheet. Sprinkle with about 2 tablespoons of graham cracker crumbs. Slide another sheet of phyllo on top of the crumbs. Brush with butter and sprinkle with powdered sugar and graham crumbs, as above. Repeat until all 6 of the pastry sheets have been used. The last sheet of phyllo should be buttered and sugared only (do not sprinkle with crumbs).

8. Using a long, nonserrated knife, cut the pastry into eleven 4-inch squares. Transfer the pastries to the prepared cookie sheets, and bake for 4 minutes. Switch the top baking sheet to the lower rack and the bottom to the top. Continue to bake for 4 to 6 minutes, or until the pastries are golden brown. The pastries can be made up to 3 days in advance, and stored in an airtight container, or frozen for up to 3 months. Those stored at room temperature can be recrisped by heating at 300°F for 5 minutes. Frozen pastries can be used directly from the freezer. *continued*

Shavuot

9. To assemble the pastries, wash the blueberries and pat dry. Place a pastry on each plate. Pipe or spoon the filling onto the pastries and then place the berries decoratively on the filling. Garnish with powdered sugar and more berries, if desired. If not serving immediately, refrigerate for up to 3 hours (you can do the pastries on a cookie sheet and transfer them to the plates before serving).

VARIATIONS

Pareve: Use unsalted pareve margarine instead of butter, and substitute soymilk for the milk. Add a pinch of saffron for color, and omit the sour cream.

Vanilla: Substitute Vanilla Pastry Cream, page 301, for the Lemon Filling.

Other fruits: Use raspberries, poached or baked pears or apples, etc., in place of the blueberries.

Napoleons: Cut the pastry into 18 rectangles, each 3½ × 2¼ inches. Use 3 rectangles per napoleon, stacking them with berries and filling between each layer, except the top. Sprinkle the top pastry with powdered sugar.

Peach Melba Varenikes

Considered an unusual dessert nowadays, dessert kreplach (dumplings) have been served by Jews since the twelfth century. These small, 2½-inch round varenikes are more traditional than the large ones made from wonton wrappers for Pear Varenikes in Chocolate Sauce (page 47). The wonton wrappers can be used as a quicker alternative for this recipe, too. The dough can be made without canola

ALSO SERVE ON
*Chanukah, Shabbat,
Yom ha-atzma'ut*

DAIRY

Light Jewish
Holiday Desserts

254

oil (reducing the fat by about 1 gram per serving), but adding the oil makes the dough very supple so there is less chance of the varenikes opening up when they are boiled. These are fun to make, and it's always amusing to see people's reaction to pasta for dessert.

MAKES 8 SERVINGS

Raspberry Sauce

One 12-ounce bag frozen raspberries, defrosted

¼ to ⅓ cup sugar

1½ teaspoons fresh lemon juice

Kreplach **Dough**

2 cups (240 grams) all-purpose flour, lightly sprinkled into a measuring cup

2 large eggs, at room temperature

2 tablespoons orange juice, or water

2 teaspoons canola oil

Filling

4 ounces lowfat cream cheese, preferably Philadelphia ⅓ Less Fat

¼ cup powdered sugar

1 teaspoon cinnamon

2 medium peaches, very ripe, or one 15-ounce can peach halves in light syrup

1 medium lemon, juiced

1. To make the sauce, press the raspberries through a food mill set over a medium bowl. Some of the seeds will get through the mill, which you can leave if not objectionable, or strain out through a fine-mesh strainer. Process the sugar in a food processor or spice grinder, until it is finely pulverized. Stir the sugar to taste and the lemon juice into the sauce. Refrigerate until cold. This makes 1 cup, and can be made up to 1 week ahead, or frozen for up to 3 months.

continued

NUTRITIONAL
NOTES
(per serving)

191 calories

4g fat (19%)

40mg cholesterol

42g carbohydrates

5g protein

36mg sodium

1g fiber

RDA %

5% vitamin A

28% vitamin C

3% calcium

10% iron

Shavuot

2. To make the dough, place the flour in a food processor bowl. Whisk together the eggs, orange juice, and oil. With the processor running, add the egg mixture through the feed tube, and continue to process until the dough forms a ball. Transfer the dough to a work surface. Knead the dough briefly into a smooth ball. Cover with plastic wrap, and let the dough rest at room temperature for 15 to 30 minutes.

3. Divide the dough into quarters. Liberally dust 1 ball with flour. Run it through a pasta machine, dusting with flour to keep it from sticking. Run through all settings, up to #4. Alternatively, you can roll the dough out until it is about 1/32 inch thick. Dust the dough with flour, cover with waxed paper, and roll the remaining dough out, piece by piece. Boil about 8 cups of water in a pasta pot. Cover and keep warm while you prepare the *varenikes*.

4. Make the filling by mixing together the cream cheese, powdered sugar, and cinnamon.

5. Peel the peaches with a knife or dip in boiling water for 1 to 2 minutes. Halve the peaches, and remove the stones. (If canned, drain well.) Dice 1 peach into 1/4-inch pieces. Cut the other peach into 1/4-inch slices. Mix the peaches with the lemon juice.

6. Place the dough onto a cutting board. Cut out twenty-six 2 1/4-inch rounds, and twenty-six 2 3/4-inch rounds.

7. Place a rounded teaspoonful of filling into the center of each smaller round. Push 3 pieces of diced peach into each bit of filling. Brush the edges of the rounds with water. Place the large rounds on top of the filling. Press and pinch the edges to seal the *varenikes*. Cover them with plastic wrap.

8. Bring the water in the pasta pot back to a full rolling boil. Drop in 1 *varenike* and boil until tender, about 7 minutes. Because you may be rolling the dough thinner or thicker than I do, you will use this one as a test to get the perfect cooking time (you have made 2 extra *varenikes* to be used for testing). Boil the remainder of the *varenikes* until tender. Drain well.

9. To serve, decoratively drizzle about 1 tablespoon of raspberry sauce onto each of 8 dinner plates. Set 3 hot *varenikes* in the middle of each plate, and garnish with peach slices.

The Jewish Sabbath, Shabbat, begins at sundown on Friday evenings and concludes with the Havdalah service on Saturday evening. Described in Exodus as the day when the Lord rested after creating the heaven, the earth, and the sea, Shabbat is a time to set aside the harried confusion of the workweek and to pay attention to our families and our spiritual needs. It is a time to rest, pray, and rejoice. Because it is a mitzvah, or good deed, to delight in Shabbat, fine foods have always been an important part of the celebration.

Throughout the ages, Jews have saved their

Shabbat

best meats, wines, and desserts for the Shabbat table. Any traditional Jewish dessert would be appropriate to serve on Shabbat, so you can choose any dessert in this book. Desserts with apples, honey, almonds, dates, and figs—the foods grown in Israel or mentioned in the Torah—would be fitting. Braided cookies and cakes that represent the tribes of Israel and circular cakes that represent the "Shabbat Queen" are also good choices. Desserts using poppy or sesame seeds represent manna, a symbol of God's covenant with the Jewish people. Sweets that one considers special or that give particular joy are also perfect for Shabbat. If you love chocolate, serve it on Shabbat! For Havdalah, desserts using sweet spices are said to help us overcome our disappointment that Shabbat is ending. Orthodox and Conservative Jews might want to make desserts for Shabbat ahead of time, so that the oven and stove do not need to be used during Shabbat. Reform Jews might also want to bake ahead in symbolic deference to the prohibition against work. Grace your Shabbat table with the following desserts:

Foods that give you particular pleasure, such as chocolate

Traditional Jewish desserts, such as rugelach, babka,

sponge cakes, and phyllo treats

Israeli foods like dates, figs, almonds, and honey

Poppy and sesame seeds

Braided cookies and cakes

Circular cookies and cakes

Sweet spices for Havdalah

Low-Cholesterol Sponge Cake

All Jewish cookbooks need to have a sponge cake recipe—bubbie's plain cake to be dunked in milk or coffee, or drowned in sauce. Traditional sponge cake contains lots of egg yolks and no additional leavening. When egg yolks are removed, however, the texture is better when a small bit of baking powder is included. We like Low-Cholesterol Sponge Cake even better than one made with many yolks because it is lighter and fluffier. It still does a great job of mopping up whatever yummy liquid you might put it in. This sponge cake is lightly scented with orange juice, so that it complements what you serve it with, rather than being assertive itself.

MAKES 20 SERVINGS

4 large eggs, at room temperature

1¼ cups sugar

¼ cup frozen orange juice concentrate, defrosted and
    at room temperature

1 cup (120 grams) all-purpose flour, lightly sprinkled into measuring
    cup

½ cup plus 1 tablespoon (60 grams) sifted cake flour,
    lightly sprinkled into measuring cup

¼ teaspoon salt

¼ teaspoon baking powder

4 large egg whites, at room temperature

1. Preheat the oven to 350°F, with a rack in the lower third of the oven. Have ready an ungreased angel food pan, or an unfluted tube pan.

2. Place the eggs in a large mixer bowl, and beat them until blended. With the mixer going, gradually beat in 1 cup of the sugar. Increase the

ALSO SERVE ON
*Sukkot, Tu b'Shevat,
Yom ha-atzma'ut*

PAREVE

NUTRITIONAL
NOTES
(per serving)

103 calories

1g fat (8%)

36mg cholesterol

21g carbohydrates

3g protein

53mg sodium

0g fiber

RDA %

1% vitamin A

8% vitamin C

1% calcium

4% iron

speed to high, and beat the eggs until very thick and off-white colored, 5 to 7 minutes. Beat in the orange juice.

3. In a bowl, mix together both flours, salt, and baking powder. In 3 additions, sift the flour mixture over the eggs, and fold it in.

4. Place the egg whites in a clean, dry, and grease, free bowl. Using clean, dry, and grease-free beaters, beat the egg whites until foamy throughout, and beater marks can just be seen on the surface. Continue to beat, gradually adding the remaining ¼ cup sugar. Increase the speed to high, and beat the egg whites until stiff but not dry. Fold the egg whites into the batter in 3 additions. Pour the batter into the pan. Bake for 45 to 55 minutes until a toothpick inserted into the center of the cake comes out with no moist crumbs attached.

5. Remove the pan from the oven, invert it, and cool upside down. (An angel food pan has feet to suspend the cake above the counter. If using a tube pan, invert it onto a bottle neck.) When cool, reinvert and cut around the sides, under the bottom, and around the inner tube of the cake. Turn upside down, and remove the cake from the pan. Wrap it in foil, and store at room temperature for up to 5 days, or freeze (defrost cake in foil at room temperature overnight).

VARIATIONS

1. If you want a more dense version which has even fewer calories, and less fat and cholesterol, substitute 2 whole eggs and 2 egg whites (mixed together) for the 4 whole eggs.

2. If you'd like a fluffier version, use 5 egg whites beaten stiffly, instead of 4.

3. For a more robust orange flavor, add 2 teaspoons of orange zest after adding the orange juice in step 2. You can also make a lemon-scented cake by using lemon juice and zest.

SERVING SUGGESTIONS: Lowfat ice cream, frozen yogurt, or Light Whipped Cream, page 299, and one of these sauces:

Chocolate Sauce, page 48; Raspberry Sauce, page 255; Fresh Strawberry Sauce, page 261; Baked Nutmeg Pears, page 222; Winter Fruit Compote, page 135; Bananas Foster, page 122; Blueberry Topping, page 210 (omit the thickener); Fresh berries

Strawberry Shortcake

Whether made the old-fashioned way with shortcakes or the typical Jewish way with sponge cake, strawberry shortcake has always been one of my favorite desserts. I confess that when I'm alone and no one is watching, I even eat it with nondairy whipped topping, a product that I never serve to company, and usually do not care for. Somehow, with berries and cake, even that tastes wonderful. Try strawberry shortcake with the Light Whipped Cream, and you'll think you are back in a time when no one counted calories or watched fat grams. A word of caution: Shortcakes are high in sodium. If this is important to you, use the sponge cake.

MAKES 8 SERVINGS

4 Shortcakes, page 231 (can be made 4 hours ahead) or
    8 three-quarter inch slices of Low-Cholesterol Sponge Cake,
    page 259 (can be made 2 days ahead)

2 pounds fresh strawberries

6 tablespoons sugar

1 tablespoon fresh lemon juice

1 tablespoon water (optional)

1 recipe Light Whipped Cream, page 299

1. After you've prepared the shortcakes or sponge cake, prepare the strawberries. If the berries are ripe and soft, wash, hull, and quarter half of them. Place them in a medium pot, and mash with a potato masher. Add the sugar and lemon juice. Let the mixture sit for 15 minutes. Cook over medium-high heat until simmering, stirring often. Remove from the heat, and let cool briefly. Refrigerate in a covered container (can be made 1 day ahead). About 20 minutes before serving, wash and slice the

ALSO SERVE ON
Shavuot

DAIRY

NUTRITIONAL NOTES
(per serving with shortcakes and 2 tablespoons of the whipped cream)

290 calories

7g fat (21%)

16mg cholesterol

54g carbohydrates

5g protein

370mg sodium

3g fiber

RDA %

3% vitamin A

100% vitamin C

11% calcium

11% iron

remaining berries. Stir them into the cold strawberry sauce, and let macerate for up to 1 hour. If the sauce is not juicy enough for your taste, stir in the optional water.

2. If the berries are very firm, proceed as above, but stir the sliced berries into the hot mixture. Cool briefly, and refrigerate until ready to serve.

3. If possible, make the whipped topping within 2 hours of serving. If made ahead (up to 1 day), some liquid will seep out. Scoop out the topping and discard the liquid. You will lose some volume if topping is made ahead (but you have ample in this recipe to allow for loss).

4. To serve, wrap the biscuits in foil and rewarm in a 350°F oven for 5 minutes. Cut the biscuits in half horizontally. Set a shortcake half on each plate. Divide the filling among the plates, letting the juice run down the sides of the shortcake. Spoon on a tablespoon of the topping. Serve immediately.

If using the sponge cake, place a wedge on each plate, top with strawberries and sauce, and spoon a tablespoon of the topping on each.

Apple Bundt Cake

This is one of those great all-around cakes that you can serve whenever dairy is acceptable. It has between half and two-thirds less fat than a typical Jewish apple cake, and yet is remarkably moist and tender.

MAKES 20 TO 24 SERVINGS

¼ cup (½ stick) unsalted butter, at room temperature

1 cup packed light brown sugar

2 large eggs, at room temperature

1 large egg white, at room temperature

1⅓ cups (160 grams) all-purpose flour, lightly sprinkled into measuring cup

1⅓ cups (140 grams) sifted cake flour, lightly sprinkled into measuring cup

½ teaspoon baking soda

½ teaspoon baking powder

¼ teaspoon salt

½ cup reduced-fat sour cream, preferably Breakstone's, at room temperature

¼ cup applesauce

1 teaspoon vanilla extract

1 cup nonfat or lowfat buttermilk, at room temperature

1 medium lemon, squeezed into 4 cups cold water

2 medium apples, any firm variety, preferably Fuji or Golden Delicious

½ cup walnuts, coarsely chopped

2 tablespoons granulated sugar

2 teaspoons cinnamon

1 whole lowfat graham cracker, crushed

Powdered sugar

continued

ALSO SERVE ON
*Rosh Hashanah,
Sukkot,
Yom ha-atzma'ut*

DAIRY

**NUTRITIONAL
NOTES**
(per serving; based on 20)

153 calories

5g fat (30%)

28mg cholesterol

24g carbohydrates

3g protein

123mg sodium

1g fiber

RDA %

3% vitamin A

2% vitamin C

4% calcium

8% iron

Shabbat

1. Preheat the oven to 325°F, with a rack in the middle of the oven. Spray-grease and flour a 12-cup fluted tube pan (Bundt pan).

2. In a large mixer bowl, beat the butter on medium speed, until creamy. Add the brown sugar and beat on medium for 2 minutes, or until they blend together and form a single mass.

3. In a small bowl, whisk together the eggs and egg white. On medium speed, beat the eggs into the butter mixture, a little at a time. Continue beating until the mixture is smooth and thickened, 3 to 5 minutes.

4. In another bowl, sift together both flours, baking soda, baking powder, and salt.

5. In another bowl, mix together the sour cream, applesauce, and vanilla. Whisk in the buttermilk.

6. In 3 additions, alternately stir the flour and buttermilk mixtures into the batter, starting and ending with the flour.

7. Peel, halve, core, and dice the apples into ½-inch pieces. Drop into the lemon-water, and then drain well. In another bowl, mix the apples with the walnuts, granulated sugar, cinnamon, and crushed graham cracker.

8. Spoon half of the batter into the pan. Smooth the top with a rubber scraper. Spoon half of the apple mixture on top of the batter. Press it lightly down into the batter. Add the remaining apples. Spoon on the remainder of the batter. Smooth it with a rubber scraper. Rap the pan on the counter to remove any large bubbles. Bake for 60 to 70 minutes, or until a tester inserted into the center of the cake comes out with no moist crumbs attached. Remove from the oven and set the pan on a cooling rack. Cool completely before inverting.

The cake can be wrapped in foil and stored at room temperature for 4 days, or frozen for up to 3 months (defrost in foil at room temperature). Sprinkle with powdered sugar before serving.

Marble Pound Cake

This moist, not too dense, pound cake is a nice ending for a dairy meal. We also like it for breakfast or for a late-night snack. Kids love it with a scoop of nonfat ice cream and a drizzle of nonfat chocolate syrup. If you're looking for a dessert that really freezes well, this is a dream come true, as it actually gets moister after being frozen. Since it contains three-quarters less fat than a traditional sour cream pound cake, you'll enjoy this dessert throughout the year.

MAKES 20 TO 40 SERVINGS

2½ cups (260 grams) sifted cake flour, lightly sprinkled into a measuring cup

1 teaspoon baking powder

½ teaspoon baking soda

½ teaspoon salt

¼ cup Dutch-processed cocoa powder, preferably Droste

¼ cup granulated sugar

¼ cup boiling water

¼ cup (½ stick) unsalted butter, at room temperature

2 ounces lowfat cream cheese (such as Philadelphia ⅓ Less Fat), at room temperature

1½ cups firmly packed light brown sugar

1 large egg, at room temperature

1 large egg white, at room temperature

1 cup lowfat plain yogurt (without added gums or gelatin, such as Dannon), at room temperature

1 tablespoon vanilla extract

¼ cup pear baby food (less than 3 ounces)

continued

SERVE ON
Shabbat, Chanukah, Shavuot

DAIRY

NUTRITIONAL
NOTES
(per serving; based on 20)

145 calories

3.5g fat (21%)

18mg cholesterol

26g carbohydrates

3g protein

131mg sodium

1g fiber

RDA %

3% vitamin A

0% vitamin C

6% calcium

7% iron

Shabbat

1. Preheat the oven to 350°F, with a rack in the middle of the oven. Spray-grease and flour a 12-cup Bundt pan.

2. In a bowl, sift together the flour, baking powder, baking soda, and salt. Set aside.

3. Place the cocoa powder and granulated sugar in a medium mixing bowl. Whisk in the boiling water a little at a time until the mixture is smooth. Cover with plastic wrap and set aside.

4. Place the butter and cream cheese in a large mixer bowl. Beat on medium speed until creamy. Beat in the brown sugar a little at a time and continue to beat for 2 minutes.

5. In another bowl, whisk together the egg and egg white. On medium speed, beat the eggs into the butter mixture, a little at a time. Beat on medium-high until the mixture is smooth, thick, and fluffy, about 5 minutes.

6. In another bowl, mix together the yogurt, vanilla, and baby food. On low, in 3 additions, alternately beat or stir in the flour and yogurt mixtures, mixing only until no flour is visible.

7. Stir 1¼ cups of batter into the cocoa mixture.

8. Spread ⅓ of the vanilla batter in the prepared pan. Drop 5 large spoonfuls of chocolate batter evenly spaced over the vanilla layer. Using a blunt knife or a rubber scraper, draw through the batter in an "s" pattern to marbleize it, making sure to go all the way to the bottom of the pan. Add another thin layer of vanilla batter, drop on 5 tablespoons of chocolate batter, cover with the remaining vanilla mixture, and any chocolate batter that is left. Repeat the marbleizing procedure.

9. Rap the pan on the counter to remove any large bubbles. Bake for 40 to 50 minutes or until a tester inserted into the center of the cake comes out with just a few moist crumbs attached. Remove from the oven and set the pan on a cooling rack to cool completely. Invert the pan and remove the cake. It will keep for about 4 days at room temperature, or can be frozen for up to 3 months (defrost the cake in the foil at room temperature). The cake can be sprinkled with powdered sugar, glazed, or served with nonfat yogurt or ice cream.

Almond Bundt Cake

This moist pound cake is terrific with coffee, for breakfast, or for a late-night snack. It travels well, and is best when made 1 day ahead or frozen.

ALSO SERVE ON
Yom ha-atzma'ut,
Chanukah, Shavuot,
Shabbat

DAIRY

NUTRITIONAL
NOTES
(per serving; based on 20)

174 calories

4g fat (19%)

17mg cholesterol

32g carbohydrates

3g protein

169mg sodium

0g fiber

RDA %

2% vitamin A

0% vitamin C

2% calcium

6% iron

MAKES 20 TO 24 SERVINGS

2⅔ cups (280 grams) sifted cake flour, lightly sprinkled into measuring cup

1 teaspoon baking soda

½ teaspoon salt

¼ cup (½ stick) unsalted butter, at room temperature

2 ounces lowfat cream cheese, preferably Philadelphia ⅓ Less Fat, at room temperature

1 cup sugar

1 large egg, at room temperature

2 large egg whites, at room temperature

1 cup buttermilk, at room temperature

½ teaspoon pure almond extract

2 tablespoons Amaretto liqueur, or water

¼ cup pear baby food, at room temperature (less than 3 ounces)

Almond Sugar Glaze

1 teaspoon pure almond extract, divided

5 tablespoons water

1⅔ cups powdered sugar, sifted, divided

1 tablespoon sliced almonds, toasted at 350°F until aromatic (about 5 minutes)

continued

Shabbat

1. Preheat the oven to 325°F, with a rack in the middle of the oven. Spray-grease and flour a 12-cup Bundt or fluted tube pan, preferably nonstick.

2. In a bowl, sift together the flour, baking soda, and salt. Set aside.

3. Place the butter and cream cheese in a large mixer bowl. Beat on medium speed until creamy. Beat in the sugar a little at a time and continue to beat for 2 minutes.

4. In another bowl, whisk together the egg and egg whites. On medium speed, beat the eggs into the butter mixture, a little at a time. Beat on medium-high until the mixture is smooth, thick, and fluffy, about 5 minutes.

5. In another bowl, mix together the buttermilk, almond extract, Amaretto, and baby food. On low, in 3 additions, alternately beat (or stir) in the flour and buttermilk mixtures, mixing only until no flour is visible.

6. Bake for 45 to 55 minutes or until a tester inserted into the center of the cake comes out with no moist crumbs attached. Remove from the oven and set the pan on a cooling rack.

7. Using a fine skewer, poke holes into the cake every ½ inch, going as deep into the cake as the skewer will allow.

8. To make the glaze, stir ½ teaspoon of the almond extract and the water into 1 cup of the powdered sugar, until smooth. Pour ⅓ cup of this mixture over the warm cake. Cover the remaining glaze and set it aside. Allow the cake to cool for 20 minutes. Invert to remove the cake from the pan. Poke holes over the entire cake. Brush the remaining glaze over the cake. Let the glaze dry.

9. Whisk together the remaining ⅔ cup powdered sugar, ½ teaspoon almond extract, and enough water to make a very thick, but flowing, glaze (2 to 2½ teaspoons water). Drizzle this over the cake. Crush the almonds and sprinkle them onto the wet glaze. When the glaze has set, wrap the cake in foil, being careful to leave a little headroom so that you don't damage the glaze. For best results, let the cake mellow overnight. If freezing, freeze after the cake has been glazed the first time. Defrost, in foil, overnight, and then add the thicker glaze.

Chocolate Tube Cake

If you love chocolate, Shabbat is a good time to serve a chocolate dessert. This one is easy to make and rich tasting. Using mostly cake flour makes it very tender. To improve freezing, a small bit of all-purpose flour is added so that the cake will not be too crumbly. For best results make the cake one day ahead.

MAKES 20 SERVINGS

½ cup miniature chocolate chips

¼ cup boiling water

One 4-ounce jar (about ⅓ cup) plum-apple or prune-apple baby food

1 teaspoon vanilla extract

¾ cup nonfat or lowfat buttermilk, at room temperature

2 large eggs, at room temperature

2 large egg whites, at room temperature

1 cup firmly packed light brown sugar

1 cup granulated sugar

¼ cup canola oil

2 cups (210 grams) sifted cake flour, lightly sprinkled into measuring cup

⅛ cup (15 grams) all-purpose flour, lightly sprinkled into measuring cup

½ teaspoon baking soda

½ teaspoon baking powder

¼ teaspoon salt

½ cup Dutch-processed cocoa, preferably Droste

continued

DAIRY

NUTRITIONAL NOTES
(per serving)

170 calories

5g fat (25%)

18mg cholesterol

31g carbohydrates

3g protein

92mg sodium

1g fiber

RDA %

0% vitamin A

0% vitamin C

3% calcium

8% iron

Shabbat

1. Preheat the oven to 325°F, with a rack in the lower third of the oven. Spray-grease and flour a 12-cup angel food pan (nonfluted tube pan).

2. Place ¼ cup of chocolate chips in a bowl. Pour the boiling water over them and let the mixture sit for a minute. Stir to melt the chocolate. Stir in the baby food and vanilla. When the mixture cools to warm, stir in the buttermilk.

3. In a large mixer bowl, lightly beat together the eggs and egg whites. Gradually beat in both sugars. Increase the speed to high and beat for 5 minutes until the eggs are thick and lightened in color. Beat in the oil.

4. In another bowl, sift together both flours, baking soda, baking powder, salt, and cocoa. Stir in the remaining ¼ cup chocolate chips.

5. In 3 additions, alternately stir the flour and the buttermilk mixtures into the eggs, starting and ending with the flour. Spoon the batter into the prepared pan.

6. Bake for 60 to 65 minutes. There may be shiny spots on top of the cake, but a tester inserted into the center of the cake will come out with only a few crumbs attached. Remove the pan from the oven and set it on a cooling rack. When cool, cut around the outside of the cake and the inner tube. Lift the tube out of the rim. Cut under the cake, then invert the tube onto a plate. Reinvert so that the cake is right side up again. For best results, wrap the cake in foil, and store overnight before eating. Sprinkle with powdered sugar before serving.

The cake will keep for 3 days at room temperature, or frozen for up to 3 months.

Chocolate-Chocolate Chip Cookies

These delicious cookies have two-thirds less fat than traditional homemade chocolate chip cookies. They're great to bring to Onegs, to pack in lunch boxes, or for afternoon snacks.

MAKES 42 COOKIES

6 tablespoons unsalted butter (or unsalted pareve margarine)

⅔ cup (110 grams) chocolate chips (dairy or pareve)

2 tablespoons boiling water

1 cup granulated sugar

½ cup firmly packed light brown sugar

2 teaspoons vanilla extract

2 large eggs, at room temperature

1⅛ cups (120 grams) sifted cake flour, lightly sprinkled into measuring cup

¾ cup (90 grams) all-purpose sifted flour, lightly sprinkled into measuring cup

1 teaspoon baking soda

¼ cup Dutch-processed cocoa, preferably Droste

⅛ teaspoon salt

¼ cup chopped walnuts or pecans

1. Preheat the oven to 350°F, with a rack in the middle of the oven. Line cookie sheets with parchment paper or nonstick Teflon liners.

2. Boil water in the bottom of a double boiler. Turn the heat off, but leave the pot on the burner. Place the butter, ⅓ cup of the chocolate chips, and 2 tablespoons of boiling water into the top of the double boiler. Set it over the hot water, and let the chocolate and butter melt, stirring occa-

DAIRY OR
PAREVE

NUTRITIONAL
NOTES
(per serving)

74 calories

3g fat (33%)

9mg cholesterol

12g carbohydrates

1g protein

59mg sodium

0g fiber

RDA %

1% vitamin A

0% vitamin C

0% calcium

3% iron

Shabbat

sionally. Scrape the melted mixture into a mixer bowl, and beat in both sugars and the vanilla.

3. Add the eggs, 1 at a time, beating well after each addition.

4. In another bowl, sift together both the flours, the baking soda, cocoa, and salt. Stir this into the chocolate mixture. Stir in the remaining ⅓ cup chocolate chips and the nuts.

5. Drop the batter by rounded teaspoonsful onto the parchment paper, spacing the cookies 2 inches apart. Bake 1 sheet at a time for 8 to 10 minutes, until the cookies are barely set and there are no more moisture beads on the surface of the cookies. Slide the parchment paper onto cooling racks and allow the cookies to cool. Repeat with the remaining dough. Cookies are at their very best if eaten the same day they are made, but will keep for 3 days at room temperature. They can also be frozen for up to 3 months (defrost cookies at room temperature).

Raisin Mandel Bread

ALSO SERVE ON
Purim,
Yom ha-atzma'ut

PAREVE

The secret to making good mandel bread is to use a soft, almost sticky dough. This keeps the mandel bread tender even when it is baked extra-crunchy. Since the oil has been greatly reduced, using less sugar prevents the cookies from becoming too hard. If you like them sweeter, sprinkle them with sugar (or cinnamon-sugar) after they are sliced and ready to go back into the oven. For a further reduction in fat, see Mocha Chip Mandel Bread, page 274.

MAKES 30 COOKIES

⅓ cup raisins

2 large eggs, at room temperature

3 tablespoons canola oil

½ teaspoon vanilla extract

½ teaspoon almond extract (or additional vanilla)

½ cup sugar

*2⅛ cups (255 grams) all-purpose flour, lightly sprinkled into a
    measuring cup*

1½ teaspoons baking powder

¼ cup almonds, coarsely chopped

1. Preheat the oven to 350°F, with a rack in the middle of the oven.
Spray-grease a cookie sheet.

2. Soak the raisins in hot water for 1 minute. Drain, squeeze dry, and set
aside.

3. In a large mixer bowl, beat together the eggs, oil, vanilla, and almond
extract just to blend. Lightly beat in the sugar.

4. In another bowl, thoroughly mix together the flour and baking powder. Dump the flour into the egg mixture, and stir (or beat on low) until
almost completely blended. Add the almonds and raisins. Stir to form a
soft dough. Divide the dough in half. On a floured board, using wet
hands, shape each half into a loaf, 1½ inches wide and ¾ inch thick
(about 10 inches long).

5. Transfer the loaves to the cookie sheet. Bake for 30 minutes. Remove
from the oven and let cool for 1 minute. Transfer the loaves to a cutting
board, and using a serrated knife, slice, on an angle, into ⅜-inch pieces.
Place the cookies cut side down on a cookie sheet and bake for 7 minutes.
Turn the cookies over and bake for another 5 to 7 minutes until the cookies are lightly browned. They will harden when they cool. Let the cookies cool right on the hot cookie sheet. Store in an airtight container for up
to 2 weeks, or freeze for up to 3 months (defrost cookies at room temperature, uncovered).

NUTRITIONAL
NOTES
(per serving)

51 calories

1.5g fat (27%)

9mg cholesterol

8g carbohydrates

1g protein

16mg sodium

0g fiber

RDA %

0% vitamin A

0% vitamin C

1% calcium

2% iron

Shabbat

Mocha Chip Mandel Bread

DAIRY OR PAREVE

NUTRITIONAL NOTES
(per serving)

56 calories

2g fat (29%)

9mg cholesterol

9g carbohydrates

1g protein

16mg sodium

0g fiber

RDA %

0% vitamin A

0% vitamin C

1% calcium

2% iron

*T*his cookie has a slightly drier and harder texture than the Raisin Mandel Bread (page 272) because more sugar and less oil is used. The extra sugar is needed to balance the bitterness of the cocoa. Chocolate chips offset the dryness by the glorious way they melt in the mouth.

MAKES 42 COOKIES

2 large eggs, at room temperature

2 tablespoons canola oil

½ teaspoon vanilla extract

½ teaspoon almond extract

¾ cup sugar

2 cups (240 grams) all-purpose flour, lightly sprinkled into measuring cup

1½ teaspoons baking powder

2 tablespoons Dutch-processed cocoa, preferably Droste

1 teaspoon instant coffee granules

¼ cup almonds, coarsely chopped

¼ cup miniature chocolate chips (or chopped pareve chocolate chips)

1. Preheat the oven to 350°F, with a rack in the middle of the oven. Spray-grease a cookie sheet.

2. In a large mixer bowl, beat together the eggs, oil, vanilla, and almond extract just to blend. Gradually beat in the sugar.

3. In another bowl, thoroughly mix together the flour, baking powder, cocoa, and coffee. Dump the flour mixture into the egg mixture, and mix (or beat on low) together until almost thoroughly blended. Add the almonds and chocolate chips. Stir to form a soft dough. Divide the dough

Light Jewish
Holiday Desserts

in half. On a floured board, using wet hands, shape each half into a loaf, 1½ inches wide and ¾ inch thick (about 10 inches long).

4. Transfer the loaves to the cookie sheet. Bake for 30 minutes. Remove from the oven and let cool for 1 minute. Transfer the loaves to a cutting board, and using a serrated knife, slice, on an angle, into ⅜-inch pieces. Place the cookies cut side down on the cookie sheet and bake for 7 minutes. Turn the cookies over and bake for another 5 to 7 minutes until the cookies are very firm. They will harden when cool. Let the cookies cool on the hot cookie sheet. Store in an airtight container for up to 2 weeks, or freeze for up to 3 months (defrost cookies at room temperature, uncovered).

Chocolate Chip Pecan Biscotti

*A*lthough most people would not quibble about a name, these twice-baked cookies can't be called mandel brot because they don't contain almonds. Children as well as adults love them, perhaps because pecans, an exceptionally buttery nut, give the cookies a wonderful richness.

MAKES 30 COOKIES

2 large eggs, at room temperature

2 tablespoons canola oil

1 teaspoon vanilla extract

½ cup sugar

2 cups (240g) all-purpose flour, lightly sprinkled into measuring cup

1½ teaspoons baking powder

½ cup pecans, coarsely chopped

¼ cup miniature chocolate chips (or chopped pareve chocolate chips)

continued

ALSO SERVE ON
Purim,
Yom ha-atzma'ut

DAIRY OR
PAREVE

Shabbat

69 calories

2g fat (30%)

12mg cholesterol

11g carbohydrates

1g protein

22mg sodium

0g fiber

RDA %

0% vitamin A

0% vitamin C

2% calcium

2% iron

1. Preheat the oven to 350°F, with a rack in the middle of the oven. Spray-grease a cookie sheet.

2. In a large mixer bowl, beat together the eggs, oil, and vanilla. Gradually beat in the sugar.

3. In another bowl, thoroughly mix together the flour and baking powder. Dump the flour into the egg mixture, and mix together until almost thoroughly blended. Stir in the nuts and chocolate chips, forming a soft dough. Divide the dough in half. On a floured board, using wet hands, shape each half into a loaf, 1½ inches wide and ¾ inch thick (about 10 inches long).

4. Transfer the loaves to the cookie sheet. Bake for 30 minutes. Remove from the oven and let cool for 1 minute. Transfer the loaves to a cutting board, and using a serrated knife, slice on an angle, into ⅜-inch pieces. Place the cookies cut side down on the cookie sheet and bake for 7 minutes. Turn the cookies over and bake for another 5 to 7 minutes until the cookies are lightly browned. They will harden when they cool. Let the cookies cool on the hot cookie sheet. Store in an airtight container for up to 2 weeks, or freeze for up to 3 months (defrost the cookies at room temperature, uncovered).

Yeast Reshicas

These crunchy, pretzel-shaped cookies are a specialty of the Sephardic community of Rhodes. The cookies are typically served on Sundays when families visit each other, on holidays, and at life-cycle events. They can be made with a yeast dough, such as this one, or with a cookie dough (see page 279). This wonderful recipe was given to me by Sarah Schreibman, a second-generation Rhodean Jew. Her mother shapes the dough by running it through a meat grinder, a method that is fast and efficient. As most people do not own meat grinders, however, my recipe calls for hand-rolling the dough into skinny ropes. The dough is so supple that this is quite easily done.

MAKES 40 COOKIES

½ cup very warm water (115° to 120°F)

¼ cup canola oil

¼ cup sugar

2 cups (240 grams) all-purpose flour, lightly sprinkled into measuring cup

1 teaspoon instant yeast, such as Fleischmann's Bread Machine Yeast (to use other types of yeast, see page 319)

¼ teaspoon cinnamon

1 large egg white, whisked with ½ teaspoon water, for glazing

1½ tablespoons sesame seeds

1. Combine the water, oil, and sugar in a mixer bowl. In another bowl, combine the flour, yeast, and cinnamon. Dump the flour into the mixer bowl. Beat on medium speed, until the dough starts to form a ball. Use your hands to gather the dough together into a ball. Very lightly oil a

ALSO SERVE ON
Yom ha-atzma'ut, Purim, life-cycle events

PAREVE

NUTRITIONAL NOTES
(per serving)

40 calories

1g fat (32%)

0mg cholesterol

6g carbohydrates

1g protein

0mg sodium

0g fiber

RDA %

0% vitamin A

0% vitamin C

0% calcium

1% iron

container that is twice as large as the ball. Place the dough in the container, turn to coat it lightly with oil, cover, and let rise for 1 hour.

2. Preheat the oven to 350°F, with the racks in the middle and lower third of the oven.

3. Divide the dough in half. Place 1 part back in the bowl and cover it. Roll the remainder into a log, and cut it into 20 even pieces. Roll 1 piece at a time into a rope, about 10 inches long and ⅛ inch wide. Transfer the rope to a cookie sheet. Make a pretzel shape (without the center twist) by bringing the two ends of the rope to the center. Repeat with the dough you have cut.

4. Brush the cookies with the egg white glaze. The easiest way to get the seeds onto the cookies without sprinkling most of them onto the cookie sheets is to dip the pastry brush (that still has egg white glaze on it) into the seeds, and then to dab the brush onto the cookies. Repeat the whole procedure with the second half of the dough.

5. Place the cookies in the oven, and bake for 5 minutes. Reverse the position of the cookie sheets, top to bottom, turn the oven off, and let the cookies stay in the oven until they are hard and crunchy, 2 to 3 hours (or overnight). The cookies should be only lightly brown.

6. Store the cookies in an airtight container for up to 2 weeks, or freeze for up to 3 months (defrost uncovered).

7. If the cookies soften, reheat them for 5 minutes, and they should re-crisp.

Cookie Reshicas

For more information on reshicas, please see page 277. This cookie dough version is a little richer than the yeasted one, and the cookies tend to stay crisper without reheating. They also take less time to make, as the dough does not need to rise.

MAKES 40 COOKIES

1 large egg, at room temperature

2 tablespoons canola oil

2 tablespoons water

½ cup sugar

2 cups (240 grams) all-purpose flour, lightly sprinkled into measuring cup

1½ teaspoons baking powder

1 teaspoon cinnamon

1 large egg white whisked with ½ teaspoon water, for glazing

2 tablespoons sesame seeds

1. Preheat the oven to 325°F, with racks in the middle and lower third of the oven. Line 2 insulated cookie sheets with parchment paper or non-stick liners (alternatively, nest 2 cookie sheets together).

2. Place the egg, oil, and water in a processor bowl. Pulse-process just to blend the ingredients. Add the sugar, and process until blended.

3. In another bowl, sift together the flour, baking powder, and cinnamon. Dump this into the processor, and process until a ball forms. The dough should be moist and supple but not sticky. If necessary, knead in a tiny bit more water or flour, as necessary.

4. Divide the dough into forty ½-inch balls. One at a time, roll each ball into a 10-inch-long rope, just slightly thicker than ⅛ inch. Transfer the

NUTRITIONAL NOTES
(per serving)

44 calories

1g fat (24%)

5mg cholesterol

7g carbohydrates

1g protein

16mg sodium

0g fiber

RDA %

0% vitamin A

0% vitamin C

1% calcium

2% iron

Shabbat

rope to the cookie sheet. Make a pretzel shape (without the center twist) by bringing the 2 ends of rope to the center, as on page 278.

5. Brush the cookies with the egg white glaze. Dip the brush into the seeds and then dab the cookies to transfer the seeds to them (using about ⅛ teaspoon per cookie).

6. Bake for 7 minutes. Move the cookie sheet on the top rack down and vice versa. Bake for another 8 minutes. Turn off the oven and leave the cookies in the oven for 15 to 20 minutes, until the cookies are hard and lightly browned. Cool before serving. Store the cookies in a container at room temperature for up to 2 weeks, or freeze for up to 3 months.

Bread Pudding

ALSO SERVE ON
Shavuot, Chanukah

DAIRY

You can make lowfat bread pudding using a lowfat challah with the crust (page 282), French bread (without the crust), or a soft, white bread with the crust (I use Arnold Lite Italian, certified Ⓤ). Contrary to the traditional baking technique for bread pudding, this lowfat version should not be baked in a water-bath, as the pudding will be too soft. Skim milk can be used, but this, too, will result in a softer set.

MAKES 6 SERVINGS

7 ounces bread, cut ¼ inch thick and into 1-inch squares
    (about 5 lightly packed cups)

⅓ cup raisins

2 large eggs

¼ cup egg substitute (such as Egg Beaters), or 2 large egg whites

⅓ cup sugar

1 teaspoon vanilla extract

1 teaspoon cinnamon

Light Jewish
Holiday Desserts

¼ *teaspoon nutmeg*

2 *to 2¼ cups 2% milk*

1. Preheat the oven to 325°F, with a rack in the lower third of the oven.

2. Place the bread on a cookie sheet, and lightly toast it in the oven for 5 minutes. (It should not brown but should become somewhat dry). Remove and let cool. If the bread is already stale, it does not need to be baked.

3. Place the bread cubes in a 2-quart baking dish (I like an 8 × 8-inch square glass baking pan). Sprinkle the raisins over the bread.

4. In a medium bowl, lightly whisk together the eggs and the egg substitute. (If using egg whites instead, you will have to whisk more vigorously to break the albumin and blend the eggs and whites thoroughly.) Whisk in the sugar, vanilla, cinnamon, nutmeg, and milk.

5. Pour 2 cups of the milk mixture over the bread. Press down on the bread with the back of a spoon. Submerge any raisins that are at the top, as they will overbake if exposed. Let the bread soak in the milk for 15 minutes, pressing occasionally with the back of the spoon. If the top does not seem to be getting moist enough, add the remaining ¼ cup milk (this will vary depending on the type of bread used, and how soft you want the finished pudding to be).

6. Bake the pudding for 60 to 70 minutes, or until puffed and set. Remove it to a rack and let cool for at least 1 hour. If you prefer a firmer pudding, refrigerate it until near serving time, and then microwave the pudding just until barely warm. If a softer pudding is desired, it can be served after it has baked, and cooled to warm. Bread pudding can be made 2 days ahead. Keep refrigerated, and before serving, microwave until warmed through.

VARIATIONS: Add or substitute other dried fruits, such as cherries or dates, for the raisins. Add diced apples, pears, chocolate chips, or coconut (adding the first 2 will make a more moist pudding; adding the last 2 will add fat).

NUTRITIONAL
NOTES
(per serving)

128 calories (165 with lowfat challah)

3g fat (17%) (4g with lowfat challah)

44mg cholesterol

23g carbohydrates

5g protein

142mg sodium

2g fiber

RDA %

3% vitamin A

1% vitamin C

9% calcium

5% iron

Shabbat

Healthy Challah

You won't notice much difference in the challah dough if you use egg substitute, but if you don't brush the crust with whole egg, it won't taste like challah.

MAKES 1 LOAF

⅔ cup very warm water (about 120°F—not hot enough to sting your finger)

2 tablespoons honey

2 tablespoons canola oil

¾ teaspoon salt

¼ cup egg substitute (such as Egg Beaters), or 2 large egg whites

3¼ cups (405 grams) bread flour, lightly sprinkled into measuring cup

1½ teaspoons instant yeast, such as Fleischmann's Bread Machine Yeast (for other types, see page 319)

Degerminated cornmeal or flour, for dusting cookie sheet

1 large egg, whisked with 1 teaspoon water, for glazing

1 tablespoon poppy seeds

1. In a large mixer bowl, beat the water, honey, oil, salt, and egg substitute, just until blended.

2. In another bowl, mix about 2 cups of the flour and the yeast. Add this all at once to the mixer bowl. Beat on low speed just until blended.

3. Change to a dough hook (or knead by hand) and add the remaining 1¼ cups flour a little at a time, until the dough forms a ball that is smooth and just slightly sticky. Transfer the dough to a floured board or a clean countertop and knead the dough a few times by hand, adding a little flour if the dough is sticky. Place in an oiled bowl, cover with plastic wrap, and let rise until double in bulk, about 1 hour. To see if the dough has doubled, flour your finger and stick it into the dough about ½ inch.

If the mark remains without puffing back up, the dough has doubled. Punch down the dough and place it on a floured board.

4. You can make a simple 3-strand braid, or a more traditional 6-strand braid as follows:

Divide the dough into 6 pieces. Roll each piece into a long skinny rope, 10 to 12 inches long. Braid the dough as follows: A. Attach 6 ropes together. Move strand #2 up past #6. B. Renumber the strands from left to right. Move strand #1 between #3 and #4. C. Renumber the strands. Move #5 up to the #1 position. D. Renumber the strands. Move #6 between #3 and #4.

    Repeat these steps until you reach the end of the braid. Pinch the ends together.

5. Place on a baking sheet that has been greased and dusted with degerminated cornmeal or flour. Cover the dough with a lint-free towel. Let rise until doubled, about 45 minutes.

6. Preheat the oven to 375°F, with a rack in the middle of the oven. Brush the egg glaze on the bread and sprinkle with poppy seeds.

7. Bake 15 minutes. Reduce the oven temperature to 350°F. Brush the loaf again with the egg glaze and bake until the loaves sound hollow when tapped on the bottom, about 15 to 20 minutes longer. Remove the loaf to a cooling rack. Do not cut until completely cooled.

VARIATIONS

Rosh Hashanah Loaves

Add 2 tablespoons raisins, after the dough has been beaten and during the early kneading stage. Shape the dough into a long rope about 1½ inches in diameter. Coil it into a loose round. Brush with glaze and sprinkle with seeds. Let rise until doubled and bake as above.

Challah Rolls

Divide the dough into 16 to 20 pieces. Roll each piece into a rope about 6 inches long. Shape the dough as if you were going to tie it in a knot, but

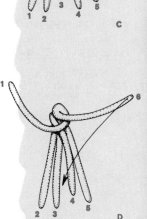

Shabbat

283

instead of pulling it tight, just leave 1 end sticking up through the center. Tuck the other end under the roll. Let rise until doubled, glaze, sprinkle with seeds, and bake for 15 to 20 minutes or until the rolls sound hollow when tapped on the bottom.

Summer Fruit Cobbler

*B*erries are the perfect fruit for cobbler because the topping soaks up the delicious juices. I like to include a couple of apples, because they do wonders for the texture of the filling. Use a quick-cooking variety, such as Rome, or you will end up with very crunchy apples. Vary the fruits and amount of sugar and spice to suit your taste. Cobbler can be served family-style from a large pan, or can be spooned into individual ramekins. Leave plenty of headroom, as the juices will splash up and can overflow the pan.

MAKES 8 SERVINGS

2 tablespoons fresh lemon juice (about 1 lemon)

6 very firm peaches

2 Rome apples

1 pound strawberries

12 ounces raspberries, washed

1 pint (2 cups) blueberries, washed

⅔ to ¾ cup sugar

1 teaspoon cinnamon

2 to 3 tablespoons cornstarch

Cobbler

1⅓ cups (140 grams) sifted cake flour, lightly sprinkled into measuring cup

ALSO SERVE ON
Shavuot

DAIRY

NUTRITIONAL NOTES
(per serving)

225 calories

2g fat (8%)

2mg cholesterol

50g carbohydrates

3g protein

211mg sodium

5.5g fiber

RDA %

7% vitamin A

16% vitamin C

8% calcium

8% iron

6 teaspoons sugar

1 teaspoon baking powder

1 teaspoon baking soda

2 tablespoons lowfat cream cheese, preferably Philadelphia
    ⅓ Less Fat

¾ cup nonfat or lowfat buttermilk

2 teaspoons canola oil

½ teaspoon vanilla extract

1. Preheat the oven to 425°F, with a rack in the middle of the oven. Have ready a decorative 8 × 10-inch baking pan, or eight 1-cup ramekins.

2. Put the lemon juice into a large bowl. Peel the peaches (plunge into boiling water for 1 minute, or just use a knife), halve, remove the pits, and dice into ¼-inch pieces. Toss with the lemon juice. Peel, halve, core, and dice the apples into ¼-inch dice. Wash, hull, and cut the strawberries into rounds. Place them, along with the rest of the fruit, into the bowl, and toss everything together. Stir in the sugar to taste, cinnamon, and 2 to 3 tablespoons cornstarch, depending on how thick you like your filling. Spoon into the baking dish or ramekins.

3. To make the cobbler batter, mix the flour, 4 teaspoons of the sugar, the baking powder, and baking soda in a large bowl. Using a pastry blender or 2 knives, cut the cream cheese into the dry ingredients until the cheese pieces are about the size of sunflower seeds.

4. In another bowl, mix together the buttermilk, oil, and vanilla. Make a well in the center of the flour mixture and pour in the buttermilk mixture. Stir until the flour is completely moistened.

5. Drop the batter by the tablespoonful over the fruit. Sprinkle the remaining 2 teaspoons sugar over the batter. Bake for 20 to 30 minutes, or until the cobbler is nicely browned. Remove it from the oven and cool on a wire rack for about 30 minutes. Eat the cobbler while it is still warm. The cobbler can be made 1 day ahead. Cover with foil and reheat at 350°F until just warm, 15 to 20 minutes. Serve with frozen yogurt, if desired.

Raised *Streusel* (Crumb) Coffeecake

ALSO SERVE ON
Yom ha-atzma'ut

DAIRY

NUTRITIONAL NOTES
(per serving)

186 calories

7g fat (34%)

17mg cholesterol

27g carbohydrates

4g protein

39mg sodium

.5g fiber

RDA %

3% vitamin A

0% vitamin C

2% calcium

8% iron

MAKE THE DOUGH 1 DAY AHEAD

The Wantuck family recipe for streusel-topped kuchen, written in German by my father's grandmother, called for "a little of this" and "enough of that." As a young woman, my mother obtained the recipe by standing at my grandmother's side and measuring everything as my grandmother assembled the ingredients and made the kuchen. I remember the cake as flat and fairly dense, topped with wonderful crumbs that would fall off in our milk, cocoa, or coffee as we dipped it into the liquid. It was a cake that we all loved as children. The family recipe contained 8 tablespoons of butter in the dough, and another 5 in the streusel, so I knew it would not be easy to make a lowfat version that would live up to the memories. On the day of the taste-test, my father took some extra insulin and then proceeded to taste and dunk. I nervously watched and waited. "Really good, Pen," my dad proclaimed. "Just like my mother used to make."

MAKES 2 CAKES, 9 SERVINGS EACH

1 recipe Kuchen Dough, page 297
Doubled recipe Streusel (Crumb) Topping, page 296
1 egg white whisked with 1 teaspoon water
Powdered sugar

1. Make the Kuchen Dough (it rests overnight in the refrigerator).

2. The next day, preheat the oven to 350°F, with a rack in the middle of the oven. Grease the bottom of two 8- or 9-inch round or square pans.

Light Jewish
Holiday Desserts

3. Make the Streusel Topping.

4. Divide the dough in half. Roughly roll each piece of cold dough to fit the bottom of one of the pans, and then press the dough into the pans to fit completely (let them rest for 10 minutes if they keep shrinking). The dough should be about 3/16 inch thick.

5. Brush the dough with the egg white mixture and then sprinkle half of the streusel crumbs over each piece of dough. Place the pans onto a cookie sheet (this is important because it provides insulation so that the bottoms do not overbake).

6. Bake for 20 to 25 minutes, until the crumbs are nicely browned and the internal temperature is about 200°F. Remove the pans from the oven. Slide a pancake turner under one of the kuchens and lift it out of the pan. Set it on a cooling rack. Repeat with the other cake. Let the cakes cool completely before eating. The cakes get stale within 1 or 2 days and are then delicious when dunked.

Apple Kuchen

Another Wantuck family favorite, apple kuchen dough has more yeast in it than streusel kuchen, making it slightly more soft and cakelike. Because the apples help to moisten the cake, less fat can be used in the dough. Make sure that you brush the apples with butter (not margarine or oil), or the cake will taste flat and uninteresting. The dough meeds to be refrigerated overnight, so plan ahead.

MAKES 9 SERVINGS

continued

ALSO SERVE ON
*Rosh Hashanah,
Sukkot,
Yom ha-atzma'ut*

DAIRY

Shabbat

NUTRITIONAL
NOTES
(per serving)

120 calories
....
3.5g fat (25%)
....
14mg cholesterol
....
20g carbohydrates
....
3g protein
....
50mg sodium
....
1g fiber

RDA %

1% vitamin A
....
3% vitamin C
....
1% calcium
....
5% iron

MAKE 1 DAY AHEAD

Kuchen Dough, page 297 (with changes, see step 1)

½ medium lemon

*2 small apples (use a nonjuicy, medium-firm to firm variety,
    such as Golden Delicious)*

1 tablespoon unsalted butter, melted

*1 lowfat graham cracker, or Stella D'oro Almond Toast,
    finely crushed (about 6 tablespoons crumbs)*

2 tablespoons sugar mixed with ½ teaspoon cinnamon

Skim milk

1. Make the kuchen dough using 2 tablespoons oil (instead of 3) and 2 teaspoons yeast (instead of 1). Refrigerate it overnight, according to the recipe directions.

2. The next day, squeeze the lemon into 4 cups cold water. Peel, halve, core, and cut the apples into ⅛-inch slices. Place the apples in the lemon-water.

3. Spray-grease an 8-inch square or a 9-inch round baking pan. Press the dough into the bottom and ¼ inch up the sides of the pan.

4. Brush the dough with the melted butter, and sprinkle the cookie crumbs over the butter.

5. Drain the apples and pat dry. Arrange in overlapping rows over the dough. Brush the tops of the apples with butter, and sprinkle generously with cinnamon-sugar. Cover the pan loosely with plastic wrap, and set aside to rise for 30 minutes. Before baking, brush the edge of the dough (where there are no apples) with skim milk.

6. Preheat the oven to 350°F, with a rack in the middle of the oven.

7. Set the kuchen on a cookie sheet (this is important because it provides insulation so that the bottom of the kuchen does not become overbaked and tough). Bake for 25 to 30 minutes, until the dough is golden and the apples are cooked. Remove from the oven, and slide the kuchen out of the pan and onto a cooling rack. The crust will get more tender over time, and is best 6 to 8 hours after baking.

VARIATIONS: Substitute for apples: pears, plums, or peaches; or alternate apples and plums, as in the Apple-Plum Galette, page 145. If prune plums are available, quarter them and use in place of apples.

Master

Recipes

Tart Pastry Dough

This crust has one-third less fat (per serving) than a standard crust. To save another gram of fat, you can reduce the butter to 5 tablespoons, but the resulting crust will be just okay—not delicious. I didn't think it was worth it. Make sure that you use cake flour, as it creates a tender crust that can be cut without breaking apart. If you chill the dough as directed, there's no need to weight it when prebaking it in a tart. Do not substitute another kind of vinegar or lemon juice for the balsamic vinegar. Others will leave an unpleasant aftertaste, while balsamic vinegar will tenderize the crust and will enhance the flavor of the pastry.

For a 9-inch tart shell

⅔ cup (70 grams) sifted cake flour, lightly sprinkled into measuring cup

⅔ cup (80 grams) all-purpose flour, lightly sprinkled into measuring cup

¼ teaspoon salt

3 tablespoons sugar

6 tablespoons unsalted butter (or unsalted pareve margarine), cold

2 tablespoons egg substitute (such as Egg Beaters), or 1 large egg white, whisked

2 teaspoons balsamic vinegar

For a 10-inch lattice pie

1⅓ cups (140 grams) sifted cake flour, lightly sprinkled into measuring cup

1⅓ cups (160 grams) all-purpose flour, lightly sprinkled into measuring cup

½ teaspoon salt

⅓ cup plus 1 tablespoon sugar

12 tablespoons (1½ sticks) unsalted butter (or unsalted pareve margarine), cold

¼ cup egg substitute (such as Egg Beaters), or 2 large egg whites, whisked

1 tablespoon plus 1 teaspoon balsamic vinegar

Glaze

2 teaspoons egg substitute or egg yolk mixed with ½ teaspoon water

For the tart

1. Spray a 9-inch tart pan with cooking spray.

2. In a medium-size bowl, mix together both flours, salt, and sugar. Using a pastry blender or 2 knives, cut in the butter until the particles of fat are no larger than lentils (you can do this in the processor, but I think it is easier not to overdo if you do it by hand).

3. In another bowl, combine the egg substitute and vinegar. Pour half of it over the flour. Stir with a fork to moisten the mixture, and then use your hands to press the dough into a ball. If necessary, add the remaining egg substitute mixture, a little at a time, pressing the dough together to form a dry, but cohesive ball (it will be moister after it rests). Wrap the dough in plastic wrap and refrigerate for at least 15 minutes.

4. Cut open a jumbo zip-top bag, leaving only 1 long end uncut. Generously sprinkle the inside with flour. Place the dough inside. Roll the dough into a 12-inch circle (the dough will be slightly thicker than ¹⁄₁₆ inch), opening the plastic and flouring the dough on both sides several times during the rolling. Turn the dough over onto the tart pan, ease it off the plastic, and fit it snugly into the pan. Press the sides of the dough gently into the grooves of the pan, and press the overhanging dough gently over the top of the pan. Roll a long rolling pin over the top of the pan to remove the excess dough (or press down on the top with a long ruler). The sides of the dough will need to be pressed back into the grooves.

continued

Master Recipes

5. Place the tart pan in a jumbo zip-top bag and put it in the freezer for at least 15 minutes, or up to 3 months.

6. Preheat the oven to 375°F. Remove the tart from the freezer. Bake the tart for 10 to 15 minutes, until it no longer looks raw. Brush the tart bottom and sides with the egg glaze and bake for 5 more minutes for a partially baked crust. For a completely baked crust, continue to bake until browned to your liking. Remove the tart from the oven, and cool on a wire rack. Can be made 8 hours in advance. Store at room temperature.

For a 10-inch lattice pie

1. Follow steps 1 to 3 for the 9-inch tart.

2. Divide the dough into 2 balls, using ⅔ of the dough for 1 of the balls. Wrap, and refrigerate the dough for at least 30 minutes. Follow the directions for lattice pie on page 290.

Nut Pastry Crust

DAIRY OR PAREVE

Do not substitute another kind of vinegar or lemon juice for the balsamic vinegar, as balsamic vinegar will complement the pastry and will leave no aftertaste.

For a 10-inch lattice pie

1½ cups (160 grams) sifted cake flour, lightly sprinkled into measuring cup

1⅓ cups (160 grams) all-purpose flour, lightly sprinkled into measuring cup

½ teaspoon salt

½ cup sugar

½ cup nuts (almonds or pecans, toasted at 350°F for 5 minutes)

6 tablespoons unsalted butter (or unsalted pareve margarine), cold

¼ cup shortening, frozen

1 teaspoon vanilla extract

2 teaspoons balsamic vinegar

¼ cup egg substitute (such as Egg Beaters), or 2 large egg whites, whisked

For an 8 × 10-inch rectangle or eight 4-inch rounds

⅔ cup (80 grams) all-purpose flour, lightly sprinkled into measuring cup

⅔ cup plus 1 tablespoon (80 grams) sifted cake flour, lightly sprinkled into measuring cup

½ teaspoon salt

3 tablespoons sugar

¼ cup almonds or toasted pecans (toasted at 350°F for 5 minutes)

3 tablespoons unsalted butter (or unsalted pareve margarine), cold

2 tablespoons shortening, frozen

½ teaspoon vanilla

1 teaspoon balsamic vinegar

2 tablespoons egg substitute, or 1 large egg white, whisked

1. In a food processor, process both flours, salt, sugar, and the nuts until the nuts are finely ground. Transfer the mixture to a large bowl.

2. Cut the butter and shortening into ½-inch chunks and place on top of the flour. Using a pastry blender, cut in the fats until they look like lentils or rice. (Alternatively, you can pulse-process the fats in with the flour until they look like small particles. I prefer doing it by hand, because I have more control.)

3. In another bowl, mix together the vanilla, vinegar, and egg substitute. Pour half into the flour mixture, and mix with a fork until completely moistened. If necessary, add the remaining egg mixture, a little at a time, pressing the dough with your hands until it forms a dry, but cohesive ball. Shape into a flattened ball. (For the lattice pie, divide the dough into 2 balls, using ⅔ of the dough for 1 of the balls.) Wrap in plastic and refrigerate for at least 30 minutes.

4. Shape and bake according to the recipe instructions.

Master Recipes

Sour Cream Muerbe Teig Pastry

FOR THE BOTTOM AND SIDES OF A 10 × 15-INCH JELLY ROLL PAN, OR FOR TWO 12-INCH GALETTES

¼ cup (½ stick) unsalted butter, at cool room temperature

¼ cup vegetable shortening, at room temperature

½ cup reduced-fat sour cream, preferably Breakstone's, at room temperature

2 tablespoons sugar

1 large egg, at room temperature

½ teaspoon vanilla extract

1⅓ cups (160 grams) all-purpose flour, lightly sprinkled into measuring cup

1⅓ cups (140 grams) sifted cake flour, lightly sprinkled into measuring cup

½ teaspoon salt

1. Place the butter and shortening in a mixer bowl. Beat on medium-low to blend together. Beat in the sour cream. Beat in the sugar. Add the egg and vanilla, and beat until well mixed. Scrape down the bowl and beat a couple of seconds.

2. Add both flours and salt. On low (use a wooden spoon if you do not have a heavy-duty mixer), beat the mixture just until it starts to ball up. Press the dough into a ball, divide it in half, wrap in plastic wrap, and refrigerate overnight.

3. Roll and shape the dough according to recipe directions.

Graham Cracker Crust and Topping

For an 8- to 9-inch square pan, or 8-inch round springform bottom

½ cup lowfat graham cracker crumbs (about 5 whole crackers)

¼ cup (30 grams) all-purpose flour, lightly sprinkled into measuring cup

1 tablespoon firmly packed light brown sugar

1 tablespoon unsalted butter, melted (unsalted pareve margarine can be substituted, but the crust will be softer)

1½ teaspoons canola oil

2 teaspoons egg substitute (such as Egg Beaters), or 2 teaspoons egg white whisked with ¼ teaspoon water

For a 9- to 10-inch piecrust or crumb topping for a 9 × 12-inch pan

¾ cup lowfat graham cracker crumbs (about 7 whole graham crackers)

⅓ cup plus 1 tablespoon (50 grams) all-purpose flour, lightly sprinkled into measuring cup

1½ tablespoons firmly packed light brown sugar

2 tablespoons unsalted butter, melted (margarine can be substituted, but the crust will be softer)

2 teaspoons canola oil

1 tablespoon egg substitute (such as Egg Beaters), or 1 tablespoon egg white whisked with ¼ teaspoon water

In a medium bowl, place the graham crackers, flour, and brown sugar. Drizzle in the butter and oil. Stir with a fork to moisten the crumbs, and then use your fingers to rub the fats in. Add the egg substitute, 1 teaspoon at a time, stirring with a fork and squeezing between your fingers until the crumbs are moistened and will just hold together. Press the

Master Recipes

crumbs firmly into the bottom of the pan. Follow the directions in each individual recipe for baking.

For graham crumb topping

For an 8-inch square pan, use only 1½ teaspoons of egg substitute. For a 9 × 12-inch pan, use 2 teaspoons egg substitute. Bake the crumbs at 350°F, for 8 minutes. Turn the crumbs over, and bake for another 2 to 4 minutes until nicely browned.

Streusel (Crumb) Topping

THICK TOPPING FOR AN 8 × 8-INCH PAN, OR ENOUGH FOR A 9 × 13-INCH PAN

¾ cup (90 grams) all-purpose flour, lightly sprinkled into measuring cup

⅓ cup firmly packed light brown sugar, or ½ cup granulated sugar

½ teaspoon cinnamon (optional)

2 tablespoons unsalted butter, melted

1 tablespoon canola oil

1. In a medium bowl, mix together the flour, sugar, and cinnamon.

2. Mix the butter and oil. Add to the flour mixture. Stir with a fork until moistened.

3. Use your fingertips to rub the fats into the flour, and then use your hands to squeeze the mixture into small lumps. Sprinkle the crumbs onto the dessert you are topping, and bake according to recipe directions. Alternatively, crumbs can be baked on a cookie sheet at 350°F for 10 to 15 minutes. The crumbs will harden as they cool.

Kuchen Dough

FOR TWO 8 OR 9-INCH ROUND OR SQUARE CAKES

½ cup skim milk

¼ cup ice water

3 tablespoons canola oil

¼ teaspoon salt

2 tablespoons sugar

1 large egg, at room temperature

*2½ cups plus 1 tablespoon (317 grams) bread flour,
lightly sprinkled into measuring cup*

*1 teaspoon instant yeast, such as Fleischmann's Bread Machine Yeast
(for other yeast, please see page 319)*

1. Place the milk in a microwavable bowl and microwave on high until the milk boils. Stir in the ice water. Set the milk in the refrigerator for about 5 minutes, until it cools to about 120°F (warm, but not hot enough to sting your finger). Pour the milk into a large mixer bowl. Mix in the oil, salt, sugar, and egg.

2. In another bowl, combine 2½ cups of the flour and the yeast. If using a heavy-duty standing mixer, add the flour mixture all at once to the mixer bowl. Beat on medium-low for 5 minutes. The dough will be very gluey and soft. (If using a hand or light-duty mixer, beat in the flour mixture a little at a time until the dough becomes too heavy for the mixer. Stir in the remaining flour mixture with a wooden spoon, and stir the dough for 5 minutes.) Sprinkle the remaining tablespoon of flour over the dough so that you can gather the dough together and remove it from the bowl.

3. Place the dough in an oiled bowl. It will be a shaggy mass, but it will come into a ball when you turn the dough over in the bowl a couple of times to coat it with the oil. Cover and set aside to rise until doubled, about 1 hour.

4. Punch down the dough; flour it lightly. Wrap in plastic wrap, making sure that there is plenty of overlap so that the dough will still be wrapped as it slowly rises. Refrigerate overnight and use according to recipe directions.

Master Recipes

Marshmallow Meringue

PAREVE

This recipe is one of the most useful items in a lowfat repertoire. It can be used alone, as a frosting, or as a base for other frostings and fillings. In my last book, Passover Desserts, I recommended that the meringue be made by beating the eggs over simmering water. The National Egg Board now recommends that the eggs be stirred, rather than beaten, because there is a small chance that the foamy part of the eggs will not reach a high enough temperature. I tried many times, in vain, to get the eggs to 160°F, but each time they overcooked. Then I read Alice Medrich's book, Chocolate and the Art of Low-Fat Desserts. Alice's method, below, is foolproof, and I always use it now. To make her meringue, Alice mixes the eggs with a smaller amount of sugar than I do. This makes a delicious but fairly soft meringue. I like to make my desserts at least one day ahead to allow for unforeseen circumstances. For these reasons, I use a higher proportion of sugar. This makes a stiffer, more marshmallowy meringue, but it is very stable and weeps very little, even after several days in the refrigerator.

MAKES 5 TO 6 CUPS

> *3 large egg whites, at room temperature*
> *¾ cup sugar*
> *1 tablespoon water, at room temperature*

1. Fill a large skillet with 1 inch of water. Bring the water to a simmer. In a small metal bowl, whisk the egg whites with the sugar and room-temperature water. Have a rubber scraper, instant-read thermometer, a timer, another mixing bowl, and a beater near the stove.

2. Place the bowl with the egg white mixture into the simmering water, and rapidly stir with the rubber scraper for 20 seconds. Remove the bowl from the simmering water and check the temperature of the egg mixture. If the eggs are not yet at 160°F, heat for 10 seconds more. Remove the bowl from the water, dip the thermometer into the boiling water (to bring it up in temperature quickly and to kill any bacteria on the thermometer) and then retest. Continue until the egg whites reach 160°F, the temperature needed to kill salmonella. Do not heat much higher, or the eggs will overcook. The time that it takes depends upon the type of bowl and pot that are being used—I've had it take from 20 to 80 seconds.

3. As soon as the eggs reach 160°F, transfer them to a cool bowl, and beat at medium-high speed until the egg whites are firm and cool. They will look like shaving cream and stand in stiff peaks when the beater is raised from them.

Light Whipped Cream

This is a variation of Alice Medrich's recipe from Chocolate and the Art of Low-Fat Desserts.

MAKES ¾ CUP

1 large egg white
¼ cup sugar
½ teaspoon water
½ cup heavy cream
⅛ teaspoon vanilla extract

1. Place a small mixer bowl and beaters in the freezer.

2. Make Marshmallow Meringue with the egg white, sugar, and water, using the instructions on pages 298-299. The egg white mixure will be very firm but will not stand in stiff peaks.

3. Beat the cream and vanilla in the chilled bowl until firm peaks form. Fold in the meringue.

DAIRY

NUTRITIONAL NOTES
(per tablespoon)

22 calories

1.5g fat (62%)

6mg cholesterol

2g carbohydrates

0g protein

4mg sodium

0g fiber

RDA %

1% vitamin A

0% vitamin C

0% calcium

Master Recipes

Lemon Filling

MAKES ABOUT 1 ¾ CUPS

1 large egg yolk

2 tablespoons cornstarch

2 tablespoons (15 grams) all-purpose flour

½ cup sugar

1 cup skim milk

½ cup fresh lemon juice (2 to 3 lemons)

2 tablespoons frozen orange juice concentrate

Finely grated zest from 1 lemon

1. Place the egg yolk in a medium bowl. Whisk it lightly, cover with plastic wrap, and set aside.

2. In a medium pot, place the cornstarch, flour, and sugar. Gradually add the milk, stirring after each addition, until the cornstarch mixture is blended smoothly into the liquid.

3. Place the pot over medium heat and cook and stir until the sugar dissolves. Raise the heat to medium-high and bring the mixture to a boil, stirring constantly in a figure eight or "s" pattern (this will ensure that the filling on the bottom of the pan does not scorch). Boil, stirring, for 1 minute.

4. Stirring constantly, add the milk mixture to the egg yolk, drop by drop, until the egg is hot. Then add the rest of the hot liquid, in a constant stream.

5. Return the mixture to the pot. Cook and stir the mixture on medium-low heat until it just starts to boil (this will cook the yolk and destroy the enzyme in the yolk that can cause the sauce to thin).

6. Remove from the heat, and stir in the lemon juice, orange juice concentrate, and zest. Strain the filling through a fine-mesh strainer into a storage container. Press a piece of plastic wrap directly onto the top of the filling. (This will prevent a skin from forming. If you are concerned about using plastic wrap, let the skin form and then scrape it off before

eating.) Place in the refrigerator for several hours until completely cool. When cool, remove the plastic wrap and cover the pudding with the container top. Can be made 3 days ahead.

Vanilla Pastry Cream

MAKES ABOUT 2 CUPS

1 large egg yolk

2 tablespoons (15 grams) all-purpose flour

2 tablespoons cornstarch

2 cups 1% milk

⅓ cup sugar

3-inch piece of vanilla bean, or 1 teaspoon vanilla extract

1. Place a medium-mesh strainer and a storage container near the stove.

2. In a medium mixer bowl, whisk the egg yolk lightly. Set aside.

3. Place the flour and cornstarch in the top of a double boiler (off the heat). Add the milk a little at a time, stirring to make a smooth paste with the starches. When smooth, add the remaining milk. Stir in the sugar and vanilla bean (if using extract, do not add now).

4. Set the double boiler over medium heat. Cook and stir until the sugar is dissolved (you will no longer feel the grains on the bottom of the pot as you stir).

5. Increase heat to medium-high, and cook and stir until the mixture boils (about 10 minutes). Continue to stir and cook for 1 minute.

6. Remove from the heat and add this mixture to the egg yolk, drop by drop, stirring constantly. As the egg yolk warms, you can add the hot mixture in a stream until it is all added.

7. Pour the mixture back into the pot. Over medium-low heat, cook and stir the custard until it just starts to boil (this will cook the egg and thicken the pudding). *continued*

Master Recipes

8. Pour the custard through the strainer into the storage container. Cut the vanilla bean in half, lengthwise, scrape out the seeds, and stir them and the bean back into the pudding. If using vanilla extract, stir it in. Cut a piece of aluminum foil that is large enough to be pressed onto the surface of the custard with enough left over to come up the container sides for a couple of inches. Press it onto the custard. Let it cool slightly. Refrigerate several hours until cold. Cover with the container top and store for up to 3 days.

Candied or Crystallized Citrus Zest

PAREVE

3 citrus fruits, washed

1½ cups water

1½ cups sugar

1. Use a vegetable peeler to peel off just the colored part of the citrus skin. To make a rose, peel off the skin in one continuous strip. For other uses the zest can be cut julienne. Place the zest, and enough water to cover, in a medium pot. Bring to a boil, then reduce the heat and simmer for 10 minutes. Drain.

2. Place the 1½ cups water and the sugar in the pot. Bring to a boil. Add the zest, reduce the heat, and simmer the zest for about 20 minutes until it is translucent and glazed. Remove the zest with a slotted spoon, and drain on paper towels. To crystallize, roll the drained peel in sugar.

3. To make a rose, use a continuous strip of candied zest. Roll the zest up, starting very tightly to form the bud, and then rolling looser and looser so that you can fan the outer layers to look like petals.

Candied zest can be stored, in the syrup, in the refrigerator. Crystallized (rolled in sugar) zest can be stored in a container at room temperature.

Baby Food

I use baby food fruit purees as a substitute for fat. Unlike prune puree, which has been available for several years, baby food fruits are not overly sweet and will not cause any intestinal discomfort. The right fruit will enhance the flavor of the dessert while adding moisture to it. Heinz and Beechnut brands carry Ⓤ certification.

Canned Milk

Carnation and Pet brand evaporated milk carry an ⓊD certification. Bordens condensed milk is also ⓊD.

Chocolate

Pareve (neither meat nor dairy) chocolate can be found in most supermarkets. Look for the words "pareve" or "parve" on the bag. If you are making a kosher-style dessert and do not care about supervision, check the label. Some of the premium brands of chocolate, such as Callebaut and Lindt, are nondairy (as evidenced by the ingredient list) even though they do not specifically say "pareve" on the packaging. Premium chocolates, though rather costly, are worth the price, as they have the best flavor and mouth-feel. Kosher for Passover chocolate usually is pareve, and in addition, does not contain lecithin, a soybean derivative. Fine chocolates can be found in some supermarkets and gourmet shops or can be ordered through mail-order houses such as these:

All Things Chocolate
P.O. Box 561
Los Gatos, CA 95031
(408) 374-4372
All brands of fine-quality chocolate.

Gourmail
(800) 366-5900, ext. 96
Fine slab chocolate (minimum order 20 pounds)
including kosher and kosher for Passover chocolate.

Williams-Sonoma
Mail-Order Department
P.O. Box 7456
San Francisco, CA 94120-7456
(800) 541-2233

Kosher supermarket brands are as follows:

Hershey's Ⓤ**D**

Nestlé's Ⓤ**D**

Bakers Ⓚ**D**

Bakers unsweetened Ⓚ**PAREVE**

Hannaford's and President's Choice chips Ⓚ**PARVE**

Working with Chocolate

Chocolate will melt more evenly if it is grated or cut into small lumps (chips are a good size). Grating chocolate in a processor makes quite a bit of noise, so you might want to use ear plugs.

Chocolate burns easily and should not be melted over direct heat.

Instead, melt chocolate in the top of a double boiler, placed over hot water (no higher than 140°F—under simmering). If the water is simmering, water from condensation may get into the chocolate and cause it to seize into a hard and crumbly mess. The water should not touch the bottom of the bowl so that the chocolate does not get too hot. Alternatively, chocolate can be melted in a microwave on medium power. Heat it for 30 to 60 seconds until it starts to look shiny. Stir and continue to heat in 10-second bursts until completely melted and smooth. Stir after each burst of heat.

Cocoa

My favorite brands of cocoa are Pernigotti (from Williams-Sonoma) and Lindt (from mail-order houses). Both are uncertified. From the supermarket, I like Droste. Regular (not Dutch-processed) cocoa is a pure product, and should not really need certification for everyday use, nor for Passover. If you prefer to use a certified product, these are my favorites (in order of preference):

Droste Ⓚ

Ghirardelli Ⓚ PARVE

Paskesz Ⓚ PAREVE

Hershey's Ⓤ

For Passover you can use any pure cocoa, or the following certified brands:

Shufra Premium Cocoa (Dutch-processed) Ⓚ PAREVE

Paskesz Ⓚ PAREVE

Cookies/Graham Crackers

Dairy
1. Nabisco—lowfat available Ⓤ D
2. Rokeach—sold in kosher food stores Ⓤ D

Pareve

1. Murray—certification Ⓤ PAREVE

2. Hannaford's (supermarket) own brand Ⓤ PAREVE

Gingersnaps

1. Nabisco Ⓤ D

2. President's Choice— Ⓚ DAIRY available at these supermarkets: Finast, Glen's, Price Chopper, Randall's, Schnook's, Star Market, Tom Thumb, and Tops

3. Murray Ⓤ D

4. Archway— △K-D reduced-fat available

Eggs

Salmonella contamination continues to be a problem with raw eggs. To reduce risk, eggs should be brought directly home from the supermarket. They should not be stored in the little compartments in the door (the door is the warmest part of the refrigerator), but left in the carton and placed in the back of the shelf where the temperature is sure to be 40°. Never use an egg that has a cracked shell. Mousses and meringues that usually use raw eggs should now be made with partially cooked eggs. Make sure to follow the cooking instructions exactly so that the eggs cook to 160°F, the proper temperature to kill salmonella.

Working with eggs

1. When a recipe calls for room-temperature eggs, the eggs can be brought to room temperature quickly by immersing them, in their shells, in a bowl of warm water. It will take 5 to 10 minutes to bring them to room temperature. Room-temperature eggs blend well with other ingredients, creating better baked goods, especially when butter is also involved.

2. When adding sugar to eggs, gradually add it as you beat the eggs, otherwise little hard lumps of egg might form. When adding hot

liquid to eggs, whisk in a little at a time so that the eggs don't cook (this is called tempering).

Separating eggs

1. Eggs are most easily separated by using an egg separator. Even a tiny bit of yolk mixed into whites will have an adverse effect upon whipping. Do one egg at a time, otherwise you may ruin an entire batch if you happen to have a bad egg, or if some yolk gets into the whites.

2. If you get a little yolk into the container you are using for separating, make sure that you discard that egg white (or save it for another use) and rinse the container before continuing to separate.

3. Bowls, too, must be dry and grease-free or egg whites may fail to whip.

Whipping eggs

1. For whipping egg whites to maximum volume, they should be at room temperature.

2. To test for soft peaks, lift up the beaters slowly. If a little peak forms and the tip slumps back over, the eggs are at soft peaks.

3. Stiff peaks stand straight up. Many recipes call for whites that are beaten "stiff but not dry." Dry eggs do not combine well with other ingredients, so that when you try to fold them in, the eggs ball up and look like little bits of Styrofoam in your batter.

4. There are three ways to help prevent eggs from becoming dry. Using cream of tartar, whipping in a copper bowl, or adding sugar to the egg whites all help to stabilize them and prevent drying. I use the sugar method, exclusively. Cream of tartar is not kosher because it is made during alcohol distillation, and I think working with a copper bowl is a nuisance. Dry eggs can be remoistened using this tip from Alice Medrich's book *Cocolat:* Scoop the first bit of egg whites out with a clean, grease-free spatula and see how well they blend. If

Ingredients

307

the eggs are too dry, add one unbeaten egg white to the remaining whites and beat briefly to combine. This should rescue the egg whites.

Egg substitutes

I use liquid egg substitute, such as Egg Beaters, in many of my low-fat recipes. Most egg substitutes are all-natural products, consisting of egg whites, natural flavorings and color, vitamins, and thickeners. Unlike eggs, however, egg substitutes contain no fat or cholesterol. Egg whites are also fat and cholesterol free, and I use them extensively, but sometimes a recipe is improved by the thickeners in egg substitutes. Egg substitutes are also convenient when only a small quantity of egg is needed, or when it would be too hard to measure out part of the egg white. For those who just don't want to use egg substitutes, an alternative is given in each recipe, but be aware that this may change the amount of fat and cholesterol listed. There are a few egg substitutes on the market that contain dairy, artificial colors and flavors, and preservatives. I would not use these products. Check labels if you are unsure. Different brands may have different flavors and different thickeners, so experiment to find your favorite brand. I like Egg Beaters because they contain added flavoring that make them taste more like eggs, but they also contain onion and garlic (in minute amounts), which some might find distressing in baked goods (I don't notice those flavors at all in the baked product). The following are all excellent products:

Egg Beaters—certified   (U)PAREVE

Egg Starts—certified   (U)PAREVE

Second Nature—certified   (K)-P

Fats

Where possible, oil has been used in these recipes because it is the most healthful fat to eat (oil has a high percentage of monounsaturated fat, no cholesterol, and no trans-fatty acids), according to Wooten,

Liebman, and Rosofsky, in "Trans: The Phantom Fat." Canola and peanut oils are my favorite, as they both have a very neutral taste. Hazelnut, almond, and sesame oils are also excellent choices, but they do have very distinctive flavors, and are only suitable for certain recipes. Not all recipes work well with oil, however, and for these I use a dairy-free, unsalted margarine for a pareve dessert, and unsalted butter for dairy desserts. I usually use Fleischmann's margarine, because I like its flavor the best. Most margarines contain dairy, so be sure to read the label if you want a pareve dessert. For Passover, use Mother's brand margarine as it is made from safflower oil and is kosher for Passover. Unsalted butter is generally of a better quality, and fresher than salted butter. I always use it when a recipe calls for butter. Butter has a unique flavor and mouth-feel, and is absolutely essential for some recipes. I've cut it down to the bare minimum in all of the recipes, and indicated when substitutions will work well. For certain pastries, shortening works best. Wesson makes a vegetable shortening that is certified Ⓚ. Choose a pan spray that is kosher, such as PAM, which carries Ⓤ certification. If you cannot find a kosher brand, grease pans lightly with margarine or oil.

Exposure to air, heat, and light causes fats and oil to spoil. If possible, buy them in opaque containers and store in a cool, dark location, or in the refrigerator. All-purpose oil, such as canola, should last for six months to one year if stored properly. Never reuse oil that has been used for frying. Nut and seed oils should always be stored in the refrigerator after opening and should last for two to four months. When refrigerated, they often turn thick and cloudy, but clear when they come back to room temperature, according to Janet Bailey, in *Keeping Food Fresh*. Margarine, even one without dairy in it, can spoil, too. Keep it frozen, or refrigerate if planning to use it within several weeks.

Measure oil in a liquid measuring cup and solid fats in dry measuring cups or tablespoons. Margarine and butter wrappers are usually marked in tablespoon increments. One stick equals eight tablespoons or ½ cup.

Flavorings

Orange flower or rose flower water can be bought at Middle Eastern and Sephardic grocery stores, at specialty shops, and by mail-order from King Arthur Flour Company or Penzey's, Ltd. See page 324 for addresses. I don't especially care for the perfumy taste of these Sephardic and Middle Eastern flavorings, but I list them as choices in recipes where they are traditional.

Flours

Although most people use cups for measuring, this is an extremely inaccurate way to measure flour. If you experiment, you will see that every time you measure a cup of flour, it weighs a different amount. Alter the way in which the flour is measured, such as "lightly spooned," or "dip and scoop," and the weight will vary. Weighed flour, however, is always the same, no matter how it is scooped, packed, or fluffed up. For all-purpose flour, for example, measuring by cups I have had results that varied from 105 grams to 140 grams per cup. In a recipe calling for two cups of flour, you could be off by over a third of a cup! If you really want good, consistent results, I urge you to buy a kitchen scale, and weigh your flour. The weights that are used in this book are:

105 grams sifted cake flour = 1 cup

120 grams all-purpose flour = 1 cup

125 grams bread flour = 1 cup

Cake flour is a finely milled, low-protein flour. It is especially useful in lowfat cakes in helping to ensure tenderness. Lowfat pastries and cookies can be too crispy unless made with some cake flour, as well. Cake flour tends to clump up, so I usually sift it first, and then I can sprinkle it into my measuring cups. Soft As Silk is certified Ⓤ

When using whole wheat for baking, always use finely milled pastry flour. It should not have any visible bran and should be powdery. Desserts made with other whole wheat flours will be overly moist and have a pronounced wheat flavor. My favorite brands are:

Arrowhead Mills
Box 2059
Hereford, TX 79045
(806) 364-0730
(Ⓚ certification)

King Arthur Flour
P.O. Box 876
Norwich, Vermont 05055-0876
(800) 827-6836, Fax (800) 343-3002
(Ⓤ certification)

Fruits

Apples

Which type of apple to use in a recipe is clearly a matter of personal choice. While one book might say that a specific apple is good only for eating, another might say that it is the preferred apple for baking. In addition, there is great variation even within types due to growing and storing conditions. Winter apples tend to be juicier than summer apples, and varieties might taste different in different parts of the country. In a pastry where the apples are all jumbled up (such as a pie), you might want to use a mixture of varieties to ensure that there will be soft and firm, and sweet and tart components.

The following general guide might help you decide which apple to use:

Quick-cooking variety:

1. Cortland—sweet, but bland

2. Gingergold—sweet and full-flavored

3. McIntosh—semi-tart, full-flavored

4. Gravenstein—tart

Medium-firm when cooked:

1. Golden Delicious (use green-colored ones)—very sweet but dryish—my favorite apple for baking when other acidic fruits are included or when there is little sugar in the recipe

2. Empire—sweet and juicy with just a touch of acidity

3. Macoun—juicy, balanced flavor

4. Granny Smith—very tart

Firm when cooked:

1. Rome—sweet but mild-flavored—for use in the fall and winter (in the summer they are softer and mealy)

2. Gala—sweet and juicy

3. Fuji—semi-tart and full-flavored—my favorite when long cooking times are required or when grated apples are called for

4. Stayman—semi-tart

5. Winesap—semi-tart and full-flavored

6. Greening—tart and full-flavored

Apricots

Because they must be picked when ripe, apricots are not often found in stores. Only 20 percent of the crop is eaten fresh, with the remainder being dried or canned. Apricots are available sporadically from May through August.

Dried apricots are dated for one year from the time they are packed, so check for freshness. Once opened, they should be stored in the refrigerator for up to two weeks. Sun-maid. the brand most commonly available in the supermarket, carries a △K-P kosher certification. Mariani is my favorite brand because the apricots are moist and plump. They are certified Ⓤ .

Berries

Because of the recent problems with bacteria on berries, I always rinse them well and then pat them dry. Don't wet them until just before using, or they may get moldy or soft. Raspberries spoil fairly fast, so buy them within a day or two of eating. Fresh, local strawberries also spoil within a day or two and should be eaten or pureed immediately. Strawberries that get shipped to market are firmer, and tend to last for four or five days. These have a mild, pleasant flavor, but may not puree well. Berries are available all year, but are very expensive in the winter. At Tu b'Shevat, use small quantities of fresh berries, or use frozen or dried berries. Shavuot is the perfect time to eat berries, as they are plentiful and inexpensive in the late spring/early summer.

Dates

Boxed dates can be bought year-round in most grocery stores. Although dried fruits are not actually perishable, quality begins to deteriorate after about one year, or sooner if they have been stored at too high a temperature. The use-date should be stamped on top of the box. Once opened, refrigerate them for up to 1 month. For convenience, buy pitted and/or diced dates. Be aware, however, that the diced dates are coated with sugar. Both Del Monte and Dromedary are certified Ⓤ.

Unboxed dates should be plump and soft with smooth, shiny skin. Store them in the refrigerator for up to two weeks. Of the three kinds of unboxed dates that I purchased, only the Deglit Noors were pitted. The Medjool dates were the sweetest of the three, and the Bachi were the driest. Unboxed dates should be stored in the refrigerator and used within two weeks.

Figs

Fresh figs are small, pear-shaped, green fruit that are rarely shipped because they spoil easily. Ripe fruit should be firm, but not hard, and should have no sour smell. Store them in the refrigerator on paper towels and eat within two days. Fresh figs are available June through October and are appropriate for Shavuot, Rosh Hashanah, or Sukkot.

Ingredients

Dried figs are available in sealed boxes or loose. Of the two varieties that I tried, I found the Calimyra figs to be drier but sweeter, and the Black Mission variety to be moister. Dried figs are available year-round and, because they are a food mentioned in the Torah, are suitable for all Jewish holidays. Sun-maid brand is certified ⚠️K-P.

Grapes

Uncooked in tarts and baked in pies, grapes add wonderful texture to pastries. I like to pair them with some of the softer fruits, such as berries or peaches. You can expect the color to dramatically fade when grapes are cooked, so don't count on them for much color. Grapes are one of the fruits mentioned in the Torah, and are abundant in Israel today. They are available year-round and are symbolic for Rosh Hashanah, Sukkot, Tu b'Shevat, and Yom ha-atzma'ut.

Lemons

To get more juice out of a lemon, prick it in several places and heat in the microwave on high for 30 seconds. Citrus skin without any of the underlying white pith attached is called zest. It can be removed from the fruit by using a sharp paring knife or a vegetable peeler. For grated zest, rub the fruit against a box grater, or grind the zest in an electric spice mill. When using the zest, consider buying organic lemons because pesticides tend to collect in the skin of fruits. In either case, make sure to wash the skin very well. Eat lemons at Sukkot to represent *etrog* and at Tu b'Shevat.

Mangoes

Buy ripe but firm fruit with some yellow and red on the skin. If you don't like the taste of the perfumy flesh, refrigerate them to suppress the flavor, or use them when very firm. At their peak, mangoes will yield to the touch. Once ripe, they should be stored in the refrigerator for three days. Overly ripe mangoes smell fermented and should be discarded. Mangoes have large, flat, odd-looking cores. To use mangoes, peel and then slice the flesh off the core. Some people are allergic to a resin in the skin of the mango so you might want to wear gloves when peeling them, writes Nicole Routhier, in *Fruit Cookbook*. Good substitutes are papaya or peach. Mangoes are plentiful from May through September and are great for Shavuot. If you can find them during the winter, they are also appropriate for Tu b'Shevat.

Oranges

Oranges taste great when freshly sliced and placed on tarts. Marinating is another way of transforming an orange without cooking away its flavor. If eating the rind, try to buy organic oranges, and wash the skin thoroughly. Oranges are eaten at Sukkot, Tu b'Shevat, and Shabbat.

Papaya

Also called paw-paws, papaya can be used in baking when very firm, or riper. Like peaches, the harder ones will not have as much flavor and will remain intact when baked. The softer the flesh, the more mushy they will get when cooked. Unripe papayas can be left at room temperature to ripen, and will then spoil very quickly. When ripe, the skin will turn yellowish and the flesh will have a perfumy flavor. To use, peel them, cut in half, and scoop out all of the little seeds (hundreds of them!). Cut flesh into chunks or slices and sprinkle with lemon juice. Good substitutes are mango or peach. Papaya are available year-round and can be used to celebrate Tu b'Shevat or Yom ha-atzma'ut.

Peaches

We get fabulous peaches here in the South, but if yours are not very flavorful, you can still use them in baking. Firm, tart peaches will hold up beautifully in a pie or pastry and will give a nice kick to the dessert. Riper peaches are best used uncooked to top tarts or cakes. Peaches tend to brown after they are cut, so be generous with lemon juice, which will keep them looking pretty. If the peaches will be used decoratively, make sure they are freestones so the flesh will come off the pit cleanly. Remove the skins by plunging the peaches into boiling water for about one minute and the skins will practically slide off. Clingstone peaches can be used in fillings. In this case the peel can simply be removed with a knife. Peaches come into season in June and are perfect for celebrating an early Shavuot, or for Shabbat.

Pears

These should be just slightly ripe for baking or they will fall apart. Bartlett and Bosc are my favorites. Pears are available year-round, but are best in the fall when they are newly harvested. Eat them at Rosh Hashanah, Sukkot, Tu b'Shevat, or for Shabbat.

Plums

There are many different varieties of plums and each will have a distinctive flavor. The texture and flavor will also vary depending upon the degree of ripeness. I like to bake with very firm plums, which hold together during baking and are very tart. If using riper, sweeter, plums, pair them with other fruits that will not get soft and mushy, such as apples. Plums are great for Sukkot or Tu b'Shevat.

Pomegranates

Often eaten as the "new" fruit at Rosh Hashanah, pomegranates are mentioned frequently in the Torah. According to the Kabbala (Jewish mystical writings), the fruit contains 613 seeds, the number equal to the commandments derived from the Torah, writes Patti Shosteck in *A Lexicon of Jewish Cooking*. For thousands of years the pomegranate has been the symbol of fertility, health, and romance. Eat the seeds in salad, or savor the juice. To extract the juice, warm the fruit by rolling it in your hands. Cut a hole in the stem end and place the fruit over a glass. The juice stains are permanent, so cover your clothing and wear gloves when handling the seeds.

Prunes

As with other dried fruits, check the date stamped on the box, to make sure they are fresh. Store at 72°F or cooler, and refrigerate after opening. Properly stored, sealed prunes will stay fresh for 1½ years. Buy pitted prunes or you may have some heavy dental bills! Del Monte brand is certified Ⓤ.

Raisins

Type of packaging and storage temperature determines the shelf life of raisins. Raisins with a bag-in-a-box will maintain quality for up to 2 years, those in canisters for 1½ years, and those in other types of packaging will last for one year. Store all dried fruits at 72°F or cooler for best results. Del Monte brand is certified ⚠️K-P . Hannaford's own and Dole are both Ⓤ.

Rhubarb

Look for rhubarb in the vegetable section of the supermarket year-round. The stalks look like reddish celery. Store rhubarb in a plastic bag in the refrigerator for one week. Make sure to remove all leaves as these are toxic, suggests Janet Bailey in *Keeping Food Fresh*. Rhubarb is another fruit that can be cooked until it is crisp-tender or soft. I prefer to combine fruits of varying texture, for example, soft rhubarb with grapes, and crisp rhubarb with strawberries. Because rhubarb is quite tart, it is not appropriate for Rosh Hashanah, but could be eaten for Sukkot, Shavuot, or Shabbat.

Gelatin

There are several different types of kosher "gelatins" on the market. Most are not gelatin at all, but substitutes that are used as thickeners. These work fine for Jell-O-type desserts, but not for mousses and other desserts where the gelatin gets added to cold or room-temperature ingredients. Fortunately, there is now a real gelatin that is kosher. Kolatin is made from kosher cows, and is processed so that it is certified as pareve by the Orthodox Union. If you cannot find it locally, call Koltech Industries, Lakewood, NJ, at (732) 364-8700. Kolatin works exactly the same as regular gelatin and can be substituted in all of your recipes. It's a wonderful ingredient for making lowfat mousses, fillings, and frostings. For thickening jam glazes, either type

Ingredients

of gelatin will work, but they need to be handled slightly differently. Gelatin substitutes do not need to be presoftened, but once liquefied they need to be used immediately, as they begin to set up at once. Kolatin, on the other hand, needs to be presoftened in double the quantity of liquid and then heated and remelted.

Nuts

The latest medical studies show that nuts are very healthful foods, although high in fat. In several studies, volunteers who ate nuts had lower blood cholesterol levels (LDL, the "bad" kind, dropped) than control groups who did not have nuts in their diets. Perhaps this is because the oil in nuts is mono- and polyunsaturated and is rich in alpha-linolenic acid, which gets converted in the body to omega-3 fatty acid (the same kind as in fish oil). They are also high in fiber and vitamin E. By the way, although the nut-eating group consumed almost 600 calories a day (from nuts) more than the control group, none gained weight during the nine-week study, reported Peter Jaret in "Good News in a Nutshell."

Opened packages of nuts can get rancid fairly quickly so it is best to store leftover nuts in the freezer. Make sure that you taste them before use or you may end up with a ruined dessert.

Working with nuts

Before processing any nuts, bring them to room temperature or they may become pasty. Adding a little sugar or flour to them before grinding will help to absorb some of the oil released so that they will chop or grind nicely.

Nuts in the shell need no certification for everyday use or for Passover. If you require shelled nuts to have certification, look for Diamond brand with a △K–P or Dole brand, certified Ⓤ PAREVE

Phyllo Dough

Phyllo (also spelled "fillo" or "filo") is a Middle Eastern pastry dough that is sold in frozen food departments of most large supermarkets.

The sheets of dough (called leaves) are paper thin and can be used to make strudels and other ultra-flaky desserts. To defrost, put the dough in the refrigerator overnight, and then let it stand (unopened) for 2 hours at room temperature. Another method is to let the unopened package stand at room temperature for 5 hours. To use, follow the instructions with each recipe, but remember to always keep the dough covered while you are working with it, or it will dry out and be unusable. Look for these brands: Athens with an Ⓚ certification, and Solo, certified Ⓚ .

Wonton and Eggroll Wrappers

Nasoya is certified Ⓚ.

Yeast

I like instant yeast because it gets mixed directly in with the dry ingredients and needs no proofing (does not need to get foamy first). It's not only easier to use, but also rises faster than regular yeast. It can be kept indefinitely in the freezer and does not need to be defrosted for use. Do not substitute rapid-rise yeast for instant yeast, as it does not have a very good aroma and flavor. If you are looking for a kosher, supermarket yeast that works very well, try Fleischmann's Bread Machine Yeast. It has a good flavor, is reliable and reasonably priced, and is certified Ⓚ. If kosher products are not important to you, you might like to mail-order either Fermepan or Saf yeast, available from either the Chef's Catalog or King Arthur Flour (see page 324). For doughs that rise overnight, I like Saf Special. Some bakers prefer active dry yeast because they feel a longer, slower rise produces a better flavor. This type of yeast has a pungent aroma that I find distressing. If, however, you do want to use regular active dry yeast, it must be mixed with a little warm liquid and sugar, and left to stand until foamy. The formula is to use ¼ cup warm liquid (which you deduct from the liquid called for in the recipe) and 1 teaspoon of sugar, for each 2 teaspoons of yeast. After it is foamy, it can be added to the flour-water

Ingredients

mixture in your recipe. When using active yeast, the liquid used should be cooler than that for instant yeast: 110°F—just lukewarm to the touch—should be perfect. Professional bakers often use fresh cake yeast. They store it in the freezer to keep it fresh, and break off as much as they need for baking. In the fifteen years that I have been actively baking and teaching, I have never seen cake yeast in any of the supermarkets that I frequent. Needless to say, I never use fresh yeast. If by some chance you find it, and want to try it, use half as much fresh yeast as the dry yeast the recipe calls for.

To mail-order the following equipment, consult the list of suppliers on page 324.

Baking Pans

Straight-sided cake pans, available in fine cooking stores and mail-order houses, are best for layer cakes. You will not have to trim the sides of these cakes to get the layers to line up. To avoid damage to nonstick cake pans, be sure to use a plastic knife when releasing the cake from the pan (a small disposable knife works fine).

Tart pans should be of the highest quality, as the inexpensive ones may warp or rust. French tart pans are excellent and are available in fine cooking stores, and can be ordered from Bridge Kitchenware or Williams-Sonoma.

Cakeboards

Cardboard cakeboards (or rounds) are very useful for getting cakes out of their pans and providing a sturdy base on which to decorate and move cakes. They are available in some craft stores, paper goods stores, and cake decorating stores, or can be ordered from Sweet Celebrations. If you are concerned about using paper products, a cake pan bottom, plate, or other flat object can be substituted.

Food Mill

It's next to impossible to make seedless raspberry sauce without a food mill. Buy stainless steel so that it won't rust. Food mills can be bought at fine cooking stores or ordered from mail-order houses.

Mixers

An expensive mixer, such as the KitchenAid, will make baking a pleasure rather than a chore. No batter will be too thick to handle, and you will save time and frustration.

Parchment Paper and Teflon Bakeware Liners

Teflon Bakeware Liners, by Dupont, are my favorite way to line pans. Nothing ever sticks to them, and they are very easy to clean. They can be cut to fit your pans, but also come in precut, standard sizes. For piped ladyfingers and cake bases, I use precut rounds, and strips that I cut from a rectangular piece—much easier than trying to draw guidelines on parchment paper every time I pipe. Teflon liners can be purchased from cooking stores. If you can't find them, call Dupont at (800) 986-2857. Parchment paper, available in most cooking stores, some supermarket or craft stores, and mail-order, can also be used.

Pastry Brushes

I like the inexpensive nylon pastry brushes that are about 1 inch wide and about ⅛ inch thick. If you are not partial to using boar bristle brushes, this is the brush you need. It is made by Fox Run Craftsmen, Ivyland, PA 18974. For brushing delicate foods, such as pastries and fruit, feather brushes are excellent. These can be purchased through fine cooking stores or mail-ordered.

Pots

Some recipes call for using a nonreactive pot. This means a pot in which no chemical reaction takes place between the metal of the pot and the food being cooked. Typically, an acidic food, such as lemon juice or vinegar, would cause such a reaction. Some pots also react to alkaline foods, such as corn and beans. Aluminum, iron, and copper are some of the metals that are reactive. The reaction of the pot and food might cause the food to change color and/or taste, and might even be harmful. Pots made of these materials are often coated to make them less reactive or nonreactive. Nonreactive materials include stainless steel (buy those with aluminum cores, which provide better heat conduction), alloys, enameled cast iron, and glass.

Processors

Because I have never used anything but Cuisinart, I cannot recommend any other brand. I own two, both of them are extra large. Buy the largest you can afford, so that you will be able to handle any dough.

Strainers

Medium- and fine-mesh strainers are both handy to have for baking. They are used for straining puddings and sauces and to remove unwanted material from your ingredients. Three-, six-, and eight-inch strainers are all useful. Buy stainless steel so that they won't rust, and try to find the ones without wooden handles so that you can put them in the dishwasher.

Spatulas and Rubber Scrapers

Rubber scrapers (commonly called spatulas) are a must when working with any batter. Try to find the plastic molded kind with a very flexible scraper. Metal spatulas are needed if you want to make a frosted cake look pretty. To spread and smooth frosting, use an 8-inch-long straight spatula (the blade is 4 inches). Offset spatulas are helpful in moving decorated cakes and for spreading frosting on a cake that stays in the pan. Very long spatulas work great with rectangular cakes, both for decorating and for moving them.

Equipment Suppliers

For food suppliers, look in the ingredient section, pages 303–320.

Bridge Kitchenware
214 E. 52nd Street
New York, NY 10022
(800) Bridge K, Fax (212) 758-5387
Extensive collection of baking equipment including excellent cake pans, tart pans, whisks, pastry bags, spatulas, and cookie cutters.

Chef's Catalog
(800) 338-3232
Strainers, parchment paper, cookie sheets in three sizes, jelly roll pans, Bundt pans.

King Arthur Flour
P.O. Box 876
Norwich, Vermont 05055-0876
(800) 827-6836, Fax (800) 343-3002
Complete supplies for the baker.

Penzeys, Ltd.
P.O. Box 933
Muskego, WI 53187
(414) 574-0277, Fax (414) 578-0278
Spices, cocoa, seeds, and extracts.

Sweet Celebrations
3244 Raleigh Ave.
Minneapolis, MN 55416
(800) 328-6722, Fax (612) 927-6215
Extensive collection of candy- and cake-making equipment, books, and foods. Especially good for cakeboards, parchment, and doilies.

Williams-Sonoma
Mail-Order Department
P.O. Box 7456
San Francisco, CA 94120-7456
Excellent baking pans, whisks, food mills, strainers, etc.

Registered symbols appear on commercially packaged products to indicate if the product is kosher, and who has done the certification. A manufacturer can put a "K" on a product even if there has been no rabbinical supervision. If you want to find out who (if anyone) has inspected the product, it is best to call the manufacturer of that specific product. There are many organizations that offer kosher certification, some of which are less strict than others. If you have any questions, consult your rabbi.

The following symbols are used on products mentioned in this book. Again, if you are very concerned, ask your rabbi's opinion about the reliability of the organization behind the symbol:

The O-U: Union of Orthodox Jewish Congregations, 45 W. 36th Street, New York, NY 10018 Ⓤ ⓊD ⓊPAREVE ⓊP

The OK: The Organized Kashrus Laboratories, 1372 Carroll Street, Brooklyn, NY 11213 Ⓚ ⓀD ⓀPAREVE

The KOF-K: Kosher Supervision, 1444 Queen Anne Road, Teaneck, NJ 07666 Ⓚ ⓀPARVE ⓀDAIRY

Triangle-K: Rabbi Joseph H. Ralbag, 225 W. 86th Street, New York, NY △K-P △K-D

Dates of Jewish Holidays
1999-2009 (5760-5769)

The first day of each holiday is listed here. Don't forget that most holidays begin at sundown the night before.

	1999/2000 (5760)	2000/2001 (5761)	2001/2002 (5762)	2002/2003 5763	2003/2004 5764
Rosh Hashanah	Sept. 11, 1 Tishri	Sept. 30	Sept. 18	Sept. 7	Sept. 27
Yom Kippur	Sept. 20, 10 Tishri	Oct. 9	Sept. 27	Sept. 16	Oct. 6
Sukkot	Sept. 25, 15 Tishri	Oct. 14	Oct. 2	Sept. 21	Oct. 11
Simkat Torah	Oct. 3, 23 Tishri	Oct. 22	Oct. 10	Sept. 29	Oct. 19
Chanukah	Dec. 4, 25 Kislev	Dec. 22	Dec. 10	Nov. 30	Dec. 20
Tu b'Shevat	Jan. 22, 15 Shevat	Feb. 8	Jan. 18	Jan. 18	Feb. 7
Purim	Mar. 21, 14 Adar	Mar. 9	Feb. 26	Mar. 18	Mar. 7
Passover	Apr. 20, 15 Nisan	Apr. 8	Mar. 28	Apr. 17	Apr. 6
Yom ha-atzma'ut	May 10, 5 Iyyar	Apr. 28	Apr. 17	May 7	Apr. 26
Shavuot	June 9, 6 Sivan	May 28	May 17	June 6	May 26

	2004/2005 5765	2005/2006 5766	2006/2007 5767	2007/2008 5768	2008/2009 5769
Rosh Hashanah	Sept. 16	Oct. 4	Sept. 23	Sept. 13	Sept. 30
Yom Kippur	Sept. 25	Oct. 13	Oct. 2	Sept. 22	Oct. 9
Sukkot	Sept. 30	Oct. 18	Oct. 7	Sept. 27	Oct. 14
Simkat Torah	Oct. 8	Oct. 26	Oct. 15	Oct. 5	Oct. 22
Chanukah	Dec. 8	Dec. 26	Dec. 16	Dec. 5	Dec. 22
Tu b'Shevat	Jan. 25	Feb. 13	Feb. 3	Jan. 22	Feb. 9
Purim	Mar. 25	Mar. 14	Mar. 4	Mar. 21	Mar. 10
Passover	Apr. 24	Apr. 13	Apr. 3	Apr. 21	Apr. 9
Yom ha-atzma'ut	May 14	May 3	Apr. 23	May 10	Apr. 29
Shavuot	June 13	June 2	May 23	June 9	May 29

Bibliography

Bailey, Janet. *Keeping Food Fresh.* New York: Doubleday, 1985.

Beranbaum, Rose Levy. *The Cake Bible.* New York: William Morrow, 1988.

Corriher, Shirley O. *Cookwise.* New York: William Morrow, 1997.

Eisenberg, Penny. *Passover Desserts.* New York: Macmillan, 1996.

Gisslen, Wayne. *Professional Baking.* 2d ed. New York: John Wiley, 1985.

Greene, Gloria Kaufer. *The Jewish Holiday Cookbook.* New York: Times Books, 1985.

Grigson, Jane and Charlotte Knox. *Cooking with Exotic Fruits and Vegetables.* New York: Henry Holt, 1987.

Jaret, Peter. "Good News in a Nutshell." *Health Magazine* (July/August 1996).

Medrich, Alice. *Cocolat.* New York: Warner Books, 1990.

_____. *Chocolate and the Art of Low-Fat Desserts.* New York: Warner Books, 1994.

Nathan, Joan. *Jewish Cooking in America.* New York: Alfred A. Knopf, 1994.

Purdy, Susan. *Have Your Cake and Eat It, Too.* New York: William Morrow, 1993.

_____. *Let Them Eat Cake.* New York: William Morrow, 1997.

Roden, Claudia. *The Book of Jewish Food.* New York: Alfred A. Knopf, 1996.

Routhier, Nicole. *Fruit Cookbook.* New York: Workman, 1996.

Shosteck, Patti. *A Lexicon of Jewish Cooking.* Chicago: Contemporary Books, 1981.

Strassfeld, Michael. *The Jewish Holidays.* New York: Harper & Row, 1985.

Wilton Enterprises. *The Wilton Way of Cake Decorating.* Vol. 3. Woodridge, IL: Wilton Enterprises, 1979.

Wooten, Liebman, and Rosofsky. "Trans: The Phantom Fat," *Nutrition Action Newsletter,* Center for Science in the Public Interest (September 1996).

apricot(s), 312
>   apple brown Betty, 140–141
>   blueberry ginger crisp, 245–246
>   chiffon cake with orange, walnut and, 133–134
>   filling, for hamantashen, 159–160
>   hamantashen, 157–158
>   rugelach, 80–84

apricot jam:
>   in apple mousse layer cake, 12–16
>   in apple-plum galette, 145–146
>   in brandied nutmeg pear tart, 58–59
>   in dried fruit and apple tart, 144–145
>   in honey spice thumbprints, 19–20
>   in Mandarin orange cheesecake, 109–111
>   in pear tart frangipane, 148–149

Ashkenazi recipes, traditional, 227

assibih bi loz (almond pistachio phyllo fingers), 84–86

ataif bi jibn (Syrian cheese pancakes), 116–117

ataif bi loz (nut-filled Syrian pancakes), 34–36

Babka, chocolate or cinnamon-raisin, 68–70

baby food, 303

baking pans, 321

baklava, chocolate or nut, 28–31

bananas:
>   in chocolate fondue with mixed fruit, 138–139
>   Foster, 122

berry(ies), 313
>   in apple butter puff tarts, 24–25
>   in apple cranberry cornmeal cobbler, 50–51
>   cheesecake, 209–212
>   in cherry vanilla trifle cups, 235
>   lemon roulade, 196–198
>   multiberry topping, 213
>   in summer pudding miniatures, 243–244

bimuelos (fried donuts in syrup), 129–130

biscotchos (crunchy orange almond cookies), 77–78

biscotti, chocolate chip pecan, 275–276

blintzes, apple caramel, 118–121

blueberry(ies):
>   apricot ginger crisp, 245–246
>   in berry cheesecake, 209–212
>   in lemon berry roulade, 196–198
>   lemon phyllo tiles or napoleons, 252–254
>   in mixed fruit trifle, 193–195
>   papaya (or peach) pandowdy, 247–248
>   strawberry sour cream tart, 250–251
>   in summer fruit cobbler, 284–285

brandy(ied):
>   in apple tart Normandy, 20–21
>   nutmeg pear tart, 58–59
>   in orange crêpe scrolls, 94–96

breadcrumb almond topping, for apple apricot brown Betty, 140–141

breads:
>   chocolate or cinnamon-raisin babka, 68–70
>   date, fig and nut loaf, 137
>   healthy challah, 282–284
>   lemon poppy buttermilk mini-loaves, 172–174
>   orange-cranberry tea loaf, 41–42
>   pudding, 280–281
>   zucchini pear loaf, 39–40

bulemas dulces (Sephardic sweet pastry rings), 165–166

butter cookie dreidels, 112–113

buttermilk:
>   in almond Bundt cake, 267–268
>   in apple Bundt cake, 263–264
>   in apple cranberry cornmeal cobbler, 50–51
>   in chocolate tube cake, 269–270
>   in Devil's food and cream cheese sheet cake, 102–104
>   lemon poppy mini-loaves, 172–174
>   in sour cream coffee cake, 100–101

>   in spiced peach shortcakes, 231–232
>   in summer fruit cobbler, 284–285

Cakeboards, 321

cakes:
>   almond bundt, 267–268
>   apple bundt, 263–264
>   apple date bundt, 11–12
>   apple mousse layer, 12–16
>   applesauce spice, 202–203
>   berry cheesecake, 209–212
>   carrot pineapple bundt, 9–10
>   cherry sour cream cheesecake, 235–237
>   chocolate nut seafoam layer, 204–206
>   chocolate nut Torah roulade, 74–76
>   chocolate tube, 269–270
>   cranberry pear *fluden*, 56–57
>   crème caramel cheesecake, 107–108
>   devil's food and cream cheese sheet, 102–104
>   honey, 5–6
>   honey coffee chiffon, 7–8
>   lemon pistachio roulade, 71–73
>   lemon poppy buttermilk mini-loaves, 172–174
>   low-cholesterol sponge, 259–260
>   Mandarin orange cheesecake, 109–111
>   marble cheesecake, 238–240
>   marble pound, 265–266
>   orange, apricot and walnut chiffon, 133–134
>   Passover *tish pishti* soaked nut cake, 207–208
>   pear zucchini loaf, 39–40
>   raised streusel (crumb) coffeecake, 286–287
>   rum raisin cheesecake squares, 105–106
>   sour cream coffee, 100–101

Calvados, in apple tart Normandy, 20–21